L. EDWARD PHILLIPS

The Purpose, Pattern & Character of Worship

Nashville

THE PURPOSE, PATTERN, AND CHARACTER OF WORSHIP

Copyright © 2020 by Abingdon Press

All rights reserved.

No part of this work may be reproduced or transmitted in any form or by any means, electronic or mechanical, including photocopying and recording, or by any information storage or retrieval system, except as may be expressly permitted by the 1976 Copyright Act or in writing from the publisher. Requests for permission should be addressed in writing to Permissions, Abingdon Press, 2222 Rosa L. Parks Blvd., Nashville, TN 37228-1306, or emailed to permissions@abingdonpress.com.

This book is printed on acid-free paper.

ISBN: 978-1-7910-0468-2

Library of Congress Control Number: 2020943317

Scripture quotations are taken from the Common English Bible, copyright 2011. Used by permission. All rights reserved.

Scripture quotations marked KJV are from The Authorized (King James) Version. Rights in the Authorized Version in the United Kingdom are vested in the Crown. Reproduced by permission of the Crown's patentee, Cambridge University Press.

20 21 22 23 24 25 26 27 28 29—10 9 8 7 6 5 4 3 2 1

More Praise for *The Purpose, Pattern, and Character of Worship*

"Ed Phillips's positing of macro-patterns, six paradigms, and portable liturgical units within present-day American Protestant worship is sheer genius and enormously helpful for students, scholars, planners, leaders, and even lay participants of worship. His insights include strategies for those who wish to effectively conflate or blend in worship seemingly antithetical elements, elements that often have historical (sometimes even ancient) precursors that serve to unite the church universal. His articulate and spirited exposition will serve to shape and empower worship leaders and committee members who are bold, intentional, informed, and unafraid as they prayerfully seek to incorporate diverse elements of worship in ways that do not clash with an overriding macro-pattern and character. Phillips's groundbreaking work can help any church from any place on the spiritual spectrum. *The Purpose, Pattern, and Character of Worship* is destined to be a classic among classics in the field of liturgical studies and is a must-read for all engaged in worship practice and related communal introspection."

—Brenda Eatman Aghahowa, associate professor of English, Chicago State University, Chicago, IL; scholar of language, literacy, and rhetoric; minister, United Church of Christ

"This book is the ripened reflection of a consummate teacher and practitioner of Christian worship, both in person and online. It belongs on required reading lists for anyone involved in planning or leading worship. With the author's permission, I have used its evolving outline with seminarians and church leaders for over a decade. They have consistently come away with fresh insights into how to understand and strengthen worship in their own settings."

—Taylor W. Burton-Edwards, ELCA pastor; former Director of Worship Resources, The United Methodist Church

"An indispensable resource for worship teams. We need to pay attention to the conduct of our worship. We too often try to heal unhealthy worship practices by sampling and conflating various worship actions. Instead, we should form a clear-headed diagnosis and conduct our worship accordingly. Doing so can protect a congregation from what Phillips calls 'liturgical whiplash.'"

—David W. Manner, associate executive director, Kansas-Nebraska Convention of Southern Baptists; author, *Better Sundays Begin on Monday*, from Abingdon Press

"Do you ever wonder why you worship the way you do? What about those services of worship that fall flat? Wonder why? This groundbreaking book answers the most urgent questions about worship. Even better, it gives us practical tools to worship with excellence in any context."

—Charley Reeb, senior pastor, Johns Creek United Methodist Church, Johns Creek, GA

"As pastors come and go, as time periods, demographics, and cultural traditions change, congregations are often left with an amalgamation of worship add-ons without careful discernment about whether it all 'works.' Scholarship and schematics combine in this book to give churches a tool for evaluating and discerning a path toward more 'coherent, compelling, and faithful' expressions of worship for their context. As for my seminary students, they will be equipped to recognize and navigate the 'character' of worship patterns wherever they are called."

—Marcia McFee, creator and visionary, Worship Design Studio; Ford Fellow Professor, San Francisco Theological Seminary, San Anselmo, CA

"Liturgical worship, which Phillips aptly observes as the primary activity identified with Christianity, exists only in actual practice, occupying a significant part of congregational ministers' work. The need for an up-to-date textbook contextualizing US Christian worship traditions solidly in history and current changing social and ecclesial contexts is great. With years of experience as a seminary educator and widely respected liturgical scholar, Phillips has provided exactly this much-needed ecumenical resource at a crucial moment."

—Bruce T. Morrill, S.J., Edward A. Malloy Chair of Roman Catholic Studies, Vanderbilt Divinity School, Vanderbilt University, Nashville, TN

"Viewing a wide (and widening) landscape of worship patterns, Professor Ed Phillips reminds us, 'almost anything done well will be more compelling than almost anything done poorly.' How true. But as he insists, there is no comprehensive standard of excellence. Every liturgical family must be understood and evaluated according to its own history, theological commitments, and spiritual goals. Working from that premise, Phillips takes us on a journey through six 'character types' found in Protestant worship, discussing both their history and contemporary manifestations. He offers analysis both insightful and generous, a discussion that can help you understand why worship in your church flourishes (when it does), and yes, why it sometimes loses its way."

—Mark W. Stamm, professor of Christian worship, chapel elder, Perkins School of Theology, Southern Methodist University, Dallas, TX

"In this accessible and insightful book, Ed Phillips helps us understand the effect that six different historic worship patterns continue to have on Protestant worship today. He provides an even-handed description of these patterns; helps us understand the end or goal each pattern seeks; assesses their strengths, weaknesses, and character; and locates them all in the worship practices of mainline Protestantism today. Not to be undone by the quick changes to worship brought about by the COVID-19 pandemic, he also includes a timely discussion of online worship practices and the new questions such raise for the identity and mission of the church. What emerges from his analysis of these patterns is a set of seven principles that, if attended to, will guide pastors and other worship leaders to shape worship in ways that are both more compelling and more faithful."

—E. Byron (Ron) Anderson, Ernest and Bernice Styberg Professor of Worship, associate dean of institutional and educational assessment, Garrett-Evangelical Theological Seminary, Evanston, IL

Contents

Preface — vii

1. Worship Today: What's Going on Here? — 1

2. Six Character Types of Protestant Worship — 17

3. Worship as Motivational Technology: The Revival — 37

4. Worship as Education: The Sunday School — 67

5. Worship, Art, and Social Class: Aesthetic Worship — 99

6. Spiritual Power and Carnal Ecstasy: Pentecostal Worship — 129

7. Democratic Worship: The Prayer Meeting — 155

8. The Catholic Model: Liturgical Ordo and Deep Traditions — 181

9. Conflated Worship: Coherence and Incoherence
    in Liturgical Order — 209

10. Worship Patterns Online — 237

Conclusion: Good Worship? — 249

Preface

Worship is the most widely recognized activity of Christian congregations. To "go to church" essentially means to "go to worship." But what Christians do when they "go to worship" encompasses a dazzling variety of pattern, practice, and style. A Haitian immigrant, urban, Methodist congregation will worship differently than a suburban, predominantly white, Episcopal congregation. A megachurch with its use of sophisticated projection media will look and feel different than a small rural church, though both may identify as Baptist.

What drives me as a Protestant seminary professor who teaches courses in Christian worship is this concern: given the complexity they may encounter in their congregations, what must my students understand about diverse liturgical practices in order to plan and lead worship well? Obviously, worship leaders need to understand and respect ethnic identity and denominational tradition. They also need to consider the size and social location of their congregations. Yet, important as these factors are, they do not account for all of the diversity.

I propose that over roughly the last two centuries, Christian churches in the United States developed six major patterns of worship that deeply influence Protestant congregations. Along with denomination, social location, and ethnicity, these six models are crucial—though largely unacknowledged—sources of liturgical practices, orders, and styles. Briefly, these six are: the Revival, Sunday School Worship, Aesthetic Worship, Pentecostal Worship, the Prayer Meeting, and Catholic Liturgical Renewal. These patterns arose in the nineteenth and early twentieth centuries to address particular social and religious concerns. They continue in the present, slightly modified, as Seeker worship, Creative worship, Traditional worship, Praise worship, Small Group worship, and Word and Table worship. Each of these patterns has a distinctive *telos* (purpose) it aims to achieve, and each also has a corresponding distinctive *ethos* (character or style) that supports its *telos*.

In this study, I provide accounts of the six dominant patterns of worship to remind us of a history that most congregations no longer consciously remember. If I succeed at this task, you will have moments of recognition: "Yes, *that's* why we do that!" I hope to show that the historical genealogies of liturgical practices continue to influence the pattern, purpose, and character of worship, even though that history has been forgotten.

I also have a practical aim: excellence in liturgical leadership. Each of the six models I describe is a more or less coherent set of practices that generates its own distinct criteria for excellent planning and leading. Leading well for a Sunday School assembly is not the same as leading well for a Revival meeting, to provide an obvious contrast. Meaning, to plan and lead a service of worship with excellence, one must know what the service of worship is supposed to do (*telos*) and lead accordingly. For whatever convictions a leader may hold about the nature and purpose of Christian worship (and we all have such convictions!), there is no avoiding this fundamental principle: almost anything done well will be more compelling than almost anything done poorly.

Finally, I want to help worship planners and leaders diagnose problems within orders of worship. Why do some liturgical elements work in your context while others fall flat? Why does a service of worship not flow well? Why is a congregation not able to engage fully in an order of worship? Why are some parts of a particular service difficult to lead well? I propose that some of these problems arise when congregations combine worship patterns without understanding the variations among them. The six models have different, quite distinctive goals and character, which means they are not reducible to each other. Crucially, for my method of analysis, they tend to clash when they are combined. To continue with my example, it is practically impossible to conduct a Revival and a Sunday School assembly at the same time! Without attention to the potential clash of purpose and character, conflated worship can become incoherent. Congregations may still experience the various parts of a conflated service as "worship"—because the elements all come from the larger repertoire of possible liturgical actions found among the six models—but such a service is not likely to flow well, and it is not likely to express the clear sense of purpose necessary for healthy congregational identity.

Writing a book that has such comprehensive ambitions is, I confess, fraught with the danger of social ignorance and academic presumption. I am a white, sixty-five-year-old American male who makes his living in the academy. My perspective is grounded in the limitations of the predominately white church and academic field in which I have mostly served. While I aspire to be helpful to pastors of congregations across the spectrum of ethnic communities in the United States, this book is inevitably more centered in the liturgical practices of white Christian congregations—a limitation of my perspective that I have not yet been able to overcome. In future work, I intend to address this limitation to the degree that it is possible for someone from my social location to do so.

As I was finishing the work on my manuscript, the world began to undergo the coronavirus pandemic. While historical accounts may not change during such times, the *meaning* of history for the present does change. Since my project is very much about the influence of historical patterns of worship on the present, I have been able to include a chapter on how this continues to be the case even as almost all congregations across the United States have, out of necessity, embraced online worship, both live-streamed and recorded. It is much too soon to know all the ways this will form the understanding and practice of worship, but I am certain the influence will be hugely important. Compared to just a few months ago, worship after the pandemic will probably look and feel different when, God willing, the pandemic has passed. Yet even as churches worship "online," they will still bring habits of thought and practice that unconsciously shape the ways they do so.

Over the years, I have had so many conversations with mentors, colleagues, students, and working pastors that it is frankly difficult to pinpoint the origins of some of the ideas in the pages to come, though I am sure of the huge debt I owe to this great cloud of witnesses.

Preface

The influence of my teachers James F. White (of blessed memory), Paul Bradshaw, and Don Saliers is on every page. Jim taught me about the richness of contemporary Protestant worship, Paul about the importance of tending to diversity of liturgical practice in the ancient churches, and Don, through his example, instructed me in the importance of liturgical performance. Jim White died in 2004, but I miss his careful advice now as I bring this project to a conclusion.

For many years, my good friends Ron Anderson and Taylor Burton-Edwards have listened to my deepest concerns about worship and have helped me shape this book. We three tend to think so much alike that I often find they help me complete my ideas as I try to form them, or perhaps I am merely co-opting theirs! Either way, I cannot imagine doing my work without their friendship.

My many colleagues at Candler School of Theology have been supportive of this project, but I especially appreciate the help of Barbara Day Miller (who is now retired), Khalia Williams, and Jimmy Abbington, all three of whom have contributed more to my work than they may know.

I also want to acknowledge current and former students who have pushed me for greater clarity and have forced me to reconsider points where I have been wrong in my analysis. In particular I have learned much from Matthew Pierce, Layla Karst, Tony Alonso (who is now a faculty colleague), Byron Wratee, and Ayisha Shields. Joshua Hilton and Jordan Grassi, my student assistants, have read drafts of chapters, corrected quotations, and fixed numerous footnotes. I am thankful for their care.

Ulrike Guthrie, professional writing editor and consultant, has shepherded me through the last stages of manuscript preparation, and I am deeply grateful for her guidance and encouragement. I thank Abingdon Press for publishing my book after such a long gestation, and I especially thank my editor at Abingdon, Connie Stella, for all the tedious work leading to actual publication.

Finally, my closest professional partner and very best friend is my wife, Sara Webb Phillips. We were married a few days before beginning seminary in 1976, and we were ordained together as United Methodist elders in 1981. My career took me to the academy, while Sara has mostly served as a pastor, preacher, and worship leader. As a parish minister she has kept me grounded in the reality of the local church when I have wandered off into theoretical fantasy. To her first of all, and to all who seek to lead congregations in faithful service of God, I dedicate this book.

CHAPTER ONE

Worship Today

What's Going on Here?

"If you mean Darcy," cried her brother, "he may go to bed, if he chooses, before it begins—but as for the ball, it is quite a settled thing..."
"I should like balls infinitely better," she replied, "if they were carried on in a different manner; but there is something insufferably tedious in the usual process of such a meeting. It would surely be much more rational if conversation instead of dancing made the order of the day."
"Much more rational, my dear Caroline, I dare say, but it would not be near so much like a ball."

—Jane Austen, *Pride and Prejudice*

Casually dressed suburbanites stream into the large, darkened auditorium as a countdown flashes on the three huge projection screens over the stage. Some hold a cup of coffee in one hand and in the other a leaflet warning those who have epilepsy about the strobe effects to come during the performance. The countdown finishes as a rock band takes the stage for the opening song. Thus they begin to worship.

As Sunday school classes dismiss, country folk enter the brightly lit sanctuary, greeting people who have been attending other classes as well as those who have only just arrived. A musician begins a hymn on the piano, and the pitch of the conversations increases. From the pulpit, the lay leader calls the meeting to order: "Who had a birthday this past week?" Someone raises a hand and everyone sings "Happy Birthday." Thus they begin to worship.

In the heart of a city, urban dwellers quietly enter the nave of the church as soft light filters through the stained-glass windows. A few whispers can be heard as the organist plays the prelude, a Bach toccata and fugue. When the organist shifts to the opening measures of a hymn, the congregation stands to sing. Garbed in their vestments, the choir processes down the central nave, followed by the processional cross, acolytes, and ministers. Thus they begin to worship.

Three different congregations, three different settings, three very different approaches to worship. How can we understand all these diverse events as "worship"? Are they essentially the same thing? Each clearly has its appeal: the excitement of the suburban church, the warmth of the rural congregation, the majesty and solemnity of the urban mass. Each has its own distinctive style, its own distinctive character. And to those of us who have visited churches in various settings, there is something recognizable about all these vignettes, something familiar. We have seen them before, or something very similar. We can discern in them patterns of sameness, though what may strike us first is their diversity.

American Christianity, of course, consists of numerous denominational and ethnic traditions, and one might expect significant differences among congregations from different traditions. Ethnicity and denomination, however, are not sufficient to account for all of the diversity in worship, for the congregations I describe above could well belong to the same denomination or ethnic group. Neither can we attribute the differences entirely to social location, though that will certainly be an important influence. These diverse expressions of worship illustrate a cultural repertoire of Christian worship in the twenty-first century that cuts across denomination and social identity.

Diversity in Worship

Diversity in worship marks the church in the twenty-first century, but it is not unique to our time. We will be examining the evolution of worship practices across the wide middle of Protestant congregations in America, but we begin with the Methodists for an example of how a tradition struggles with matters of liturgical identity and difference.

Methodists. In 1784, John Wesley sent the newly formed Methodist Episcopal Church the *Sunday Service*, an abridgment of the English *Book of Common Prayer*, containing fully realized orders for morning and evening prayer, Holy Communion, baptism, and ordinations, along with a lectionary and various pastoral rites and prayers.[1] Adherence to the *Sunday Service*, however, was spotty at best, and one year after John Wesley's death in 1791, Methodists abandoned it. The 1792 *Discipline of the Methodist Episcopal Church* contained only brief prescriptions for the content of "Public Worship":

> *Quest.* What directions shall be given for the establishment of uniformity in public worship amongst us, on the Lord's day?
>
> *Answ.* 1. Let the morning-service consist of singing, prayer, the reading of a chapter out of the Old Testament, and another out of the New, and preaching.
>
> 2. Let the afternoon-service consist of singing, prayer, the reading of one or two chapters out of the bible, and preaching.
>
> 3. Let the evening-service consist of singing prayer, and preaching.
>
> 4. But on the days of administering the Lord's supper, the two chapters in the morning-service may be omitted.
>
> 5. Let the society be met, wherever it is practicable, on the sabbath-day.[2]

Urban preachers followed the directions for public worship, but many frontier preachers did not even follow these simple rules because they

---

1. John Wesley and Methodist Episcopal Church, *John Wesley's Sunday Service of the Methodists in North America*, Quarterly Review Reprint Series (Nashville, TN: Quarterly Review, 1984).

2. *Methodist Episcopal Church, The Doctrines and Discipline of the Methodist Episcopal Church in America* (Philadelphia, PA: Printed by Parry Hall, 1824), 40–41. Cited by William Nash Wade, "A History of Public Worship in the Methodist Episcopal Church and Methodist Episcopal Church, South, from 1784 to 1905" (PhD dissertation, University of Notre Dame 1981), 122.

found them too confining in the missionary context of the American frontier. Frontier preachers held preaching services at any time that they could gather a group of Methodist recruits, and they often treated the Lord's Day as merely another preaching occasion, with even scripture reading optional.[3] By 1824, some Methodist leaders grew concerned about the lack of uniformity in pastoral leadership of Sunday worship across the denomination. That year a committee on the appointment of pastors gave the following report to General Conference:

> In regard to public worship and the administration of the ordinance, it appears there is a great want of uniformity. The reading of the Scriptures, the Lord's Prayer, and the apostolic benediction are frequently omitted; and in the administration of the ordinances [i.e., the sacraments] some use the form in the Discipline, some mutilate it, and others wholly neglect it.[4]

From this description of what is "omitted," we can surmise that the services of these circuit riders may have consisted simply of singing, extemporaneous prayer, and preaching, with preaching taking up the majority of time. This was a pattern of worship born out of the contingencies of frontier evangelism and replicated as seasoned itinerants passed on their practical wisdom to neophyte preachers settling on the frontier. It contained hardly a trace of John Wesley's *Sunday Service*, especially for those preachers who "wholly neglected" the disciplinary form for administering the sacraments.

The issue of "uniformity" was not resolved in 1824, though as the American populations settled into towns over the course of the nineteenth century, Methodists gradually turned away from frontier austerity. Larger congregations in county seat towns began to reintroduce liturgical practices that previous generation of Methodists had abandoned, and this created a different problem in regard to uniformity. At the 1888 General

---

3. Karen B. Westerfield Tucker, *American Methodist Worship* (New York, NY: Oxford University Press, 2001), 9–10.

4. *Journal of General Conference* (1824): 298–99. For a discussion of this, see Wade, "History of Public Worship," 218–22.

Conference of The Methodist Episcopal Church, the bishop offering the Episcopal Address complained on behalf of his fellow bishops:

> In "traveling through the Connection at large" we often experience embarrassment upon discovering that we do not know how to conduct public worship in the congregation. We either sit as spectators, joining in the worship as best we can, or keep before us a written programme, and proceed with grave apprehension lest a blinder be perpetrated. The remedy is a form of public worship which shall be uniform and imperative in its essential features.[5]

We may not have much pity for the bishop, for I suspect that few pastors and worship leaders (now or then) would want to organize their regular weekly worship services for the benefit of bishops' occasional participation. He was speaking for the episcopacy; we might question whether the rank-and-file circuit rider had any concern for the "great want of uniformity" either in 1824 or in 1888. Indeed, when denominational leaders complain about some "abuse" of the practice of worship in an official statement, especially if they forbid a particular practice, this is good evidence that the practice is fairly widespread. Likewise, when denominational leaders strongly encourage a practice, this is good evidence that it is not being done often enough to suit them. Otherwise, why would the leaders feel the need to make such comments?

Note an important difference, however, between the 1824 and 1888 General Conferences. In 1824, the reported concern was for what was being *left out* of public worship: ample reading of scripture from the Old and New Testaments, the Lord's Prayer, and the apostolic benediction. Even the most austere Methodist services, the leaders declared, ought to contain these hallmarks of Christian worship. Sixty years later in 1888, on the other hand, the bishops complained that Methodists were beginning to include *too much*. The 1888 Episcopal Address cited above continues, "Cultivated music and responsive readings are not objectionable;

---

5. Methodist Episcopal Church, General Conference, *Journal of the General Conference of The Methodist Episcopal Church* (New York, NY: The Church, 1888): 56–57. See Wade, "History of Public Worship," 330–42.

but when they consume time needed for general hymns, prayer, and sermon, they become monotonous."[6] By the latter decades of the nineteenth century, as Methodists became established in towns in what was no longer the frontier, the more conservative bishops grew concerned that Methodist worship was becoming so "cultivated" that it had lost its focus on the more humble core practices of singing, preaching, and praying.

Whether the concern was too little tradition or too many liturgical practices, nineteenth-century Methodists clearly exhibited a diversity in worship. The official denominational guidelines made up only a part of the content of worship in Methodist congregations. With so much diversity of practice, it may look as if order and style in Methodist worship were arbitrary, with congregations or pastors doing their own thing without historic norms or patterns.

This conclusion is wrong.

Patterned Diversity: The Character of Worship

As this historical case study demonstrates, Methodists do not have a *single* identifiable form of worship. However, this is not because they lack patterns. As we expand our study to Presbyterians, Baptists, and Congregationalists, we will find that these American denominations, like the Methodists, have *several* identifiable, historical patterns of worship, though most pastors and congregations are not conscious of them as patterns. They are present simply as implicit expectations held by worship leaders and congregations whenever they plan and participate in worship. Congregations have patterns—they just don't realize they do.

This book brings to conscious awareness the implicit patterns in the worship of Protestant congregations in the United States. The metaphor I employ to talk about these patterns is *character*. As for people, so for worship, character indicates distinctive traits, style, and manners of being in the world.

---

6. *Journal of General Conference* (1888): 57.

Within the distinctive individuality of each person, moreover, we can recognize "character types." We may refer to "the character of a father" or "the character of a mother" and know implicitly what that means. We speak of "the character of a leader" or "the character of a soldier." Though every single leader or soldier, father or mother fulfills the role uniquely, we can discern a pattern that draws its shape from the purpose that a leader, soldier, father, or mother must fulfill. In the same way, worship has character because worship has distinctive traits, styles, and patterns. It can have strong character, which lends to participants a sense of its power. Or worship can have a weak character that leads participants to experience it as trivial.

Over my years of teaching, I have read evaluations of worship services in numerous congregations. In all that time, no one has ever complained about an experience of worship being *too* purposeful. I have, on the other hand, received many complaints about worship that felt irrelevant or incoherent. Obviously, no one ever *intends* a worship service to be irrelevant or incoherent. Most of us long for worship that is purposeful and engaging; we desire worship that has strong character. I am counting on this longing for strong character in worship among the readers of my book. While a good bit of what follows will illustrate worship as it takes place in congregations, I am not merely interested in providing descriptions of the character of worship practices and patterns, for description is not enough. Worship can (and almost always does) have character flaws, places where it lacks integrity, where its practices do not match its goals. Wise and faithful worship planners will want to tend to these flaws of character, and this will require more than description; it will require evaluation. Furthermore, if Christian worship is always supremely significant, as I will argue, then worship leaders, planners, and congregations will need to seek more than coherence between practices and goals. Not all goals are of equal value, and this will require another level of evaluation. Strong, coherent character is not enough; we must also strive for *good* character.

In this study, I lay out a set of methodological principles to assist pastors and worship teams in their planning of congregational worship. I hope these principles will equip pastors and leaders with critical tools to help evaluate worship in their congregations so that it can have integrity of character and be more coherent, more compelling, but above all more faithful to the gospel.

Principles for Understanding the Character of Worship

1. All worship follows patterns.

Without identifiable patterns, we would not be able to recognize our actions as worship rather than, say, a business meeting or bridge club. While it is logically possible to conceive of a worship service that does not follow any established pattern, in actual practice congregations do not gather for worship and then begin to figure out what to do, nor do worship planners start with a blank slate. Regular services of worship could not continue for long without some sort of structure that the congregation recognizes, such as the use of the Bible or the time and place for the gathering. Even the classic Quaker meeting, with its "un-programmed" procedures for waiting on the movement of the Holy Spirit, is a highly structured pattern of gathering in silence at a specific time with certain rules for conduct of the meeting.

Years ago, I conducted an unscientific experiment in a campus ministry setting that illustrates this principle. Worship at this campus ministry took place in a multipurpose room with a movable lectern, communion table, and folding chairs set up in semicircular rows. One Sunday morning when I was responsible for leading the worship, I intentionally placed all of the chairs and furniture randomly around the perimeter of the room. As the congregation began to arrive, I informed them I was not going to impose a seating arrangement. Instead, I wanted them to exercise the freedom to sit wherever they wished and to arrange the furniture however they felt led. Gradually, this congregation of students began to move the chairs and furniture into an arrangement for worship that turned out to be a rather sloppy version of our usual arrangement of chairs, with almost exactly the same orientation of the table, lectern, and seating. Without intending to do so (even being discouraged from doing so!), we had conformed to our established pattern of seating.

2. *The patterns of worship work on two levels: the liturgical unit and the macro-pattern.*

The macro-pattern is made up of several liturgical units, usually placed in a standardized order. Liturgical units are blocks of liturgical action that have a particular shape and content.[7] For instance, most congregations have a liturgical unit of reading scripture followed by a sermon:

Scripture Reading(s)

Sermon/Message

Such a concise statement of this simple pattern will be so obvious that it may seem banal. This simple pattern, however, is remarkably durable and flexible, and it expands in a rich variety of ways. In any given congregation, there may be one or several readings of scripture. Usually there will only be one sermon, though in some congregations, perhaps more than one speaker will address the congregation, as occurred recently in my home congregation when the pastor preached a sermon and a layperson gave a "personal testimony."

Typically, this liturgical unit will include several pieces of liturgical action that separate the readings from the sermon. Here is one possible arrangement:

Old Testament Reading

Psalm

Epistle Reading

---

7. I am adapting the concept "liturgical unit" from the Comparative Liturgy school of liturgics. For a good introduction to the comparative method and analysis of liturgical units, see Robert Taft, S.J., "The Structural Analysis of Liturgical Units: An Essay in Methodology," in *Beyond East & West: Problems in Liturgical Understanding* (Washington, DC: The Pastoral Press, 1984), 151–64.

Chapter One

    Children's Message

    Gospel Acclamation/chorus/hymn

    Gospel Reading

    Hymn

    Sermon

Or in a more "contemporary" vein:

    Scripture

    Skit illustrating the reading

    Message

There are congregations that occasionally do not have a sermon. Yet, if there is no sermon, something almost always takes its place, such as a play, a set of musical pieces (e.g., a Christmas or Easter cantata), or extended silence. In other words, the basic pattern remains. Rarely will we find a worship service in which there are no readings or in which the reading of scripture follows preaching, though we do find examples where the reading of scripture is interspersed throughout the sermon.

    As we go on, I will say much more about how liturgical units function, but for now it is important to recognize that liturgical units are components of macro-patterns. The macro-pattern includes the overall structure of a service of worship: how the order begins, how it organizes liturgical units, how it concludes. As stated above, *the macro-pattern is made up of discrete liturgical units, usually placed in a recognizable order.* The two most widely used descriptions of macro-patterns today are "traditional worship" and "contemporary worship." While I will show how these two descriptions are inadequate, they do helpfully convey some important differences among macro-patterns. In the examples above of the scripture-preaching liturgical unit, one could easily identify which would be more at home in a traditional service (Gospel Acclamation/Gospel Reading/Hymn/Sermon) and which would fit a contemporary service (Skit illustrating the reading/Song/Message).

My illustrations, thus far, have been examples of words and actions arranged in a particular sequential order. While sequential order is a feature of the macro-pattern, it is only one feature among many. In fact, for some macro-patterns the actual sequential order of liturgical units is less significant than other factors. These other factors include environment and aesthetics (art, music, architecture), as well as emotions that characterize participation in the service.

Since congregational worship is not an occasional but a regularly repeated practice, once a particular macro-pattern is established it tends to continue without a great deal of change. As a pattern, it functions as a sort of "default mode" that does not require the conscious awareness of those who lead or participate in the worship service.[8] Macro-patterns do evolve, but they tend to do so slowly, unless a strong personality commandeers the worship life of the congregation. More than a few eager worship leaders have learned from a failed attempt at liturgical reform that it is less disruptive to add something (a liturgical unit) to a congregation's order of worship than it is to subtract something or change the macro-pattern fundamentally.

3. A macro-pattern of worship has a telos *(goal) it aims to achieve.*

Historically, patterns of worship arise to address particular concerns about church life, something the church lacks or is doing poorly. At the time of the Reformation in the sixteenth century, Christians in Europe addressed the problems of the church not only by reforming church teaching but first of all by addressing various concerns about worship: preaching, sacraments, use of vernacular language, and so forth. The reformers developed new patterns of worship that embodied these concerns. Not all shifts

---

8. I have in mind here sociologist Pierre Bourdieu's concept of *habitus*. He defines habitus as "systems of durable, transposable dispositions, structured structures predisposed to function as structuring structures, that is, as principles which generate and organize practices and representations that can be objectively adapted to their outcomes without presupposing a conscious aiming at ends or an express mastery of the operation necessary in order to attain them." A significant point in this difficult definition is that a habitus does not require conscious awareness of individuals for it to do what it does. See *The Logic of Practice,* trans. Richard Nice (Stanford, CA: Stanford University Press, 1990), 53.

in patterns of worship are as cataclysmic as those that occurred in the sixteenth century, but the principle still applies. The meteoric rise of the Seeker church with its rejection of traditional forms of worship is a good example of this principle. The *telos* of the Seeker church is to reach out to the "unchurched." The problem the Seeker church addresses is that the unchurched are not attracted to "traditional" churches.

Worship, of course, always has the primary goal of serving God. As the Catholic Church's *Constitution on the Sacred Liturgy* declares, worship aims for "the sanctification of humanity in Christ and the glorification of God."[9] I take this to be utterly uncontroversial. But worship also serves a variety of other important, if secondary, purposes: reaching the unchurched, the need for human community, formation of group identity, help facing the struggles of life, and education in Christian virtue, to name a few.[10] Each of the various patterns of worship I will describe has a distinctive *telos* that motivates its particular approach to serving God and sanctifying humanity.

4. A macro-pattern has a particular ethos, a "character," or in some cases we might say "style," that fits with its particular telos.

In addition to addressing a particular problem in the church, the distinctive *telos* of a pattern of worship will be connected to a congregation's predominant concept of God, and a congregation will expect the conduct of worship that fits this concept. In his study *Congregations in America*, sociologist Mark Chaves cites a study by Lynn Smith Lovin and William Douglass to make this point:

---

9. *The Constitution on the Sacred Liturgy* 10 (1963), http://www.vatican.va/archive/hist_councils/ii_vatican_council/documents/vat-ii_const_19631204_sacrosanctum-concilium_en.html, accessed July 5, 2011.

10. As liturgical scholar Lester Ruth has shown, all orders of worship intend to mediate the presence of God, but some congregations will emphasize the transcendence of God expressed though a "cosmic story," while other congregations will emphasize God's immanence through the telling of "personal stories." Ruth goes on to show how the worship in various congregations also mediates the presence of God primarily through music, through reading and preaching the Word, or through the Lord's Supper. See "A Rose by Any Other Name," in *The Conviction of Things Not Seen: Worship and Ministry in the 21st Century*, ed. Todd E. Johnson (Grand Rapids, MI: Brazos, 2002), 47ff.

> [Lovin and Douglass] accurately predict the ritual content of worship in two congregations solely from information about how congregants view themselves and God. In a congregation in which individuals consider God to be more supremely good, active, and powerful, worship was predicted to be informal and personal, with congregants "applauding" and "amusing" God while God attempts to "satisfy" congregants. In a congregation of individuals who view God in a less active and powerful way, congregants are predicted to "speak to" and "admire" God rather than "applaud" or "amuse" the deity, and the deity is expected to "counsel" and "reassure" rather than "satisfy" or "like" the congregants. The remarkable thing about these predictions is that *they are made by a computer algorithm* solely on the basis of a social-psychological theory holding that individuals' ideas about themselves and others shape interpersonal interactions because people act to keep those ideas intact.[11]

In other words, if a congregation primarily understands God as the creator and ruler of the universe, they will probably desire worship to conform to that understanding by employing more elevated language and actions. If a congregation thinks of God primarily as a close friend, they will expect more personal, colloquial language and actions. This is what I mean by the particular *ethos* or character of worship. We might also think of this as "style," though that word may sound a little trivial. There is nothing trivial about the *ethos* of worship, since it directly connects to a congregation's deep theology.

The *ethos* of worship both expresses and *shapes* the ways Christians understand God, since worship is a primary way we learn about God. It is not the only way we learn about God, however. We learn about God from all sorts of interactions in the world, including from family and friends, various social institutions, television, and the music we enjoy. If our engagement in Christian worship is limited to a couple of hours each week, it is not likely to have a very strong role in shaping our understanding of God. Nevertheless, if Chaves is right that we seek worship that confirms what we already know (or think we know) about God, this raises a host of issues for anyone who thinks, as I do, that the *telos* of Christian worship is

---

11. Mark Chaves, *Congregations in America* (Cambridge, MA: Harvard University Press, 2004), 140.

to form a congregation to be the body of Christ in the world. A great deal is at stake in the *ethos* of worship; content and style are not trivial.

Another way to understand the coherence of the *telos* and *ethos* of worship patterns is to think of them as analogous to the rules of games. It is common these days for theologians to talk about systems of religious belief as language games. Church doctrines, similar to the rules of games, are not founded on anything other than their own system of procedure. For example, there is no independent, universal reason an infield fly is an "out" in baseball. Such a rule only makes sense within the game of baseball itself. It relates to all the other rules that make baseball a game distinct from soccer. There is no infield fly rule in soccer—it would not make sense. Similarly, there is no independent, universal reason any human community would hold the Bible as scripture or preach or sing hymns or baptize or break bread in the name of Jesus *apart from* the belief system of Christianity. We learn these rules by participating in churches that practice and teach them.

We could say that the final *telos* of team sports such as baseball, basketball, and football is to outscore the other team through the fair use of athletic ability and strategy. All three of the sports I have mentioned require team cooperation and all use balls of some sort. But that would not tell us much about any particular sport, really. In baseball, winning is accomplished by scoring runs. In basketball, the players score baskets; and in football, touchdowns and field goals. Each of these sports is played on very different sorts of "fields," and each kind of team has different numbers of players with different roles. The uniforms are quite different—caps, helmets, no cap at all, cleats or rubber-soled shoes, pads, gloves, and so on. And as I noted already, each has a distinct set of rules that only makes sense within the structure of the particular game. They share the ultimate *telos* of winning but through runs, baskets, or touchdowns and by very different styles and procedures of play. In much the same way, all the patterns of worship I describe may share the ultimate *telos* of glorifying God and sanctifying humanity, but this does not tell us much about them. Each pattern has a distinctive set of rules of procedure, and even dress and architecture, for accomplishing its particular *telos*.

The coherence of *telos* and *ethos* in worship functions not only at the macro-level; the liturgical units that make up the macro-pattern also participate in the overall *telos* and *ethos*. As an organizing system, the macro-pattern will attract units of liturgical material that fit its system—its *telos* and *ethos*. When the liturgical units fit the macro-pattern, the order of service will be (and, importantly, will "feel") coherent. If, however, a specific liturgical unit does not work well within a macro-pattern, the liturgical unit will tend to subvert the *telos*. Unfortunately, as I will demonstrate, an incompatible liturgical unit can find its way into an order of worship. When it does, it not only subverts the *telos*, it clashes with the overall *ethos*; it will be a "character flaw." I will say more about this in the next chapter.

> **In summary, here are the first four principles of method for understanding the character of worship:**
>
> 1. All worship follows patterns.
>
> 2. The patterns of worship work on two levels: the liturgical unit and the macro-pattern. The macro-pattern is made up of several liturgical units, usually placed in a standardized order.
>
> 3. A macro-pattern of worship has a *telos* (goal) it aims to achieve.
>
> 4. Each macro-pattern has a particular *ethos* (character or style) that fits with its particular *telos*.

We return to our overarching metaphor: character. The distinctive character of worship for each congregation has identifiable character types, just as (to mix my metaphors) the character of baseball is different from the character of soccer. It is essential for us to understand worship character types in order to get a handle on character flaws.

To move beyond generalities, in the next chapter I will provide an overview of six character types of worship that we find in Protestant worship in the United States.

CHAPTER TWO

Six Character Types of Protestant Worship

[T]he performers of rituals do not specify all the acts and utterances constituting their own performances. They follow, more or less punctiliously, orders established or taken to have been established, by others.

—Roy Rappaport, *Ritual and Religion in the Making of Humanity*[1]

The principles I have described thus far address three important features of worship: pattern, *telos*, and *ethos*. A **pattern** is the order of worship, both the overall configuration of a service (the macro-pattern) and the order of particular blocks of liturgical material (liturgical units). ***Telos*** is the goal that a pattern seeks to achieve, the "end" to which it aims, such as reaching seekers or forming the saints. ***Ethos*** is the character of the pattern (such as intimacy or enthusiasm), the identifying qualities or style of a pattern that, ideally, fit the *telos*. The character of worship is unique to each congregation's local tradition of worship, but it also exhibits something like "character types," stereotypical macro-patterns of *telos/ethos* that can be found across a wide range of congregations. According to principle two, an order of worship is a macro-pattern made up of liturgical units, and this principle also applies to the character types of worship. Liturgical character types have dististinctive macro-patterns and liturgical units.

The prevailing way to categorize liturgical character types is to label them "traditional worship" and "contemporary worship."[2] These descriptions are useful to a point, and even I employed them for illustrative

---

1. Roy Rappaport, *Ritual and Religion in the Making of Humanity* (Cambridge, UK: Cambridge University Press, 1999), 32.

2. This classification of worship types into "Traditional" and "Contemporary" is so prevalent it was accepted without any qualification by the United Methodist *Call to Action Report (2010)*, http://www.umc.org/who-we-are/call-to-action, accessed September 6, 2018.

purpose in chapter 1. The problem with the "traditional worship/contemporary worship" dichotomy is that it does not distinguish enough variety in historical development or current practice.[3] Therefore, I want to offer an observation that expands on the principles I have given so far:

Observation A: Six dominant character types exist in Protestant worship in the United States.

I state this as an observation rather than as a principle because it does not have the universal applicability of the principles I have thus far enumerated. Rather than being universal, these six character types arise within the particular history of American churches over the past two centuries.[4] They are: the Revival Meeting, Sunday School Worship, Aesthetic Worship, Pentecostal Worship, the Prayer Meeting, and Catholic Liturgical Renewal.[5] These patterns have historic roots in the nineteenth and early twentieth centuries, but each of them continues in the present in slightly altered forms. The current form of the Revival is the Seeker Service. Sunday School Worship is the antecedent to the Creative Worship movement that began in the 1960s. Pentecostalism spawned the Praise Service, while the Aesthetic Worship movement is largely what today we would call Traditional Worship. The intimacy of the Prayer Meeting underlies the current House Church/Small Group pattern. The Catholic Liturgical Renewal pattern is often called Word and Table.

In what follows, I give an overview of these six character types of worship.

---

3. Robb Redman identifies four important "New Ways to Worship": The Seeker Service, The Praise and Worship Movement, the Contemporary Worship Music Industry, and the Liturgical Renewal Movement. See *The Great Worship Awakening: Singing a New Song in the Postmodern Church* (San Francisco, CA: Jossey-Bass, 2002), 3–92. James F. White, to whom I am greatly indebted, identifies at least nine patterns of Protestant worship that continue to show influence. See *Protestant Worship: Traditions in Transition* (Louisville, KY: Westminster John Knox, 1989).

4. With the growth of immigrant populations of Christians in the United States, other patterns may be entering into the liturgical repertoire of American congregations.

5. Due both to missionary activity and to modern communication technology, these patterns are also influential throughout the world, though our focus in this study will be on congregations in the United States.

i. The Revival

The Revival will be familiar particularly to older Protestants in the southern United States. When many of us think of "old-fashioned" church, this is what comes to mind. However, the Revival is not really all that old. While there have been several sorts of revivals in the history of the church, the Revival pattern I describe here, and which continues to exert influence on twenty-first-century American churches, arose in the early nineteenth century during the Second Great Awakening. Briefly, the pattern of the revival is:

Preliminaries. This included welcoming of the "audience," hymn singing, perhaps a testimony or two of someone who has experienced conversion, introductions of the song leader and evangelist, and so forth. (Some southern American church buildings may still have three big throne-like chairs on the chancel stage. I grew up in a church that had these three chairs, and as a child I thought they represented the Trinity—the Father, Son, and Holy Spirit! This is, incidentally, an illustration of a tendency we often see among Christian worshipers: we tend to make up theological explanations for the things we do in worship if we do not know the original meaning and purpose. These three chairs, however, did not originally represent the Holy Trinity—nor did anyone ever tell me they did, for that matter. Rather, a Revival needed three chairs for the leaders of the service: the pastor, the song leader, and the visiting evangelist.[6])

The preliminaries were followed by:

The message. Note "message" rather than "sermon." This term was significant because it established a relationship between the preacher, who delivered the message, and the congregation (conceived primarily as an audience), which received it. In a standard Revival, the message was not given by the pastor but by the visiting evangelist, who would be an "expert" in delivering messages that were emotionally effective. A Revival message contained stories of persons who had experienced a conversion to

---

6. I thank my former, much beloved professor, James White, for setting me straight on this!

Christ or whose faith had become deepened through an encounter with Christ (possibly through hearing the visiting evangelist!).

After the message came:

The altar call. The evangelist concluded the message with a strong invitation for people to make a decision or respond by giving their hearts to Christ (to use the terminology of Revivals) or by rededicating themselves to Christ if they had lost their first love for God or had "backslidden" in their commitments. While the congregation sang an emotionally moving song, the evangelist continued to ask (and often to beg or to threaten!) people to respond. The new converts or backsliders came forward to kneel at the front of the chancel stage or at the communion rail, and to give their hearts to Christ.

As I said, this should sound familiar to many readers. Anyone who ever watched a Billy Graham crusade on television would be familiar with this pattern. I grew up in a small town in Tennessee in the 1960s, and my little United Methodist church still had yearly Revivals. As a young man, I preached a few myself.

The *telos* or goal of the Revival service was conversion, to bring people into a saving relationship with God. Because this required rhetorical skill, the *ethos* or character of the Revival worship was emotional effectiveness and theatricality through efficient technique. That's why Revivals employed experts—the visiting song leader and the evangelist who led the service. The idea of a Revival service is to set a mood that will move people to give their hearts to Jesus Christ. Revivals employ experts to do this as effectively as possible.

The modern form of the Revival is the Seeker Service, which also uses technological excellence with an emphasis on the "expert" leader to move people to make a response to Christ. "Seekers" are those unchurched folk who are curious enough about Christianity to try it out but who are not particularly attracted to church. A Seeker Service does not look much like traditional church, since unchurched folk (especially of the baby boomer demographic) are not drawn to traditional church architecture, language, and symbols. Rather, Seeker Services use projection screens, stage bands with amplified instruments, popular music styles, professional-looking singers and musicians, skits, and very basic, personally engaging preaching. Most Seeker Services, however, tend to soft-pedal the "altar call," since seekers tend not to like such hard-sell tactics. Rather than concluding with an invitation to "Give your heart to Jesus," Seeker Services end with an invitation to come again next week or to check out at the visitor kiosk what the church has to offer. Nevertheless, the basic pattern is still that of the Revival: preliminaries, message, open-ended invitation to learn more.

ii. The Sunday School

About the same time that the Revival movement was gathering steam in the early nineteenth century, the Sunday School movement was also capturing the attention of American Protestants. The first Sunday Schools focused on the education of children, and the setting was conceived as a classroom. By the middle of the nineteenth century, in addition to the classroom experience, the Sunday School also had plenary assemblies that included acts of worship. The pattern of the Sunday School Worship assembly could be as loose as the preliminaries of the Revival, but it almost always contained these elements:

Opening exercises. This included the singing of songs and choruses that taught lessons, such as "Jesus Loves Me," often done as a march or with hand movements. Typically, there would be a devotional reading from a book, a group recitation of a memory exercise, or even a responsive reading of a scripture lesson or psalm.

Theme of the day. The opening exercises focused on a theme, such as family, abstinence from alcohol, or patriotism.

Announcements. The Sunday School was a venue for informing children of upcoming events. An important part of announcements was welcoming newcomers, taking attendance, and (at least once a year) awarding attendance pins.

Collection for mission fund. From the beginning, the Sunday School stressed the importance of foreign and domestic mission work.

Dismissal and benediction. Children were dismissed to their classes, or if the Sunday School took place in the morning and the classes came first, they went to congregational worship.

These were standard elements of a Sunday School assembly. The sequential order of the elements was less significant than the overall order for a Revival, but the macro-pattern was clear in its central concern. The *telos* of Sunday School Worship was the formation of Christian character, or we might even say, the Christian citizen, for there was a strong element of civic duty in a great deal of early Sunday School programming. Whereas the Revival sought conversion through emotional effects, the Sunday School sought conversion of the individual by teaching lessons and practicing exercises that enlightened children in the ways of faith and civic duty.

The *ethos* of Sunday School Worship was didactic, that is, educational, and *very* participatory. If the Revival was aimed at the gut to move people, the Sunday School aimed at the mind and body to educate them. Revivals got people to feel. Sunday Schools got children (and eventually adults) to think and do. Members of a Sunday School Assembly were less an audience than a team. The children might process around the room singing a song, such as "Onward Christian Soldiers," after which everyone would join in a responsive reading or recite the Apostles' Creed as a memory exercise. Significantly, the Sunday School was not led by professional experts but by local laypersons. The superintendent (a very important role) and the teachers came from the congregation. Even if by the early twentieth century some larger congregations had professional ministers of education, the focus was still on the laity and lay leadership. Furthermore, Sunday School assemblies tended to be very wordy and sometimes a little trivial. This was probably directly connected to the fact that Sunday Schools began as education for children rather than adults.

The modern equivalent is what I call Creative Worship.[7] This is a style of worship that many seminaries promoted in the 1970s and 1980s. Creative Worship is theme-oriented (drawing on the Sunday School pattern of the "theme of the day"), and it is *very* wordy, with printed, modern

---

7. The phrase "Creative Worship" appeared in the titles of several books and articles on worship in the 1970s.

prayers of confession, responsive readings, or calls to worship. The whole concept of "worship resources" (i.e., ad hoc liturgical materials) originates in the Sunday School tradition. To illustrate the didactic quality of Creative Worship, a typical call to worship might be: Leader: "Good morning"; Response: "Good morning"; Leader: "Why are we here?" Response: "We are here to worship our God."

iii. Aesthetic Worship

As the frontier era of American history drew to a close, many Protestant church leaders became concerned about matters of decorum and art in worship environments. They constructed church buildings that drew upon Gothic Revival forms, and they began to publish orders of worship that more or less followed the general outline and terminology of the Order for Morning Prayer adapted from Anglican prayer books. I call this pattern Aesthetic Worship.[8] A chief identifier of Aesthetic Worship was the use of more formal-sounding words such as "Introit" and "Doxology," especially when these were used by churches with historically less-formal worship. Here is an example of Aesthetic Worship order:

> *Organ Prelude.* This is a piece of classical music.
> *Processional Hymn.* The choir, in choir robes, process down a central aisle to a loft in the chancel.
> *Introit or Call to Worship.* This contains printed responses for the congregation.
> *Prayer of Confession.* The congregation reads this prayer in unison.
> *Anthem.* The choir performs.
> *Prayer.* The minister offers the pastoral prayer.
> *Scripture Reading.* The lesson for the sermon.
> *Doxology.* The congregation sings, "Praise God from whom all blessings flow. . . ."
> *Confession of Faith.* The congregation reads in unison a historic creed or modern affirmation of faith.
> *Gloria Patri.* This concludes the recitation of the confession of faith.

---

8. I derive the term from White, who describes the "aestheticism" of this period in American worship. See White, *Protestant Worship*, 165–66.

Offertory. Ushers take up the collection and present it at the altar.
Hymn. This concludes the first half of the service and transitions to the sermon.
Sermon. Note the use of "sermon" rather than "message."
Benediction. Spoken by the pastor, it can be a closing prayer rather than a blessing.
Recessional Hymn. The choir processes out of the choir loft.
Organ Postlude. This is another piece of classical organ music.[9]

Notice how much more detailed and scripted this order of worship is compared with previous examples. Envision this order of worship being used in a Gothic Revival church building. The order of worship told only part of the story. From its early development, the *telos* of Aesthetic Worship was to shape worshipers into more spiritually sensitive persons who are more culturally sophisticated. It did this by using fine art (rather than popular, folk art) and more formal language. Thus, the *ethos* of Aesthetic Worship was a particular form of aestheticism: the use of high art and language drawn primarily from the European tradition. Here we have robed choirs, robed clergy, formal-sounding prayers, and restrained emotion. In this pattern, a key for Protestants was the presence of a "sermon," rather than a "message," separated from the scripture reading by several liturgical sub-units. Another marker was the "offertory" located among the liturgical units that separated the reading of scripture from the sermon. This offertory (as opposed to a collection) entered into Protestant worship once Protestants acquired Gothic-style altars to replace their humble communion tables.

Let me be clear: by using the label "aesthetic" I am not categorically speaking of art in worship, nor am I suggesting that only the Aesthetic Worship pattern does or ought to pay attention to art. Yet I do suggest that the aesthetics that characterized this pattern were a particularly narrow understanding of art as a signal of class—that is, high art and architecture in the European tradition, especially in the Medieval and Baroque eras.

---

9. This order, with only slight modification, comes from Von Ogden Vogt, *Art and Religion* (New Haven, CT: Yale University Press, 1921), 254. Vogt was an important voice in the aesthetic worship movement.

By the middle of the twentieth century, Aesthetic Worship was the dominant model for middle-of-the road Protestants in urban and county-seat congregations all across the United States. The use of more formal liturgical terminology, European-style hymnody, and a fine art aesthetic is roughly what people today mean with they talk about Traditional Worship. Ironically, though, the "tradition" of this pattern is only a century old.

iv. Pentecostal Worship

Pentecostalism took its classic form in the early twentieth century, and it continues to be a growing force in world Christianity.[10] This form of Christianity gave rise to worship that is especially participatory, with vigorous singing of songs that are very rhythmic to facilitate bodily movements. The roots of Pentecostal Worship were in African American congregations that brought to Christianity an African awareness of the mind-spirit connection. Other precursors included the frontier Camp Meeting, with its various exercises such as being slain in the spirit, running, dancing, barking, and so forth. Pentecostal Worship made a strong connection between spiritual ecstasy and the body. In a sense, it shared this focus on the body with Sunday School Worship. However, Pentecostal Worship was much more expressive and much less regimented.

Central to early Pentecostalism was the belief that worship, as all of life, must be open to the movement of the Holy Spirit, and therefore Pentecostals generally resisted the idea of fixed order. Therefore, improvisation was important for Pentecostal Worship, but it did not mean that it was utterly unpredictable. Like the musical improvisations of a jazz ensemble, Pentecostal Worship was freedom within certain established conventions.

The order of a standard Pentecostal service has not changed much since the early twentieth century and follows roughly this pattern:

Praise and Worship. Pentecostal services entail lots of singing, most of it praise songs. Singing almost always involves the congregation, even if it is led by a choir, a band, or a single vocalist. Moreover, singing usually

---

10. Philip Jenkins, *The Next Christendom: The Coming of Global Christianity* (Oxford, UK: Oxford University Press, 2002), 7–8.

continues with several songs in sequence without interruption until this portion of the service comes to an end.

Prayer and Prophecy. As the singing subsides, the congregation engages in prayer. Even if (as is usually the case) the pastor or another leader prays aloud, the congregation will engage in simultaneous prayer with lifted hands, kneeling, weeping, looking up to heaven, or other bodily gestures. Once praying subsides, someone in the congregation may offer a "prophetic word" or extemporaneous message to the congregation prompted by the Holy Spirit.

Message. The preacher addresses the congregation extemporaneously (meaning led by the Holy Spirit) with the congregation participating by calling out "Amen." Congregational responses increase and begin to involve more expressive body gestures as the message builds in tempo to its conclusion, which flows seamlessly into the last part of the service.

Altar Call. The altar call is very open in Pentecostal Worship. People come forward for all sorts of concerns, ranging from the need for conversion to requests for intercessory prayer.

Superficially, the order of Pentecostal Worship looks like a Revival service. Yet there are significant differences. First of all, while revivalism treats the congregation as an audience with relatively little required of them in terms of participation until the altar call, Pentecostal Worship requires full congregational interaction from the beginning. Second, whereas revivalism focuses on conversion, Pentecostalism pushes beyond this to what is typically called "baptism in the Holy Spirit," a concept I will discuss in a later chapter.

The *telos* of Pentecostal Worship is spiritual union with God, with strong feelings of emotional elation and oneness. The focus is on an intensity of the believer's relationship with God, and a dominant mode of expressing this in music is praise. The *ethos* of Pentecostal Worship is embodied ecstasy, the physical experience of giving oneself over to the Holy Spirit, "lost in wonder, love and praise," to quote a Charles Wesley hymn. Indeed, the holiness tradition in Methodism is one of the sources of contemporary Pentecostalism.

Praise Worship is the more recent, softer version of Pentecostal Worship. Superficially, it is similar to the Seeker Service and both often get lumped together under the label Contemporary Worship due to the similarity of musical style. However, on close examination there is significant difference. For example, Seeker Services do not typically require much singing. Praise Worship, on the other hand, encourages people to raise their hands and sing vigorously, requiring a more exuberant ritual participation. For seekers or for those who are new to the faith, Praise Worship can be a little overwhelming.

v. The Prayer Meeting

The Prayer Meeting was an important feature of Protestant life in the nineteenth century. Daily prayer was a regular part of the family life of many Anglo-American Christian families, with parents leading children in evening "devotions" that included scripture readings, singing of simple hymns by heart, and extemporaneous prayers that included confessions, thanksgivings, and requests for blessings of the coming day. The domestic aspect of such meetings carried over into other regular gatherings for prayer within congregations. The African American Christian prayer meetings had a very different origin and intensity. In a secret "hush harbor" or "brush arbor" away from and outside the control of plantation owners, slaves blended traditional African worship practices of singing, dance, and group interaction with Christian scripture. In both hush harbors and in meetings of white Christians, a preacher might offer a reflection on scripture or a sermon. However, group interaction and prayer, not preaching, was the central purpose of these meetings.

A typical Prayer Meeting in the early nineteenth century had this shape:

Gathering. Informal greetings were shared among participants.

Singing one or several songs (hymns or spirituals). The songs were selected for the devotional content and ease of singing, that is, their appeal to popular religion rather than their doctrinal content.

Scripture lesson. The lessons were typically brief.

Testimonies and/or preaching. The pastor or a lay leader often would begin testimonies with some reflections on the readings from scripture. However, the primary focus of this was to prompt testimonies and other responses from other participants. These testimonies included personal stories of God's goodness to the individual but often contained elements of confession of sin and repentance, as well as requests for prayer.

Extemporaneous prayer. Prayer was offered by the leader of the service, but others were encouraged to voice prayer spontaneously. Actual leadership would circulate among participants.

Concluding songs. Closing hymns or spirituals were sung, typically from memory.

Prayer Meetings were immensely popular occasions of intense personal sharing, both for "seasoned" Christians and for recently converted believers who appreciated the opportunity to share their enthusiasm for their newfound faith. The *telos* of the Prayer Meeting was democratic equality before God. Closeness with God corresponded to intimacy with fellow believers in a community of mutual support. Testimonies shared at Prayer Meetings were personal stories of faith, victory over temptation, feelings of love for God and neighbor, and palpable accounts of the power of God at work in the lives of individuals. These testimonies provided an intense group experience. The *ethos* of the Prayer Meeting was psychological openness through interpersonal intimacy, including the sharing of potentially embarrassing aspects of personal life in a communal setting. Sharing of personal information in a communal worship service is the novel contribution of the Prayer Meeting to Protestant worship.[11]

While the popularity of the Prayer Meeting dwindled in the late nineteenth century, in the second half of the twentieth century we find the concept resurfacing in retreat settings, small group settings, and in the house church movement. In many smaller Protestant congregations, we

---

11. The Methodist Love Feast of the eighteenth and nineteenth centuries drew upon the personal sharing of prayer meetings; indeed, the Love Feast was, in many respects, an expanded form of prayer meeting.

see remnants of the testimony period in the liturgical unit "Sharing of Joys and Concerns."

vi. Catholic Liturgical Renewal

The sixth pattern, Catholic Liturgical Renewal, has antecedents in the Oxford and Cambridge movements in England during the nineteenth century but begins to take shape in the early twentieth century. It was fueled by the discovery of several important early Christian liturgical texts, such as the so-called *Apostolic Tradition of Hippolytus* (ca. 230–400, though the date is hotly contested), which prompted church historians and liturgical scholars to re-examine many of the other known liturgical texts from the early church. The Catholic Liturgical Renewal movement wanted to reclaim the ancient shape of Christian liturgy,[12] which had an order of Word and Table for Sunday worship. Protestants, of course, had always included preaching in worship, but by the last third of the twentieth century, there was a growing awareness that the Lord's Supper had been a regular and essential part of Christian worship in the early history of the church. Consequently, in the last quarter of the twentieth century, when many of the mainline Protestant churches revised their liturgies and hymnals, the new books emphasized the Lord's Supper, with Word and Table becoming the standard order for Sunday worship.

The Word and Table pattern in bare outline is, obviously:

Word
Table

But this can be further delineated:

WORD

Gathering of the people. The gathering concludes with an opening prayer.

Readings from the Old and New Testaments. Between the readings, this unit includes a psalm, which functions as a hymn.

---

12. Perhaps the most influential book for Protestants was Gregory Dix's *The Shape of the Liturgy*, first published in 1945 but still in print (New York, NY: Continuum, 2007).

Preaching. The word of God read is followed immediately by the sermon, or the word proclaimed.

Prayers of the congregation. The congregation offers intercessions for the world.

Kiss of peace. The congregation kisses one another to seal their spiritual unity as brothers and sisters of Christ. Note, this is *not* a friendship ritual but a family ritual.

TABLE

Offertory. The Table part of the order begins with the offertory, which is, first of all, the bringing up of the elements for the Lord's Supper along with the collection of resources (money, etc.) for the charitable work of the church.

The Great Thanksgiving/Eucharistic Prayer. This is the prayer for offering the Lord's Supper, which has an ancient structure going back to at least the fourth century. The prayer ends with a trinitarian doxology and the congregational "Amen."

Communion of the congregation. All of the faithful partake of both bread and wine.

Dismissal. The assembly is dismissed to go out into the world to live as Christian disciples. Communion is taken to those unwillingly absent.

In this order the Catholic Liturgical Renewal movement saw an organic wholeness of life and worship that transcended the divisions of the Reformation as well as the division of the church, West and East. The *telos* of the Word and Table pattern is to unite the worshiping congregation with the historic and cosmic body of Christ so that the congregation may serve as Christ in the world, for the salvation of the world. The use of historical forms that go back to the earliest days of the church expresses this unity. The *ethos* is what I call "universal" or "catholic." It tends to suppress individualism and idiosyncratic styles, both of particular congregations and individual pastoral leaders, to join worshipers into the great praise of the universal church, using patterns of worship and prayer that are consistent over the broad course of the church's history.

As I noted above, the Word and Table pattern is what we find in liturgical books in most mainline Protestant churches in the West. Moreover, this order is broadly similar among all of the historic Christian churches around the world—Catholic, Orthodox, and Protestant. To be clear, I am only referring to the orders in the *official* liturgical books of Protestant denominations. Few mainline Protestant congregations in the US are obligated to follow the official orders in their liturgical books. Among United Methodists, for example, denominationally approved orders of worship often are used piecemeal or even ignored.

These, then, are the six dominant character types of worship among Protestants in the US today: Revival, Sunday School, Aesthetic Worship, Pentecostal Worship, Prayer Meeting, and Catholic Liturgical Renewal. There are other patterns that may influence congregations—patterns that come from various ethnic groups or patterns that arise in geographic localities but have not spread widely. Other character types, such as Quaker worship, may have a long historical pedigree but are not particularly influential in the broad middle of American churches. Without denying the existence and influence of numerous additional macro-patterns, I suggest that the six I describe are the predominant influences on Christian worship in the United States.

19th to early 20th-century type	*Telos*	*Ethos*	Present form
Revival Meeting	Conversion	Emotionally effective/Technologically efficient/Theatrical	Seeker Service
Sunday School Worship	Christian character/citizenship	Didactic	Creative Worship
Pentecostal Worship	Spiritual union	Embodied/Ecstatic/Enthusiastic	Praise Worship
Aesthetic Worship	Sophisticated spirituality	High Art Aesthetic	Traditional Worship
Prayer Meeting	Equality before God	Personally Intimate	Share Group/House Church
Catholic Liturgical Renewal	Participation in Christ	Catholic	Word and Table

Each of these character types of worship has a distinctive, identifiable *telos* and *ethos*. Furthermore, following principle two above, each character type is a macro-pattern made up of liturgical units of worship that contribute to the *telos* and *ethos* of the macro-pattern of which they are a part. Indeed, I suggest the character types (as a macro-pattern) provide the essential character for the liturgical units that constitute it. Nevertheless, this is complicated by the following principle that I now add to our list:

Principle 5. Liturgical units are portable blocks of liturgical action.

Since a liturgical unit in an order of worship is a relatively discrete block of liturgical action, it can break free from the macro-pattern in which it originates. Even so (continuing the genetic metaphor) a liturgical unit will continue to carry much of the DNA of its original macro-pattern—its *telos* and *ethos*—even though it may also undergo mutations. The example of the "offering" of money demonstrates this principle. Historically, the collection of money in worship originated in the early church as part of a general offering that primarily entailed the presentation of bread and wine for the Lord's Supper. During the Reformation, when many Protestant churches ceased a weekly practice of the Eucharist, the collection of money might still follow the sermon, but the offertory no longer included the presentation of bread and wine for the Eucharist. In the nineteenth-century Revival pattern, the preaching came late in the service and was followed immediately by the altar call, which concluded the order. The money ritual moved into the preliminaries part of the service and was called a "collection," since it no longer had any perceived association with the offertory of the Eucharist. By the early twentieth century, however, under the influence of the Aesthetic Worship pattern, the money collection was renamed "offering" and became one of the most highly ritualized moments in the majority of Protestant services. In short, even though the money ritual went through various permutations, it nevertheless kept some of its original DNA of being a ritually significant offering to God, and this trait eventually re-emerged in the twentieth century.

The portability of liturgical units gives rise to a second observation:

Observation B: Typically, patterns of *telos/ethos* become conflated in contemporary practice.

This is an observation and not a principle because, as I will later show, there is nothing that compels patterns to be conflated. However, given the fact that most Protestant churches are not required to follow a fixed order of worship, the resources pastors and leaders use for preparing orders of worship tend to be ad hoc. Resources include not only denominational books but also patterns and liturgical materials that leaders bring in from other congregations (often from various denominations or traditions). They also may come from varieties of unofficial resources in the form of books, articles, or online materials. All worship employs patterns (principle one), yet pastors and worship leaders will rarely be able to develop patterns entirely from whole cloth. The patterns almost always come from somewhere other than the creative imagination of leaders. I suggest that the six patterns described above function as the dominant available paradigms, *though they are not often recognized as paradigms, either by congregations or worship leaders*. For that matter, they are not often recognized by publishers of liturgical resources. Rather, the liturgical units that comprise the six paradigms *all together constitute an undifferentiated repertoire of available liturgical units for Protestant worship*. As I will demonstrate, worship planners and congregations construct orders of worship (usually over the course of several years or even decades) from this repertoire of liturgical units but without awareness of the paradigms that originally grounded the liturgical units. For example, a congregation might begin worship with this series of units in this order:

Organ Prelude. A classical organ piece.

Choral Introit. A choral setting of a psalm verse.

Welcome. The pastor welcomes the congregation and acknowledges visitors.

Friendship Ritual. The pastor tells people to share the peace of Christ, though almost everyone in the congregation actually shakes hands with exchanges of "Good morning," "Good to see you," rather than making a reference to Christ's peace.

Call to Worship. The pastor calls the congregation back to order and asks them to read the responses from the bulletin:

> Pastor: We come from many places to gather here and offer our praise to God.
> Congregation: We come from homes, from work, from school, from other places of distraction. We come to focus on God.
> Pastor: Let us turn our hearts and minds to God our maker.
> Congregation: Amen! God is with us!

Songs of Praise and Worship. Two praise hymns—one a contemporary praise song, the other a hymn of praise from the hymnal—are projected on a screen.

An order like this does not fit a single paradigm. Rather, it contains liturgical units that originate in four different historic patterns. The organ prelude and choral introit come from the Aesthetic Worship model. The welcome and friendship ritual come from the Sunday School model. The pastor's direction to share the "peace of Christ" comes from the Liturgical Renewal model. The call to worship comes from Sunday School/Creative Worship model. The singing of two praise hymns (in a row) is adapted from the opening praise singing of the Pentecostal model.

If a congregation were to use such an order for several years, to them it probably would seem to be an acceptable way to begin worship, since it would be familiar. Nevertheless, while an order that conflates several historic macro-patterns may become the status quo for a congregation, I want to offer one more methodological principle:

Principle 6. *The telos/ethos of various patterns are not interchangeable with each other and tend to clash when combined.*

In our example, the *ethos* of the prelude and choral introit is formal, classical art. The informal welcome and friendship rite are casual, warm, and interactive. The call to worship is heavily didactic and provocative, possibly raising some discomfort as people read aloud these awkward phrases. This will put worshipers into a mindset that makes it difficult to give themselves fully to the rousing, ecstatic songs of praise that follow. A congregation may find this order to be familiar. They may even find that it fulfills their expectations about worship since all of the elements come from patterns of worship that congregations have known for decades. However, they probably will not find it to be compelling because it *will lack coherence of character.*

Here is our growing list of *principles* for understanding Protestant worship in North America:

Principle 1. All worship follows patterns.

Principle 2. The patterns of worship function at two levels: the liturgical unit and the macro-pattern.

Principle 3. A macro-pattern of worship has a *telos* (goal) it aims to achieve.

Principle 4. Each macro-pattern has a particular *ethos* (character type or style) that fits with its particular *telos*.

Observation A: There are several identifiable character types in Protestant worship in the United States: The Revival, Sunday School, Aesthetic Worship, Pentecostal Worship, Prayer Meeting, and Liturgical Renewal.

Principle 5. Liturgical units are portable blocks of liturgical action.

Observation B: Typically, patterns of *telos/ethos* become conflated in contemporary practice.

Principle 6. The *telos/ethos* of various patterns are not interchangeable with each other and tend to clash when combined.

In the next six chapters (3–8), I offer a more detailed history of the six dominant paradigms of Protestant worship, including a more expanded description of the *telos* and *ethos* of each pattern, and I will give examples of the liturgical units that make up these patterns. I will show what is most valuable and even compelling about each of the patterns. I will also indicate problems with each of the patterns, for just as each pattern will arise to address a perceived lack or excess in the worship practices of congregations, so too each pattern will give rise to its own set of difficulties. From my experience of consulting with congregations, I have found that worship planning and evaluation are often done at the level of subjective impressions—what "seems natural" or what "works." However, what "seems natural" or what "works" will almost always be a practice with a history. The aim is to give an account of this history to raise to a conscious level what has become implicit but hidden from view, so that congregations may then be able to evaluate liturgical practices more wisely.

In chapter 9 I will discuss the tendency to conflate patterns in Protestant worship. Conflation of worship practices is neither categorically good nor bad, but it can be problematic. When it is done carelessly, worship will seem awkward, lack flow, or even become incoherent. Yet, some degree of conflation may be unavoidable, and I will offer suggestions on how to manage conflation to avoid awkward shifts in *ethos*.

Chapter 10 looks at the explosive surge of "online worship" and considers ways the six patterns are helpful for understanding and evaluating the success of such experiences. Indeed, I will argue that the standards of excellence required for video production can expose orders of worship that do not have a strong, overarching character.

Finally, in the conclusion I will give an "altar call," to draw on the language of the Revival pattern. For though we will have waded through a good bit of history and descriptive analysis, our task is not merely to have a detached appreciation of history or ritual flow. Rather, our fundamental task as leaders is the same as for all believers: obedience to the awe-inspiring and fearful task of serving God and the world as faithful disciples of Jesus Christ. To give our hearts to Christ in union with the saints of God who make up the body of Christ as church: this is our aim. Understanding our worship more fully and planning it more carefully are steps down the aisle in that direction.

CHAPTER THREE

Worship as Motivational Technology

The Revival

God has found it necessary to take advantage of the excitability there is in mankind, to produce powerful excitements among them, before he can lead them to obey.

—Charles G. Finney, "What a Revival of Religion Is"[1]

Now a church is like everything else,—it's got to have a boss, a head, an authority of some sort, that people will listen to and mind. The Catholics are different, as you say. Their church is chuck-full of authority—all the way from the Pope down to the priest—and accordingly they do as they're told. But the Protestants—your Methodists most of all—they say "No, we won't have any authority, we won't obey any boss." Very well, what happens? We who are responsible for running the thing, and raising the money and so on—we have to put on a spurt every once in a while, and work up a general state of excitement; and while it's going, don't you see that THAT is the authority, the motive power, whatever you like to call it, by which things are done? Other denominations don't need it. We do, and that's why we've got it.

—Speech by "Sister Soulsby" in *The Damnation of Theron Ware* by Harold Frederic[2]

Case One: "I end with this: what is at stake here is your very soul. With every head bowed and every eye closed, I want to ask you a question. If you died tonight, where would you spend eternity?"

Case Two: "We are glad you came to our service today. If you would like to know more about what a difference following Jesus would make in

---

1. *Lectures on Revivals of Religion*, 2nd ed. (New York, NY: Leavitt, Lord & Co., 1935), 2.

2. Gutenberg Project (eBook), March 8, 2006, 431. First edition published by Stone and Kimball, 1896.

Chapter Three

your life, please go to our visitor kiosk where we have some information to share with you."

Two very different ways to end a worship service: the first, emotionally manipulative and frightening; the second, low-key and inviting. Yet both ask, "If you . . ." Both call for a response to a message that has preceded it. These two ostensibly different cases are examples of the Revival model of worship, the most influential of all of the patterns of worship to arise in the North American context. Not only did the Revival model change the forms of worship that many American congregations employed, it fundamentally altered the ways churches construed the meaning of worship. To see just how influential this pattern became, we will need to compare the Revival pattern to the dominant patterns of Protestant worship in the previous century.

Worship Patterns in the Eighteenth Century

In 1906, Yale church historian Williston Walker observed that "the non-liturgical churches of America" followed an order of public worship based on the 1645 *Westminster Directory of Publick Worship* of the Scottish and English Puritans.[3] The *Westminster Directory* was not a written liturgy such as found in the Anglican *Book of Common Prayer*. Rather, it described the order and contents of the various elements for worship. In outline, the order of worship in the 1645 *Westminster Directory* was:

> Call to worship and invocation
> Scripture reading—a chapter from each Testament
> Singing of a psalm
> Long prayer containing an acknowledgment of sin, confession,
>   thanksgiving for the Gospel, prayer for the spread of the
>   Gospel, general intercessions, and blessing upon the sermon
> Sermon
> Briefer prayer of thanksgiving and petition, and the Lord's Prayer
> Singing of a psalm

---

3. Williston Walker, "The Genesis of the Present Customary Form of Public Worship in the Reformed Non-Prelatical Churches of America," *Papers of the American Society of Church History*, second series, vol. 1 (1909).

Benediction
Dismissal with Apostolic Benediction (2 Cor 13:14)[4]

The *telos* of this order of worship was biblical purity, stripping away every practice, ceremony, and prayer that was not grounded in the Bible. Reading of scripture and preaching took the largest amount of time in the service. But the prayers of confession and thanksgiving also drew on biblical quotations, and even the hymns were metrical versions of psalms. The *ethos* of this order was sensual austerity; it pared away any action that did not focus attention on the word of God. According to Walker, the *Westminster Directory* continued to be the basic order of worship for New England churches well into the nineteenth century.

For a nineteenth-century example, Walker then cites the 1829 edition of the *Constitution of the Congregational Churches*, which descended from the Puritan tradition.[5] Even the Methodists breathed the air of New England's Puritan austerity, at least in their published order of worship, as this comparison with the *Doctrines and Discipline of the Methodist Episcopal Church* of 1824 demonstrates:[6]

MEC Discipline 1824	Congregationalists 1829
Singing	Invocation (invoking the blessing of God)
Reading (one chapter of the OT and one chapter of the NT)	Reading of Scriptures
[Singing?]	Singing
First prayer concluding with Lord's Prayer	A long prayer of supplication and thanksgiving
Preaching	Preaching
[Second prayer?]	Short, concluding prayer
[Singing?]	Singing
Apostolic Benediction	Benediction
*Items in square brackets indicate some ambiguity in the directions.	

4. The *Westminster Directory* is available online at several websites. See, for example, https://www.covenanter.org/reformed/documents/the-directory-for-the-publick-worship-of-god, accessed June 5, 2020.

5. Walker, "The Genesis of the Present Customary Form of Public Worship," 90.

6. *Doctrines and Discipline of The Methodist Episcopal Church* (New York, NY: N. Bang and J. Emory, 1824), 72.

Yet neither the 1824 *Discipline* nor the 1829 *Constitution of the Congregationalists* give the entire story. On the frontier, Americans convened camp meetings that embraced wildly exuberant practices of singing and shouting, preaching and repenting—definitely *not* Puritan austerity. By the early nineteenth century, the somber worship of the *Westminster Directory* was losing influence.

The Revival and Its Prophet, Charles G. Finney

Changes in worship had been brewing for decades prior to the period described by Walker. The First Great Awakening in the eighteenth century, with such notable figures as Jonathan Edwards and George Whitefield, introduced American Christians to "flamboyant and highly emotional preaching" that moved listeners from "staid and routine formalism" to embrace a more experiential, personal faith.[7] Whitefield in particular was noted for preaching at meetings outside of regular public worship, which was a type of Revival meeting.[8] However, the form of Revival that has had the most enduring influence on Protestant worship developed in the nineteenth century during the so-called Second Great Awakening. Several important figures were associated with the Second Great Awakening, but the most famous and influential was Charles Grandison Finney. Finney went beyond Edwards and Whitefield to embrace the emotionally exuberant practices of the frontier circuit riders and camp meetings—the intense focus on conversion, the pragmatic use of space, and preaching that used ordinary, personal illustrations rather than doctrine or exposition of scripture. As James F. White has noted, Finney's genius was his domestication of these frontier practices to make them palatable and workable for urban congregations. Furthermore, he developed a vigorous intellectual defense

---

7. Sydney E. Ahlstrom, *A Religious History of the American People* (New Haven, CT: Yale University Press, 1972), 287.

8. At that time, the word *revival* was not generally used to describe meetings for preaching but the results of them. One did not "attend a revival" but experienced revival—i.e., the "revival of religion" in the hearts of men and women.

of his systematic approach to Revival whose fundamental principles continue to be persuasive.[9]

Born in 1792 to a farming family in Connecticut, Finney spent his early adult years training to become a lawyer. In 1821, he experienced a profound religious conversion that led him to abandon his legal aspirations to pursue the ministry. Although the Presbyterians licensed him (and eventually ordained him) as a preacher, he was actually more of a free agent minister who chafed at the core Presbyterian doctrine concerning God's election of the saints, otherwise known as predestination.

Finney's perspective on predestination offers a good window into his methodology for revivals. His argument with election of the saints was not theological but practical:

> If election and Sovereignty are *too much* preached, there will be Antinomianism in the Church, and sinners will hide themselves behind the delusion that they could do nothing.[10]

How should a preacher make the right impression on sinners? In the previous century, both Edwards and Whitefield, the giants of the First Great Awakening, had preached the doctrine of election of the saints, and both of them had been wildly successful at converting the lost. Yet, the reason for their success, Finney argued, was not the truth of the doctrine but the social context in which they preached it:

> Then [at the time of Edwards and Whitefield] the churches in New England had enjoyed little else than Arminian preaching, and were all resting in themselves and their own strength. These bold and devoted servants of God came out and declared those particular doctrines of grace, Divine sovereignty, and election, and they were greatly blessed. They did not dwell on these doctrines exclusively, but they preached them very fully. The consequence was, that because *in those circumstances* revivals followed from such preaching, the ministers who followed *continued to preach these doctrines*

---

9. I concur with White's suggestion that Finney "may be the most influential liturgical reformer in American history." James F. White, *Protestant Worship: Traditions in Transition* (Louisville, KY: Westminster/John Knox Press, 1989), 176.

10. Charles G. Finney, *Lectures on Revivals of Religion* (New York, NY: Leavitt, Lord & Co., 1835), 174. Italics original.

almost exclusively. And they dwelt on them so long that the church and the world got entrenched behind them, waiting for God to come and do what he required *them* to do, and so revivals ceased *for* many years.[11]

In other words, Edwards and Whitefield were successful because their preaching struck the unconverted as novel—it got their attention. Many American ministers continued to imitate Whitefield and Edwards, preaching the same ideas in the same ways until those ideas and ways lost the power to arouse a response. Election became a stale doctrine that made the unconverted feel helpless and hopeless in the face of their sins. As Finney analyzed the situation, the problem with preaching election was *not* that the doctrine was wrong *but that it no longer worked* as a method to convert sinners, which was the chief goal of the preacher.[12]

By the late 1820s, Finney was a famous and highly effective revivalist, and in 1832 a group of laymen in New York City called him to be the pastor of a church that met in the Chatham Street Theatre, which they had renovated to serve as an auditorium-style church building. Within a few months of taking the pulpit at Chatham Street, Finney delivered a series of lectures that was published under the title *Lectures on Revivals of Religion*. These lectures retold the history of the church as a progressive story of "new measures" for drawing attention to the message of the gospel. Unlike what previous generations of ministers had been taught, faithful Christian ministry was not about receiving and handing on a tradition, he said. Instead it was a systematic innovation of techniques for getting and holding attention. In short, ministry was (and always has been) an evolving technology.

Revival as Machine-Age Technology

By technology I mean the systematic cultural or scientific principles for the tools and techniques humans develop for work and art. Technology, like religion, is as old as human culture itself. Moreover, technology not only expresses culture but also shapes it. Consider, for example, the practices of mu-

---

11. Finney, *Lectures on Revivals of Religion*, 189.

12. See Ted A. Smith, *The New Measures: A Theological History of Democratic Practice* (New York, NY: Cambridge University Press, 2007), 75–85.

sic. Music is a supremely expressive form of human culture, but music often is expressed through the use of musical instruments, which is a technology. Once a musical instrument is developed, composers create music with that instrument in mind, and the range of instruments composers have available to them inevitably shapes the music they compose and perform. It would be unthinkable for a musician to produce a sonata if all she had access to were a drum but not unthinkable if she had access to a piano. Drums existed long before the invention of keyboard instruments, but once keyboard instruments became available, they shaped what was musically possible.

Beginning with the Industrial Revolution of the eighteenth century, technology began to take on expanding power through the development of machines, and like all technology, machines shaped culture.[13] As a result, Western culture began to express itself according to principles made possible by machines. To be very general, before the Industrial Age, work was judged by pride in a job well done. Standards for evaluation came through continuity with standards handed down by tradition, parent to child. As Susan White has shown, this began to change by the beginning of the nineteenth century, for with the rise of the machine, different standards came into effect. For example, the production of cloth became dramatically more efficient and productive with the invention of power-driven looms. The value of "skillful weaving" became irrelevant since a machine took care of the precision aspects of weaving. The values of traditional skill were supplanted by the values of productivity and efficiency. Furthermore, the standards made possible by machines began to have an effect on more than the material production of consumer goods. According to White, as Western cultures embraced industrialization, "efficiency, productivity, and progress became the goals in almost every department of life"—including religion.[14]

Finney's *Lectures on Revivals* are a testimony to the influence of "efficiency, productivity, and progress" in nineteenth-century American Christianity. Previous generations of Christians understood faith as a response to God's divine initiative. "Wait upon the Lord" was their slogan.

---

13. Susan White, *Christian Worship and Technological Change* (Nashville, TN: Abingdon Press, 1994), 18.

14. S. White, *Christian Worship and Technological Change*, 20.

Christians must be patient, receive what God gives, and then respond. In the first of his lectures, Finney turns this slogan upside down: "*Religion is the work of man. It is something for man to do.*"[15] Hence, it comes under the scrutiny of principles of productivity:

> [A Revival] is not a miracle according to another definition of the term miracle—*something above the powers of nature*. There is nothing in religion beyond the ordinary powers of nature. It consists entirely in the *right exercise* of the powers of nature. It is just that, and nothing else. When mankind become religious, they are not *enabled* to put forth exertions which they were unable before to put forth. They only exert the powers they had before in a different way, and use them for the glory of God. . . . It is not a miracle, nor dependent on a miracle, in any sense. It is a purely philosophical result of the right use of the constituted means—as much so as any other effect produced by the application of means.[16]

This is a long way from the well-known American Congregationalist preacher and theologian Jonathan Edwards, who titled his account of the First Great Awakening, "A Faithful Narrative of the Surprising Work of God." *For Finney, conversion was not something surprising* at all; rather, conversion increases with the systematic use of the right techniques. The Revival was similar to a productive, efficient machine from which one gets results.

New Measures for Revival

With this technological approach to religion, Finney was fearless in breaking with traditional approaches to conversion, formation, and worship. In his lecture on "Measures to Promote Revivals," he argued for "new measures" that would achieve results:

> If we examine the history of the Church we shall find that there never has been an extensive reformation, except by new measures. Whenever the Churches get settled down into a norm of doing things, they soon get to rely upon the outward doing of it, and so retain the form of religion while they lose the substance. And then it has always been found impossible to

---

15. Finney, *Lectures on Revivals*, 9.
16. Finney, *Lectures on Revivals*, 12–13.

arouse them so as to bring about a reformation of the evils, and produce a revival of religion, by simply pursuing that established form. Perhaps it is not too much to say, that it is impossible for God Himself to bring about reformations but by new measures.[17]

Even God needed continually fresh measures to keep the attention of congregations! Finney described measures, such as female prayer meetings, that were a genuinely novel development, and others measures, such as protracted meetings, that had historical precedents. New measures need not be entirely novel, but they had to be *experienced* as novel in order to get and keep people's attention.[18]

Getting attention: that was the key Finney discovered for how ministry could be effective. The desired effect of new measures was to enable people to hear the gospel in a world of competing demands for attention:

> Without new measures, it is impossible that the church should succeed in gaining the attention of the world to religion. There are so many exciting subjects constantly brought before the public mind, such a running to and fro, so many that cry "Lo here," and "Lo there," that the church cannot maintain her ground, cannot command attention, without very exciting preaching, and sufficient novelty in measures, to get the public ear. The measures of politicians, of infidels and heretics, the scrambling after wealth, the increase of luxury, and the ten thousand exciting and counteracting influences that bear upon the church and upon the world, will gain their attention and turn all men away from the sanctuary and from the altars of the Lord, unless we increase in wisdom and piety, and wisely adopt such new measures as are calculated to get the attention of men to the gospel of Christ.[19]

Pastors must be wise to the devices of the world and counter these devices with measures "calculated to get the attention of men." From this perspective, worship was a collection of tools that pastors could employ for getting and sustaining attention. Compare this to the understanding of

---

17. Finney, *Lectures on Revivals*, 249.

18. Smith, *The New Measures*, 97–99. Smith comments: "Charles Finney could not imagine that novelty itself might become boring," 99.

19. Finney, *Lectures on Revivals*, 251–52.

worship found in the *Westminster Confession of Faith* of the Presbyterian and Reformed churches in the early nineteenth century:

> XXI. Of Religious Worship and the Sabbath-day
>
> The light of nature showeth that there is a God, who hath lordship and sovereignty over all; is good, and doeth good unto all; and is therefore to be feared, loved, praised, called upon, trusted in, and served with all the heart, and with all the soul, and with all the might. But the acceptable way of worshipping the true God is instituted by himself, and so limited by his own revealed will, that he may not be worshipped according to the imaginations and devices of men, or the suggestions of Satan, under any visible representation or any other way not prescribed in the holy Scripture.

According to the *Westminster Confession*, the impulse to worship God is a natural response to God's sovereignty and goodness to all. Left to their own natural desires, however, human beings would worship God "according to the imagination and devices of men, or the suggestions of Satan." Therefore, the natural impulse is not enough for proper worship, for God must be worshiped according to the ways God has instituted and revealed through scripture.

Finney essentially turned this article on its head. God revealed to the ancient Jews a form of worship for the temple, but in the New Testament God did not reveal a *liturgy* but a *message* of salvation through Jesus Christ. Consequently, the New Testament was utterly silent on the forms of public worship employed by the apostles:

> We are left in the dark as to the measures which were pursued by the apostles and primitive preachers, except so far as we can gather it from occasional hints in the book of Acts. We do not know how many times they sung and how many times they prayed in public worship, or even whether they sung or prayed at all in their ordinary meetings for preaching. When Jesus Christ was on earth, laboring among his disciples, he had nothing to do with forms or measures.... His object was to preach and teach mankind the true religion. And when the apostles preached afterwards, with the Holy Ghost sent down from heaven, we hear nothing about their having a particular system of measures to carry on their work, or one apostle doing a thing in a particular way because others did it in that way. Their commission was, "Go and

preach the gospel, and disciple all nations." It did not prescribe any forms. It did not admit any. . . . Do it—the best way you can—ask wisdom from God—use the faculties he has given you—seek the direction of the Holy Ghost—go forward and do it. This was their commission. And their object was to make known the gospel in the *most effectual way*, to make the truth stand out strikingly, so as to obtain the attention and secure the obedience of the greatest number possible. No person can find any *form* of doing this laid down in the Bible. It is *preaching the gospel* that stands out prominent there as the great thing. The form is left out of the question.[20]

Since the New Testament was silent on the subject of measures, preachers needed to employ their own creative genius to devise effective new techniques for spreading the gospel. From his own experience Finney knew that God blessed the use of measures if they were *effectual* in presenting the truth of the gospel. Thus, he concluded, the means or measures themselves were utterly arbitrary, *except insofar as they achieved results*. While the *Westminster Confession* had forbidden performing worship "according to the imaginations and devices of men," Finney proposed that the devices of men were really all the church had at its disposal. Of course, ministers should "ask the wisdom from God" and "seek the direction of the Holy Ghost" in adopting new measures, but the primary assignment was "Do it—the best way you can."

Revivalism: A Shift in the *Telos* of Worship

If preaching for conversion of sinners was the central task of the church, Finney assumed that everything the church did must be aimed at that goal. Public worship was essentially a set of tools for evangelism, and the *telos* of Revival worship was conversion. While Finney argued that this had always been the case, it was a major shift in the Christian understanding of the purpose of worship. Proclamation of the gospel for the conversion of the world had been a central task of the church from the time of the New Testament, but earlier generations of Christians presumed that divine worship was the obligation of the already converted. The early church did not even allow neophyte Christian believers to participate in the common prayers

---

20. Finney, *Lectures on Revival*, 233.

or to recite the Lord's Prayer until after they were baptized.[21] In later centuries, the church became less restrictive regarding who was allowed to be present during worship, but the church kept the fundamental assumption that worship of God was for the already converted. Thus, according to the seventeenth-century *Westminster Confession*, worship was not immediately accessible to all. New believers must be taught to worship in "the ways God had ordained." Over the centuries churches disputed "the ways God had ordained" for worship, and the order and content varied in different times and places. Before Finney, however, no one proposed that historical differences meant worship was arbitrary, nor had anyone argued that the whole meaning of worship was its practical effects. Yet Finney proposed that the value of worship was nothing more than its effectiveness in leading sinners to repentance.

Revival worship, moreover, entailed perpetual progress—always seeking a better way to affect the congregation. This was not progress toward practices that are genuinely, eternally good in the theological sense because the changes are more or less arbitrary. Whereas earlier generations of Christians sought worship that was *right* (in the sense that it was what God wanted), the Revival strove for worship that was *successful* (in the sense of what attracted people). The *telos* of Revival worship was conversion by any means that worked; this was progress merely as novelty, something new and therefore interesting. In short, for Finney, worship was anthropologically potent but theologically trivial.

Revivalism: A Shift in the *Ethos* of Worship

The Revival used worship for effect, and different worship styles were employed to the degree that they made an emotional impact on an audience. This required expertise in the use of techniques, that is, a technology of worship. Here we see another important shift in the understanding of worship. Previous generations of Christians understood ordained ministry

---

21. See, for example, *The Apostolic Tradition* 18: "When the teacher has finished instructing, let the catechumens pray by themselves separated from the faithful." Paul F. Bradshaw, Maxwell E. Johnson, and L. Edward Phillips, *The Apostolic Tradition: A Commentary* (Minneapolis, MN: Augsburg Fortress, 2002), 100.

as an office of the church, established by God. A sermon preached or sacrament administered by an incompetent minister was just as "effective" as one administered by a competent minister because the "effect" had to do with what God intended rather than what individual worshipers felt. Obviously, competent ministers were better able to hold the attention of congregations, but that was not particularly crucial to the meaning of worship. Finney inverted this understanding: the effect on the congregation was the whole of worship, and this meant that the effectiveness of leadership could not be arbitrary—it was everything.

An expert leader had to know how to pray effectively in public: "A man may be pious, but so weak that his prayers do not edify, but rather disgust, the people present. When this is so, he had better keep silence."[22] An expert leader must know how to use music appropriately, calling out the right sort of song or hymn appropriate to the tone of the meeting. The singing of praise songs, for example, was out of place when the spirit of the meeting turned serious: "Christians never feel less like singing, than when they have the spirit of prayer for sinners."[23] Here is his example of music used to good emotional effect:

> I once heard a celebrated organist produce a remarkable effect in a protracted meeting. The organ was a powerful one, and the double bass pipes were like thunder. The hymn was given out that has these lines:
>
> See the storm of vengeance gathering
> O'er the path you dare to tread;
> "Hear the awful thunder rolling,
> Loud and louder o'er your head."
>
> When he came to these words, we first heard the distant roar of thunder, then it grew nearer and louder, till at the word "louder," there was a crash that seemed almost to overpower the whole congregation.[24]

---

22. Finney, *Lectures on Revivals*, 120–21.
23. Finney, *Lectures on Revivals*, 122.
24. Finney, *Lectures on Revivals*, 123.

The point of music is, thus, to concentrate emotional impact: "It should always be such as not to take away feeling, but to deepen it."[25] Finney is one of the first Christian leaders to pay attention to what contemporary worship leaders will call the experience of "flow" in worship. The discrete acts of worship should all come together to produce a sustained experience in the worshipers, and skilled musical leaders must use music accordingly.

Perhaps nothing so clearly illustrates Finney's pragmatic *ethos* as his recommendations concerning the public reading of scripture. As noted above, the previous standard for scripture in public worship in most Protestant churches was to read aloud one chapter from each of the testaments. Finney opposed this practice:

> Do not drag in the word of God to make up part of the meeting as a mere matter of form. This is an insult to God. It is not well to read any more than is applicable to the subject before the meeting, or the occasion. Some people think it always necessary to read a whole chapter, though it may be ever so long, and have a variety of subjects. . . . Wandering over a large field, hinders and destroys this design.[26]

Rather than adapting worship to the reading of scripture, he said, scripture should be adapted to its use in public worship. For Finney, scripture, like prayer and music, was a tool and its use a technique. As a result, the Revival employed a minimal amount of scripture reading in public worship, sometimes only a verse or two as a springboard for the message.

Preaching was the focal skill of Revival worship, as it had been in Protestant worship for centuries. However, the kind of expertise required for Revival preaching was not theological expertise but rhetorical skill. A preacher should emulate the expert lawyer who argues a case to "convert" a jury.[27] A good lawyer uses simple words to explain difficult concepts so that the least-educated juror can understand. Likewise, an "expert" minister should avoid complicated theological terms and present the gospel in the simplest language possible, using homespun illustrations and a con-

---

25. Finney, *Lectures on Revivals*, 123.
26. Finney, *Lectures on Revivals*, 116.
27. Finney, *Lectures on Revivals*, 205.

versational style to which the average listener could easily relate. Finney recommended a theatrical style of preaching to communicate the emotional content of the message, like a stage actor who skillfully communicates emotions in the lines of a play:

> Now what is the design of the actor in a theatrical representation? It is so to throw himself into the spirit and meaning of the writer, as to adopt his sentiments, make them his own, feel them, embody them, throw them out upon the audience as living reality. And now, what is the objection to all this in preaching? The actor suits the action to the word, and the word to the action. His looks, his hands, his attitudes, and everything are designed to express the full meaning of the writer. Now this should be the aim of the preacher. And if by "theatrical" be meant the strongest possible representation of the sentiments expressed, then the more theatrical a sermon is, the better.[28]

A sermon must not only be delivered, it must be *acted out* with appropriate gestures that flow naturally from feeling. Such preaching would elicit in the congregation their own emotional response—just like an actor elicits tears or laughter from an audience. Preachers must communicate their sincere belief in the gospel, and that required an actor's skill. It was not enough to *be* sincere; one had to cultivate the ability to *act* sincere.[29]

The explicitly theatrical approach to worship that Finney advocated required a shift in liturgical architecture. Neither a Puritan-style meetinghouse with its box pews nor a church with a screened chancel and center aisles would suffice. Revivals required a space that suited a theatrical production, and indeed Finney's first church in New York met in a renovated theater building.[30] Like theaters, Revival churches contained curved

---

28. Finney, *Lectures on Revivals*, 204.

29. Finney believed that sincerity should be genuine, but how can anyone ever know that for sure? This brings to mind the quotation often attributed to George Burns: "The key to acting is sincerity; if you can fake that you've got it made" (http://www.quotedb.com/quotes/1773, accessed August 15, 2011). For an extended treatment of the problem of sincerity in ritual and modern religion, see Adam B. Seligman et al., *Ritual and Its Consequences: An Essay on the Limits of Sincerity* (New York, NY: Oxford University Press, 2008).

30. See Jeanne Halgren Kilde, *When Church Became Theatre: The Transformation of Evangelical Architecture and Worship in Nineteenth-Century America* (New York, NY: Oxford University Press, 2002).

pews or rows of seats and side aisles, with little room for congregational movement. Instead of chancels with simple pulpits and obscured choirs, Revival churches had pulpit stages with proscenium arches, clearly visible choir lofts, and organs.[31] Earlier reformed Protestants had placed the emphasis on the ear—worship was meant to be heard but not gazed upon. Revival worship kept an emphasis on hearing and placed an equally strong emphasis on seeing. Proscenium arches and pulpit stages focused visual attention on the preacher and other worship leaders. Revival auditoriums often had raked seating on the main floor and galleries on three sides so that the congregation, like an audience, could have unobstructed views of the pulpit stage and choir from any seat in the room. In short, Finney's new measures brought an end to Protestant liturgical austerity; the character of the Revival church was unashamedly ostentatious and performative.

The Revival Macro-Pattern of Worship

Finney never gave a definitive list of new measures, nor did he provide a standard order for a Revival service. He did not want to give the impression that the new measures were a set order of practices to emulate. Once a measure became an established method, it lost its effectiveness. This did not stop revivalism from developing stereotypical patterns.[32] As I state in principle one: all worship follows patterns.

The macro-pattern of the Revival began with an informal welcome and song service aimed at warming up the audience. The music was at turns lively, touching, and sentimental. Almost all of it was aimed at the subjective experience of the worshiper: "I come to the garden alone, while the dew is still on the roses"; "Leaning on the everlasting arms . . . safe and secure from all alarms." Songs with choruses and refrains were especially popular because they were easy to sing. If a church was large enough to

---

31. Finney, *Lectures on Revivals*, 67, 138.

32. We do not have detailed descriptions of the order of Revivals until well into the twentieth century. Wesleyan Methodist Luther Lee produced a widely used aid, *The Revival Manual* (New York, NY: Wesley Methodist Book Room, 1850), which gave some general directions about the use of music and prayer in Revivals. By the late nineteenth century, we find several references to the preliminaries (or preliminary exercises) and to altar calls.

have an organ or musical ensemble, the service might begin with an overture of instrumental music. An important feature of the music in Revival worship is that it is well prepared and led by the most skilled musicians available. A song leader directs the congregation and leads the choir. Ensembles and soloists perform entertaining music. The terms *special music* or *selection* identify this liturgical unit:

> **Special Music/Selection**
> Introduction of the soloist/choir
> Musical performance
> Applause ("Amens" or other acclamations from the audience)[33]

After the song service came a prayer led by a minister or lay leader who was proficient at emotionally engaging prayer. While the music part of the service was well rehearsed, the prayer and testimonies were extemporaneous, though skillfully executed. Finney completely rejected any reading of prayers from books. Prayers should be from "the heart" and use simple, conversational language. To heighten the dramatic effect of prayer, an organist or pianist would softly play a hymn (such as "Sweet Hour of Prayer") as background music. Extemporaneous prayer accompanied by music was another distinctive liturgical unit of Revival worship:

> **Extempore prayer with music**
> Introduction to the prayer
> Musician begins soft music
> Extempore prayer by leader as music continues

The prayer was followed by a collection, which might be called a "love offering" if the preacher were a visiting evangelist. A musician would also play during the collection. Often this was followed by a piece of "special music" by the soloist or choir, particularly if a "special" had not been performed earlier. Personal testimony is a liturgical unit that could appear in this part of the service, if not earlier.

---

33. Note the term *audience* rather than *congregation*, which underscores the performative aspect of worship.

The first part was often caricatured as "the preliminaries."[34] The purpose of the preliminaries was to get the congregation into an emotionally receptive mood. Preliminaries were the warm-up to the main event, which was the message. While Finney used both *sermon* and *message* to refer to preaching, the latter term became standard for Revival worship since it more clearly fit the purpose of revival preaching. He discouraged doctrinal preaching (except for practical application of doctrine, such as God's love or mercy) and expository preaching. The message usually was preceded by the reading of a verse or two of scripture at most, since a Revival message was not particularly based on a passage of scripture. It was not uncommon for Revival preachers to develop a sermon and then look for a short verse to append at the beginning. Revival sermons usually began with preliminary remarks as a warm-up to the message. These remarks could be humorous (such as a joke) but were meant to establish a connection between a preacher and audience.

Finney opposed the use of written texts for messages. A brief outline of main points the preacher wanted to address was sufficient.[35] Revival preaching used ordinary conversational language and evocative human-interest stories. Since the aim was to arouse people to make a decision to follow Christ, the preacher adapted the message during the delivery to make sure congregations understood. Finney instructed preachers to keep eye contact with congregations and to listen for their verbal feedback. If the listeners did not seem to be getting the point, the preacher should repeat it using different words. Extemporary speaking was effective for this style of preaching since the preacher's gaze was not focused on a written text. Preaching without a manuscript was a central feature of this distinctive liturgical unit:

Message
    Preliminary remarks
    Short scripture text (a verse or two at most)
    Message (preached without written text)

---

34. Finney himself never used this term. As far as I can find, it arose in the late nineteenth century and was often used in a dismissive sense by early twentieth-century liturgical reformers.

35. Finney's few published sermons were recorded by a secretary, as he preached extemporaneously.

The message concluded with a call for the congregation, and especially the unconverted, to make a decision to follow Christ and to do so by coming forward to a designated sitting area called the "anxious seat" or "anxious bench." Coming forward to the anxious seat was, for the lost, "a public manifestation of their determination to be Christians."[36] A sinner could come forward to sit on the anxious seat at any time during the service, but typically this took place after the message. The anxious seat provided a place for those who were "anxious" about their salvation to indicate their desire to be saved, and it allowed the ministers and other lay leaders to pray with them to help them "break through" to an experience of conversion as a singular event. Finney strongly believed that conversion was an immediate event rather than a gradual process.[37] The "conversion of sinners [was] the work of men,"[38] and preachers should be direct and forceful in asking sinners to make immediate decisions for Christ. For Methodists, communion rails could function as the anxious seat, with sinners kneeling before the communion table for prayer with a minister. Probably due to the influence of the Methodists, by the end of the nineteenth century the anxious seat began to be referred to as the "altar call." To this day, some Methodist congregations refer to the communion rail (rather than the communion table) as "the altar." By the same token, small Southern Baptist congregations in the rural South, where the Revival pattern is still in use, often refer to the front of the church as "the altar."

Altar Call
>Call for decision/response to the message (issued by preacher)
>Demonstration of response ("Come forward," "Raise a hand," etc.)
>Invitational song (for example, "I Surrender All." This may be sung by a choir or a soloist.)
>Prayer and counseling with responders (leader[s] interacting individually with those who respond)

---

36. Finney, *Lectures on Revivals*, 248.

37. Finney: "The truth is, Regeneration, or conversion, is not a progressive work. What is regeneration? What is it but the beginning of obedience to God? And is the beginning of a thing progressive? . . . When persons talk about conversion as a progressive work, it is absurd" (*Lectures on Revivals*, 312).

38. Finney, *Lectures on Revivals*, 180.

Despite the fact that Finney did not propose a pattern for the Revival, a threefold service of preliminaries, message, and altar call became the standard, not only for the protracted meetings that churches held once or twice a year but also for Sunday worship. Local pastors imitated the preaching styles of traveling evangelists. In many Protestant congregations, especially among Baptists and rural Methodists, Sunday worship became Revival worship focused on conversion.

The Evolution of Revival Worship

Just as Finney predicted, once the churches got "settled down into a norm of doing things," the Revival began to lose the power of novelty. However, the Revival has been "revived" many times since the mid-nineteenth century. Such internationally known evangelists as Dwight L. Moody (1837–1899) and Billy Sunday (1862–1935) employed audience-friendly music, emotionally compelling preaching, and the altar call. The Revival employed television as a new measure in the Billy Graham crusades, which were immensely popular well into the late twentieth century. By 1970, pioneers of the Contemporary Christian Music genre, such as Larry Norman, Randy Stonehill, and Randy Matthews, gave concerts that mixed musical performance with personal testimony and ended with an altar call during the final song.

The Seeker Service

The most successful current reincarnation of the Revival as public worship is the Seeker Service as developed in the 1980s at Willow Creek Community Church in Barrington, Illinois.[39] Bill Hybels, founder and senior pastor of the congregation, came from the evangelical, nondenominational line of churches that was thoroughly steeped in the methods of

---

39. In 2007, Willow Creek published a self-study, which found that participation in the numerous programs of the congregation, including the Seeker Services, did not correlate with growth in discipleship. As a result, Willow Creek has been restructuring its various ministries, including the weekend services. The model of Seeker Service I describe here is the model that was in place before this study. See Greg L. Hawkins and Cally Parkinson, *Reveal: Where Are You?* (Barrington, IL: Willow Creek Association, 2007).

Finneyite revivalism. He began his ministry as a youth pastor at a non-denominational church in suburban Chicago, where he first began to experiment with styles of evangelism that could reach youth who had no experience of church. Hybels continued this focus when he left his successful youth ministry to start his own congregation. From its beginnings, Willow Creek was a church for those who knew little about "church."

As developed at Willow Creek, the goal of the Seeker Service was to appeal to "the unchurched," those who do not have a vital relationship to Christ and little or no churchgoing experience. This meant that leaders of the Seeker Services had to be knowledgeable about the likes and dislikes of potential attendees. Willow Creek had been unapologetic in the use of marketing principles to design services that unchurched people would find attractive.[40] G. A. Pritchard's study of Willow Creek describes a survey of Barrington suburbanites conducted by Hybels and other "Creekers" as the congregation was forming to find out what the young and middle-aged unchurched persons found distasteful about church. Six concerns rose to the top of the list of complaints:

1. The church is always asking for money (most common answer).

2. I am unable to relate to the music.

3. I am unable to relate to the message.

4. The church does not meet my needs.

5. The services are predictable and boring.

6. The church makes me feel guilty.[41]

Willow Creek structured a service that addressed these complaints. They used the "soft rock" songs of the burgeoning Christian music industry. They used multimedia technology to give the services the visual

---

40. "[Willow] Creekers argue that they are in the business of God's work. They believe that like any business, if their business is going to be successful they need to understand their customers (and their needs), clarify a target market profile, and develop or package products to meet these needs." G. A. Pritchard, *Willow Creek Seeker Services: Evaluating a New Way of Doing Church* (Grand Rapids, MI: Baker, 1996), 241.

41. Pritchard, *Willow Creek Seeker Services*, 55.

interest of a rock concert and to use media clips that emulated the rock videos of MTV. The video presentation is a distinctive feature of Seeker worship. They always projected lyrics to the songs, but the congregation was not ordinarily invited to sing along on more than one or two of the several songs during the service. Instead the stage band performed the music for an audience. To provide a close-up view of the performers, the entire service was televised and simultaneously broadcast onto large projection screens. Musicians and other leaders dressed very casually (no ties or suits), though the preacher of the day might wear a sport coat and tie. Willow Creek had resident artists write and perform short dramatic sketches related to the theme of the message. Preaching was practical and simple, with preachers using props for illustrations. Though the messages were still long by some standards (about thirty-five minutes on average), the object was to make the unchurched visitors feel immediately at home, able to understand everything they might experience from the moment they set foot in the building.

So far, this was right out of the playbook of the Revival: entertaining preliminaries and engaging message. Yet, the Willow Creek Seeker Service diverged from the Revival pattern by omitting an explicit altar call. The Barrington suburbanites disliked the pressure and guilt that an altar call might produce. In place of a confrontational altar call, the Seeker Service concluded with a nonconfrontational invitation to find out more about what the church had to offer. While this might seem like radical departure from the Revival model, it actually was a "new measures" approach to the altar call rather than an abandonment of it altogether. Willow Creek discerned that a soft-sell approach got a better response in the long run, and the proof was in the large numbers who came to the visitor center to find out more about what the church had to offer. Willow Creek did not ditch the altar call; they found a more successful method for achieving it.

The first complaint of the unchurched was that churches were always "asking for money." Willow Creek continued to take up collections at the weekend services, but they asked newcomers not to put anything in the plastic baskets being passed through the audience. However, the most important information that Willow Creek drew from this complaint is that suburbanites are concerned about the value of their money; they are willing to pay (and to devote time) only if the product they receive is first rate. Therefore, Willow Creek made sure that music, media, drama, and message were of the highest technological and professional quality possible and that the building and grounds always *looked great.*

Since the Barrington suburbanites found traditional churches "predictable and boring," Willow Creek decided to avoid anything that might give the appearance of a traditional church. Willow Creek first met in a theater in Barrington (an echo of Finney's congregation at the Chatham Theater in New York), and when they built the first auditorium on their Barrington campus, the inside looked much like a large, modern television studio. Like a television studio, the auditorium had absolutely no traditional Christian symbols or church-like decoration that indicated a distinctly religious setting.

It is important to note that the leadership of Willow Creek did not consider the Seeker Service to be worship for the members of the church.[42] Seeker Services were aimed at nonmembers. The actual membership at Willow Creek was much smaller than the numbers who came on the weekends. The members of the congregation (until recently at least) attended worship services on Wednesday or Thursday evenings. As worship, these weekday services involved much more congregational participation, including Holy Communion once a month.[43]

The Willow Creek Seeker Service is the gold standard for the pattern, and countless congregations around the world have emulated it. This is a service in the Revival tradition that has the goal of converting the lost, now more politely called the "unchurched." It has the Revival character of theatrical, emotionally effective, technology-driven worship. Components of the service are arbitrary "new measures," evaluated according to the

---

42. Pritchard states: "The church staff recognizes that the weekend service is not a worship service," *Willow Creek Seeker Services,* 25. See also Joe Horness, "Contemporary Music-Driven Worship," in *Exploring the Worship Spectrum, 6 Views,* ed. Paul E. Engle (Grand Rapids, MI: Zondervan, 2004), 107.

43. In recent years as a result of the *Reveal* study, the congregation has moved Communion services to the weekends.

results they produce. Like the Revival, the Seeker Service rejects traditional liturgical practice and embraces novelty.[44]

The Revival Macro-Pattern

Revival	Seeker Service
Preliminaries	*Preliminaries*
Welcome	Opening song, performed by band
Congregational songs led by leader	Welcome
Special music, solo or ensemble	Song, sung with congregation
Prayer, accompanied by music	New song, performed by band
Special music	Prayer, as music continues
Collection/music	Collection/music
[Testimony]	[Video presentation]
	[Dramatic sketch]
Message	*Message*
Preliminary remarks	Preliminary remarks
Scripture text/verse	Scripture text/verse
Preaching	Preaching
Altar Call	*[Altar Call]*
Closing prayer	Closing prayer
Call for decision	Closing song, performed by band
Closing music, as people respond	[Invitation to come next week]
	[Invitation to visitors' center]*

*Components in [ ] are optional.

---

44. William Dyrness provides a slightly different comparison chart, though the overall outline is the same, in *Primer on Christian Worship: Where We've Been, Where We're Going, and Where We Can Go* (Grand Rapids, MI: Eerdmans, 2009), 62.

> **Distinctive Liturgical Units and Character Features of the Revival/Seeker Pattern**
> Special music/selection sung by a soloist, ensemble, or choir
> Personal testimony
> Message (preaching aimed at the needs of the congregation)
> Invitation to learn about church
> Limited congregational verbal participation and gestures
> Use of novelty and entertainment to attract attention
> Dramatic sketch related to theme of message
> Video presentation, usually with music
> Audience oriented
> Designed for easy participation by the "unchurched"
> Collection for regular members only

Assessment of the Revival Macro-Pattern

From the days of Finney up to the present, the Revival has been both praised and vilified. Yet, once one accepts the principles of effectiveness and progress for evaluating churches, revivalism's consumerist approaches to Christianity seem irrefutable. The sales figures for church growth manuals, the popularity of marketing strategies for churches, the development of "brand" churches—evangelical, contemporary, Gen X, liberal, emerging, progressive—are all based on technological and consumerist principles of productivity, efficiency, and progress. Revivalism continues to be a major influence in American Christianity for congregations across the theological spectrum.[45]

What happens to the character of worship when congregations design services *according to the consumer preferences of the attendees*? Critics argue that the marketing style of American revivalism leads churches to adapt their ministries to the human beings as consumers of manufactured

---

45. Stephen Ellingson's study of West Coast Lutherans shows, in the face of declining attendance, that Lutherans are being thoroughly won over to the megachurch/Seeker model as a way to grow churches, despite the incongruence of this model for historic Lutheranism. See *The Megachurch and the Mainline: Remaking Religious Tradition in the Twenty-First Century* (Chicago, IL: University of Chicago Press, 2007), 178–90.

goods, which distorts the meaning of the gospel.[46] Earlier generations of Christian believers may have wondered, "How do I make my life fit to worship God in the company of the church?" A Revival/Seeker model leads attendees to ask, "How well does the worship of this church fit me?" Such worship no longer requires a sense of obligation or obedience, something I ought to do regardless of how I might feel about it at any particular moment. From the perspective of the congregation, the most important criterion for judging worship becomes: Do I like it?

Audience-centered worship requires a large investment of human and financial resources. Preachers and liturgical leaders are under tremendous pressure to come up with novel and entertaining presentations, and this takes time. Audience-centered worship also requires excellent multimedia equipment, technicians to run it, and an auditorium in which such media will work well. One common misconception about Seeker Services is that they are "casual." While a well-done Seeker Service may *feel* casual to the audience, there is nothing casual about it from the standpoint of leadership. A Seeker Service is planned down to the second. The lights come up, and a well-rehearsed band begins the first song. The preacher comes on stage and the lectern and props appear as if by magic. Actors in skits do not flub their lines. Sound, lights, projections all work perfectly. I can say from experience that it can be painful to worship with small, under-equipped, under-staffed congregations using cheap, inadequate equipment in hopes of emulating a megachurch. Technological and theatrical excellence is essential to the *ethos* of the Seeker Service, and without such excellence, a Seeker Service will likely fail to achieve its goal of being attractive to the unchurched.

Despite such problems, however, there is much to admire in the Revival/Seeker model of worship,[47] for it engages the democratic and populist *ethos* that has become indigenous to North American life and recognizes that North America is inescapably a *consumer* culture. Just as the church has

---

46. See, for example, Philip D. Kenneson and James L. Street, *Selling Out the Church: The Dangers of Church Marketing* (Nashville, TN: Abingdon Press, 1997).

47. For a critique of the "Sunday's Coming" video that emphasizes why this approach to worship can be compelling, see Taylor Burton Edwards, "'Sunday's Coming': A Companion Ritual Analysis," part one: http://www.gbod.org/site/apps/nlnet/content.aspx?c=nhLRJ2PMKsG&b=5609115&ct=8398993, accessed August 22, 2011; part two: http://www.gbod.org/site/apps/nlnet/content3.aspx?c=nhLRJ2PMKsG&b=6745269&ct=8402463, accessed August 22, 2011.

engaged with various cultures throughout history to become the Church of Jesus Christ in a particular location, American congregations cannot ignore the democratic habits and consumerism that Americans bring with them to church, even as they challenge these habits.[48] This is especially important for the work of evangelism, which means first engagement with the host culture.

The Revival/Seeker model also takes seriously the performance of worship leadership. While this may put pressure on liturgical leaders, put positively it challenges them to do their best. There is nothing salutary about sloppy leadership, even if it is sincere. If worship is the central and most visible activity of congregations, as a matter of respect it ought to be done well. Even a congregation that uses a fixed liturgy from a prayer book deserves ritual leadership that is competent.

Furthermore, while the Revival's obsession with novelty can be problematic, modern brain science has shown that there is, in fact, a strong correlation between the experience of novelty and human ability to pay attention. Finney was right about that. Science also shows that too much novelty can be overwhelming and provokes a drop in attention.[49]

Finally, even if some critics charge Revival/Seeker churches with wholesale accommodation to American culture, one may reach the opposite conclusion. By putting conversion first among its goals, the Revival/Seeker model challenges congregations to resist the assumption that they live in a Christian culture where the default mode of life and religion is Christianity.[50] Congregations that spawned the Seeker Service did not assume that they could put up a building and expect people to show up out of habit. They developed the model to attract people who were not believers, and since they were not already converted, the church did not

---

48. Vincent J. Miller, *Consuming Religion: Christian Faith and Practice in a Consumer Culture* (New York, NY: Continuum, 2003), 20–31.

49. Daniel T. Washington, *Why Don't Students Like School: A Cognitive Scientist Answers Questions* (San Francisco, CA: Jossey-Bass, 2009), 8–10. The need for novelty also correlates to how one understands the nature of a particular activity. This raises the problem about how we understand worship and ritual: is it more like entertainment, where a large amount of novelty might be desired, or is it more like the routines of daily life, where a little novelty goes a long way to keep routines fresh?

50. I think that the use of the neologism "unchurched" for people who are not actively Christian is a problem, however. It sounds as if being in church is the default way of life. That only makes sense in a hegemonic Christian culture.

expect them to do the things that experienced Christians would know how to do or want to do. It is highly significant that from its earliest days Willow Creek Church leadership has considered the Seeker Service to be only the first step into the life of faith. To be a full member of the church means joining a small discipleship group, receiving the sacraments, and making further commitments to support the work of the congregation. In short, the Seeker model recognizes that congregational worship cannot do everything; the unchurched require something more rudimentary.

Telos/Ethos of the Revival/Seeker Model (Expanded)

	Telos (Goal)	*Ethos* (Qualities of Character)
Nineteenth-century type: Revival	Convert the lost Revive the unmotivated	Emotional effectiveness Technological excellence Motivational expertise Disregard for traditional norms Novelty Confrontational interaction Audience-centered content "Stage" theatricality
Present form: Seeker Service	Reach the unchurched	Emotional effectiveness Technological excellence Motivational expertise Disregard for traditional norms Embrace of novelty Casualness (for audience) Nonconfrontational interaction Consumer-focused content Market-driven Multimedia dependent "Television" theatricality

Love it or hate it, the influence of the Revival/Seeker model of worship has been profound. Even critics of "new measures" often default to Finneyite arguments about genuine efficiency, productivity, and progress in worship. Motivation of congregations, effectiveness of leadership, meeting personal needs, being relevant to culture, suspicion of traditional practices and ways of thinking—these are the hallmarks of revivalism, and both liberal theological progressives and conservative technological progressives embrace them. As we look at other models of worship in subsequent chapters, we will continue to see the influence of Charles G. Finney.

CHAPTER FOUR
Worship as Education

The Sunday School

The supreme court of Illinois, in a decision rendered recently, seems to take the ground that the Sunday-school is not a service of worship in the sense contemplated by the law, exempting church property from taxation. . . . We do not think the argument of the court, that the Sunday-school is not part of worship, is correct. The Sunday-school, as those who have been connected with one know, is to a large extent the service in which children engage in public worship. There would be as much reason for an opinion on the part of the court that the sermon is not a part of public worship as it is to assume that the Sunday-school is not a part of public worship.

—*Northwestern Christian Advocate*,
"Illinois Supreme Court Decides That a Sunday School Is Not Public Worship"[1]

On Tuesday morning, the pastor prepares the worship bulletin for the following Sunday. She thinks to herself, *What shall we say for the unison prayer? We just finished our pledge campaign. Perhaps we should say something about our financial giving. It's also the first week in Advent; we need to acknowledge that.* She types "stewardship campaign Advent worship resources" into her web browser, and with a few short clicks, she finds this:

> Gracious God, we offer you thanks and praise for this season of anticipation, this season of Advent. As we prepare for the birth of your son, we share our tithes and offerings with the joy and excitement that is common as one anticipates the birth of a new child.[2]

---

1. Vol. 38, no. 2 (Jan 8, 1903): 54–55.

2. http://www.gbod.org/site/c.nhLRJ2PMKsG/b.3784705/k.A0D8/Stewardship.htm, accessed December 6, 2011.

Just about perfect, she thinks. *Anticipating Christmas and excitement in giving. All I need to add is a line about our successful campaign and we're good to go.*

Where did the pastor get the idea that planning worship meant composing ad hoc didactic prayers for her congregation to recite in unison? Though among many contemporary Protestant ministers this has become standard procedure, for most of the history of the church no pastor would have dared take such authority. This modern idea arose in the Sunday School over the course of the nineteenth century.

The Rise of the Sunday School

The church has not always had Sunday School. This may be surprising to many Protestants for whom the Lord's Day is synonymous with attending classes, or at least bringing their children to classes before or after worship. Yet nothing quite like it existed until the late eighteenth century. In 1780, Englishman Robert Raikes established the first Sunday School for the children of poor working-class families in his hometown of Gloucester. Raikes's school used the one free day a week to inculcate Christian values in the young poor, teaching them to read in order to learn the Bible and the Anglican catechism. Not only did the Sunday School have the evangelical goal of bringing poor children into a saving relationship to Christ, it also attempted to form useful, law-abiding subjects of the British Crown.[3] This social experiment in Gloucester caught the attention of the British press, and other cities soon began their own schools. Growth was astounding, and by 1787 Sunday School enrollment in England reached 250,000, according to best estimates.[4]

Word of the British Sunday School soon spread to the recently established United States of America. By 1790, church leaders of several denominations in Philadelphia started the "First Day Society" for the education of poor children. The following year, Methodist Bishop Francis Asbury recommended Sunday Schools for all the children of members of Methodist

---

3. Edwin Wilbur Rice, *The Sunday-School Movement and the American Sunday-School Union: 1780–1917* (Philadelphia, PA: American Sunday-School Union, 1917), 13–17.

4. Robert W. Lynn and Elliott Wright, *The Big Little School: 200 Years of the Sunday School* (Nashville, TN: Abingdon Press, 1980), 27–28. For standard histories of the Sunday School, in addition to Lynn and Wright, see Anne M. Boylan, *Sunday School: The Formation of an American Institution, 1790–1880* (New Haven, CT: Yale University Press, 1988).

societies, not only for the poor, and other denominations also adopted this more comprehensive approach.[5] Thus, in the United States, the Sunday School developed as a democratic institution spanning the social classes.

By the early nineteenth century, American Protestant congregations enthusiastically embraced Sunday School, and by the middle of the century many churches had also organized classes for adults.[6] In 1824, the American Sunday-school Union reported that its member churches enrolled 48,681 children, or roughly 1.5 percent of the population of children in the United States.[7] By 1833, that number had ballooned to 760,000 "scholars," and 80,913 volunteer teachers.[8] In 1890, the Methodist Episcopal Church alone claimed to have 300,000 teachers and 2.5 *million* scholars.[9] Not only was the Sunday School movement ecumenical, it also spanned the ethnic divide. The African Methodist Episcopal Church, Zion, for example, claimed a roll of 100,000 scholars in 1872, though their membership totaled only twice that number.[10]

Due to such rapid growth, the Sunday School movement had a huge effect on congregational life in the United States. First, it provided a significant new venue for the ministry of the laity. Among Episcopalians and Lutherans, clergy conducted the catechism classes for children preparing for confirmation, but other denominations did not have such a built-in system and depended on parents to catechize their children. The Sunday School movement changed this emphasis by placing the formal religious education of children in the hands of adult volunteers.

Second, the Sunday School required large amounts of time in planning and implementation, and this crowded an already full schedule of Lord's Day meetings. Some of the biggest debates in the movement were about

---

5. James E. Kirby, Russell E. Richey, and Kenneth E. Rowe, *The Methodists, Student Edition* (Westport, CT: Praeger, 1998), 171.

6. The Methodist Episcopal Church General Conference of 1860 mandated adult classes in the Sunday School. See Kirby, Richey, and Rowe, *The Methodists*, 202.

7. Boylan, *Sunday School*, 11.

8. *Ninth Annual Report of the American Sunday-school Union* (Philadelphia, PA: American Sunday-school Union, 1933), 3.

9. Kirby, Richey, and Rowe, *The Methodists*, 201.

10. *The Methodist Almanac* (New York, NY: Carlton and Lanahan, 1872), 19. *The Methodist Almanac* reports a similar Sunday School attendance to membership ratio for other historically black denominations.

Chapter Four

finding the ideal time for holding classes in relationship to the Sunday services. By the mid-nineteenth century, a few congregations experimented with holding classes at the same time as public worship, with Sunday School serving as a substitute "children's service."[11]

Third, the Sunday School required meeting space. Before the nineteenth century, Protestant churches were primarily places to gather for worship. As churches adopted a graded system of Sunday School curriculum, congregations expanded their facilities to accommodate the need for children's classrooms. Lewis Miller, a Sunday School superintendent in Akron, Ohio, planned, and his congregation built, the first Sunday School building in 1872. This Akron Plan (as it became known) was the most widely used pattern for church architecture for fifty years in the United States.

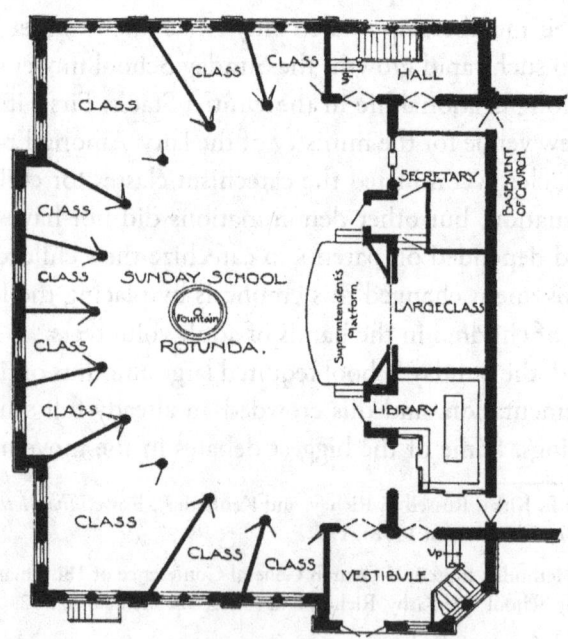

The Akron Plan[12]

---

11. "On Public Worship Suitable for Sunday School Children," *The Sunday School Teachers' Magazine and Journal of Education,* third series, vol. 1 (Jan 1844): 185–87.

12. Marion Lawrance, *Housing the Sunday School* (Philadelphia, PA: The Westminster Press, 1911), 87.

Nothing quite like it had ever existed, and both the religious and secular press of the day reported on Miller's Sunday School building.[13] With its movable partitions for classrooms and central rotunda for plenary exercises, the Akron Plan proposed the innovative concept of "multiuse" space for church architecture, including spaces formerly dedicated to worship alone. The Akron Plan fell out of favor by the early twentieth century, but by that time it was unimaginable for a congregation to undertake a church building project without considering appropriate meeting rooms for the Sunday School.

The adoption of the Sunday School added to the cost of being a church, not only the monetary cost of building construction and educational curriculum but also the cost of human resources necessary for making the educational programs work. The considerable requirements of the Sunday School had an inevitable influence on all aspects of church life, including the conduct of public worship.

The Sunday School Assembly: Opening and Closing Exercises

In 1828, at a meeting of the American Sunday-school Union, noted Congregationalist preacher Lyman Beecher offered a motion that neatly summarized the goal of the Sunday School:

> *Resolved,* That this meeting regard this Institution [the Sunday School] with high satisfaction, as eminently adapted to promote the intellectual and moral culture of the nation, to perpetuate our republican and religious institutions, and to reconcile eminent national prosperity with moral purity and future blessedness.[14]

---

13. Prominent architect George Kramer gushed about the Akron Plan Sunday School model: "It marked an era and an advance in church or ecclesiastical architecture such as had not been made for centuries." George W. Kramer, *The What, How, and Why of Church Building* (New York, NY: n.p., 1897), 218.

14. "Annual Report," in *The Fourth Report of the American Sunday-school Union* (Philadelphia, PA: American Sunday-school Union, 1828), 13.

Chapter Four

The *telos* of the Sunday School was to develop Christian knowledge and character in children and to strengthen these qualities in adults. In nineteenth-century America, this included formation in civic as well as religious virtues. The *ethos* of the Sunday School was didacticism, using the various "exercises" to effect spiritual and civic formation. This *ethos* pertained not only to classroom instruction but also to opening and closing exercises of the assemblies, such as the singing, praying, and unison reading that framed each session.

The "exercises," as they were called, brought elements of public worship to Sunday School assemblies. According to an 1839 teachers' manual of the American Sunday-school Union, "The usual introductory exercises are singing, reading the Scriptures and prayer."[15] The manual recommended that about twenty minutes be allotted to the devotional exercises, which were varied and accessible to children. The superintendent read the scripture lesson for the day, carefully pausing to explain difficult words or phrases. The key requirement for the readings, prayers, and hymns was their suitability for the sensibilities and capacities of the children.

As the Sunday School matured, the worship exercises gradually became more elaborate. At a training event in 1871, John Vincent, a leading proponent of the Sunday School, who would eventually become a Methodist bishop, provided this example of an order for the exercises:

I. Opening.

1. Singing.
2. The Beatitudes read by the assistant superintendent and the school. (Matt. v, 1–10.)
3. Prayer (the entire school standing.) Close by repeating in concert the Lord's Prayer.
4. Singing.
5. Roll of teachers.

---

15. Frederick Adolphus Packard, *The Teacher Taught, or an Humble Attempt to Make the Path of the Sunday-school Teacher Straight and Plain* (Cincinnati, OH: The American Sunday-school Union, 1939), 183ff.

II. Bible Study.

1. Announcement of the lesson.
2. Preparatory prayer.
3. Study for thirty minutes.
4. Recitation of the Golden Text [Matt. 5:6, 8]
5. General Review.

III. Closing.

1. Singing.
2. Closing service.

> Let the whole school rise at the signal and repeat the following: "Let the words of my mouth and the meditation of my heart be acceptable in thy sight, O Lord, my strength and Redeemer."
> Then the superintendent shall say: "The Lord watch between me and thee when we are absent one from the other."[16]

Vincent's order illustrates how certain memory exercises became a fixed part of the order: the Lord's Prayer, the Golden Text and, in this example, the concluding response between the students and the superintendent.

What is not obvious from Vincent's order is that the reading of the Beatitudes would also have been done responsively between the school and the superintendent. British Anglicans and American Episcopalians had long been accustomed to the responsive reading of psalms, but other Protestant churches avoided this practice, which required both access to books (a prayer book or Bible) and the ability to read well out loud with others. In 1855, an anonymous review essay by a Congregationalist minister in *The New Englander and Yale Review* stated what was a widespread concern regarding responsive readings in public worship:

---

16. John H. Vincent, *The Sunday-school Institutes and Normal Classes* (San Francisco, CA: K. Thomas; Cincinnati, OH: Hitchcock & Waldern, 1872), 80–81.

> The responsive reading of the Psalms, and of other devotional parts of Scripture, between the minister and the congregation, or the repetition of the Lord's Prayer by the whole assembly, would be quite certain to break down, if attempted in any of our churches. Anything of that sort, we are sure, will be a failure. The Methodist responses in prayer—each worshiper uttering his own *Amen*, to express his participation in the petitions offered—would be more consistent with Scriptural indications of primitive usage, and therefore more consistent with the genius of our system.[17]

Despite such protests, the Sunday School embraced the responsive method as a way to enliven the reading of scripture with direct student engagement. Students were already acquainted with the question and answer format of the catechisms and scripture lessons, and responsive reading was very similar in form. By the end of the century, hymnals printed specifically for the Sunday School contained lessons set out in responsive format. At countless conventions and workshops, both ecumenical and denominational, Sunday School leaders presented examples of responsive readings. Gradually, Sunday School teachers in "nonliturgical" churches throughout the United States and Canada embraced this very Anglican, liturgical method of reciting.

In 1872 the American Sunday-school Union adopted a series of uniform lessons to facilitate the preparation and dissemination of literature. The uniform lessons enabled publishers of church literature to produce aids based on the standard lesson series that included lesson plans, along with hymns, prayers, and responsive readings composed specifically for children and keyed to the scripture text for each Sunday. The promotion of this literature in conferences and workshops increased the spread of liturgical materials among nonliturgical denominations. Baptist, Methodist, Presbyterian, and Congregationalist leaders accepted the uniform lesson plan quite warmly. Ironically, the very churches that were adamantly opposed to the notion of a fixed lectionary for worship and preaching adopted a fixed, ecumenical lectionary for the readings, prayers, and hymns in the Sunday School.

Once the gate was open, Sunday School teachers in nonliturgical traditions began to borrow other bits of liturgical practice, such as the use

---

17. "The Puritan Ritual," *New Englander and Yale Review*, vol. 13, no 4 (1855): 461.

of chant, fixed benedictions, sung doxologies, the Lord's Prayer, the Ten Commandments, and the Apostles' Creed.[18] By the beginning of the twentieth century, the use of responsive readings expanded to include the call to worship and various litanies composed according to themes for the day's class. In short, nonliturgical denominations embraced standardized scripture readings, responsive reading of psalms, scripture passages, calls to worship, and written prayers as devotional exercises in the Sunday School.

From Devotional Exercises to Enrichments of Worship

Today it might seem counterintuitive to suggest that the modern use of responsive readings, chants, creeds, recitations, and doxologies originated in children's Sunday School assembly. Yet in the nineteenth century, these devotional exercises of the Sunday School were participatory and engaging in ways that the typical sermon-centered worship service would not be. In historical context, the devotional exercises were "child-appropriate," and children, reportedly, enjoyed them. Perhaps the best evidence that the devotional exercises succeeded is that children, formed in the devotional exercises of the Sunday School, brought these participatory practices with them as they matured into adult worshipers. By the late nineteenth century, Methodists, Baptists, and Presbyterians incorporated the devotional exercises into the Sunday service by calling them "enrichments of worship."[19] Indeed, "the united prayings and praisings and recitings of the Sunday-school" (as educator Clay Trumbull described them)[20]

---

18. John J. Matthias, *The Sunday School Manual* (New York, NY: Lane & Scott, 1848).

19. For example, from a popular weekly paper: "Closely allied to the matter of Scripture-reading is the matter of a responsive service. Indeed, when the enrichment of our public worship is spoken of, this is what is generally intended—this and a multiplicity of printed prayers." *Public Opinion*, vol. 8, no. 20 (Feb 22, 1890): 476.

20. In his influential Yale lectures on the Sunday School, H. Clay Trumbull commented: "Many, very many children have thus been helped into Christ-likeness by the influence of the united prayings and praisings and recitings of the Sunday-school." *The Sunday-school: Its Origin, Mission, Methods, and Auxiliaries, Yale Lectures on the Sunday-school* (Philadelphia, PA: John D. Wattles, 1888), 198.

had become training in the use of ad hoc liturgical material for adult worshipers in nonliturgical churches.[21]

Larger, more affluent congregations incorporated Sunday School practices and liturgical books and materials into the Sunday service as enrichments of worship, but for smaller, rural congregations, the use of Sunday School exercises for congregational worship was less intentional. Few small or ethnic minority congregations could afford to build separate auditoriums for the children's programs. For these churches, both the Sunday School assembly and public worship took place in the same space. Moreover, many rural congregations did not have the luxury of employing a pastor for a preaching service every Sunday morning. Since the Sunday School assembly did not require a pastor, congregations would have their weekly Sunday School meeting on those weeks when the preacher was elsewhere. For many of these congregations, the Sunday School assembly, conducted by laity, became the regular weekly opportunity for worship, and even when a preacher came, the preaching service began immediately after the Sunday School assembly in the same room. Well into the twentieth century, it was not uncommon for the closing reports, devotional readings, prayers, responses, and songs of the Sunday School assembly to function as the first part of the preaching service in rural congregations, or to take the place of the preaching service if a pastor was not scheduled to preach.[22] Some larger African American congregations still begin the Sunday service with reports and devotions that are remnants of the Sunday School assembly.

Preaching for Children

As noted above, disputes arose early in the Sunday School movement about the relationship of the children's meeting to the public worship of congregations. Most leaders at the national level strongly discouraged calling the Sunday School "the children's church," as if it could substitute for

---

21. The Methodist bishop who complained about the diversity of worship orders (chapter 2 above) was referring to these "enrichments" that came from the Sunday School.

22. In the 1980s I served a circuit of three rural United Methodist congregations that began Sunday Worship with the closing devotions of the Sunday School.

public worship. Children were expected to attend both Sunday School and public worship, and since the Sunday School assembly was not a full service of public worship, it did not ordinarily have a place for preaching. Nevertheless, superintendents or teachers would offer child-appropriate illustrations while teaching the lessons, and Sunday School journals and books of the day abound with examples of such illustrative material. Though this was not preaching, it did suggest the usefulness of sermons using illustrations that children could understand.

The first examples of preaching for children by pastors took place not in Sunday School assemblies in the morning but in monthly "concerts" for children sponsored by the Sunday School program. For these meetings, the pastor would deliver a sermon that incorporated illustrations similar to those employed by teachers. As one Sunday School leader described a typical example: "[The] pastor takes the skeleton of a discourse preached to the adult members of his congregation, and fills it up with teachings, illustrations, and facts comprehensible to the most juvenile mind, and so makes a children's sermon."[23] Initially, few pastors were adept at doing this, and complaints abound in Sunday School journals of preachers' awkward attempts with children's sermons. This did not keep the practice from growing in popularity, even among adult listeners who reported enjoying hearing their minister preach in simple language using simple illustrations.[24] Under the pressure of revivalism, preachers sought to be more challenging and theatrical, but under the influence of the Sunday School their sermons became more friendly and practical. By the 1880s, many American pastors of congregations across the spread of denominations were inviting the young to come forward for a brief children's message during the Sunday morning service itself. The modern children's sermon, with its short scripture reading and practical illustrations, is a liturgical unit that originated with the Sunday School.

---

23. Erwin House, *The Sunday School Teacher*, vol. 3 (1868): 70.

24. A typical observation: "The children's sermons have sometimes been spoken of as the best part of the day's service." *Minutes of the Seventy-Eighth Annual Meeting of the Congregational Churches of Massachusetts* (Boston, MA: Congregational Publishing Society, 1880), 17.

Chapter Four

Twentieth-Century Developments

Throughout the nineteenth century, religious education largely followed a schooling model that emphasized reading, recitation, and rote memorization. By the early twentieth century, educational theory began to stress the importance of the students' experiences in the event of teaching. For religious educators, the discussion developed under the category of "the psychology of religion," which sought a scientific basis for its methods. The pragmatist philosophies of William James and John Dewey lent intellectual heft to the exploration of experience as a scientific category.[25] Educators proposed that experience, approached scientifically, could more effectively shape the moral life of the individual, which was the implicit *telos* of the Sunday School. Before long, the new science of education found its place in the curricula of theological seminaries, which began training professional religious educators in the educational methods of the time. Experience-based religious education aimed to do more than teach the Bible and catechism; it sought to shape individuals, both children and adults, to take a role in "creating a more ethical society."[26]

As we have seen, the nineteenth-century Sunday Schools had already incorporated experiential activities through the devotional exercises of the assemblies. Sunday School leaders justified the use of devotional exercises as ways to keep children's attention, to develop their piety, and to train them to join in the Sunday worship with the rest of the congregation. In the twentieth century, the importance of worship as an experiential activity received even greater emphasis as a way of shaping the social values of young people. Hugh Hartshorne, a professor of religious education at Union Seminary in New York, stressed the social significance of worship in numerous essays and books on worship in the Sunday School. Hartshorne acknowledged the importance of devotional prayer and singing for producing religious feelings, but he stressed the practical (and ethical) effects these

---

25. William James, *The Varieties of Religious Experience* (London: Longmans, Green, and Co., 1911); John Dewey, *Democracy and Education* (New York, NY: MacMillan, 1916).

26. David Ralph Bains, "The Liturgical Impulse in Mid-Twentieth-Century American Mainline Protestantism" (Harvard University unpublished PhD dissertation, 1999), 46.

practices had on the attitudes and ethical habits of worshipers. For him, worship was "a means by which a leader may control the social experience of a group so as to conserve and develop social values."[27]

According to Hartshorne, it was the task of worship planners, both in public worship of the congregation and in the preparation of worship in the Sunday School, to plan orders of service that would achieve ethical social formation by changing attitudes:

> The minister has a definite purpose and a definite plan. He wishes to bring the congregation to a new point of view or to a new resolve. To this end he selects music, hymns, prayers, Scripture, and addresses, and weaves all into a harmonious whole which shall, in its total effect, induce the desired change in the minds of the audience.[28]

As radical as his rhetoric may sound, Hartshorne's book of resources for Sunday School worship largely drew from historical liturgical material of the Anglican tradition. Even the modern children's hymn texts he recommended fit traditional European hymn tunes.[29]

Soon, however, religious educators proposed more innovative approaches to worship. In 1935, Marie Cole Powell, a Methodist Christian educator at Boston University, used experience-based educational methods in her book, *Guiding the Experience of Worship*. She stated bluntly that "worship itself is not primarily a form; it is an experience. . . . The most important thing about it is its experience quality."[30] According to Powell, successful worship planning constructed a meaningful experience of God. Like Hartshorne, Powell believed this required more than an understanding of the Bible and theology: "The one who is to plan worship programs must be something of a scientist and also of an artist as well as a

---

27. Hugh Hartshorne, *Worship in the Sunday School: A Study in the Theory and Practice of Worship* (New York, NY: Teachers College, Columbia University, 1913), 28. See also Bains, "The Liturgical Impulse," 46.

28. Hartshorne, *Worship in the Sunday School*, 115–16.

29. Hugh Hartshorne, *The Book of Worship of the Church School* (New York, NY: Charles Scribner's Sons, 1916).

30. Marie Cole Powell, *Guiding the Experience of Worship* (Cincinnati, OH: The Methodist Book Concern, 1930), 14. For the term "worship experience," see page 22.

religionist."[31] Rather than using historical liturgical material to construct meaningful worship experiences, however, Powell promoted the use of entertaining stories, talk-back sessions, music, pictures, and even projected slides synchronized with worshipful music. Presciently, in that 1935 book she further suggested that future churches would use "moving pictures" to produce experiences in worship.[32]

The Organization of Sunday School Worship throughout the Year

Controlling the formative experiences of Christians, thus, became a central problem of planning worship programs, and for churches that were not wedded to a prayer book tradition, this raised the problem of the organization of worship for each Sunday throughout the calendar year. The uniform lesson series of the American Sunday-school Union provided one form of organization, and various denominational and independent publishing houses published lesson helps based on the series that included printed prayers and suggestions for illustrative hymns for individual graded classes. Such devotion aids, however, were not always suitable for worship in the plenary assembly of the Sunday School. Hartshorne was among the first to propose that Sunday School worship could be profitably organized according to themes. In his first book on Sunday School worship, he suggested the fundamental Christian attitudes of "gratitude, goodwill, reverence, faith and loyalty" as the thematic framework for a six-week series covering the period from Thanksgiving through Easter.[33] The practice of organizing Sunday School worship according to a thematic series waned in the mid-twentieth century as the Sunday School assembly itself gradually fell into disuse. However, the idea was taken up by Protestant preachers in the form of the sermon series, and in this form entered

---

31. Powell, *Guiding the Experience of Worship*, 30.
32. Powell, *Guiding the Experience of Worship*, 159–60.
33. Hartshorne, *Worship in the Sunday School*, 50–51.

into public worship. Today, the megachurch movement has revived the practice of thematic, sermon-series worship.

Another way the Sunday School movement began to organize worship thematically is through the promotion of standard "special days" during the year. The first of the special days promoted by the American Sunday-school Union emphasized the work of the Sunday School itself, with schools commemorating Rally Day each fall, when students advanced in the graded school. By the late nineteenth century, Sunday Schools recognized Children's Day (which emphasized education) and Decision Day. While the historic Christian festivals of Christmas and Easter were widely (but not universally) celebrated by Protestants, the Sunday School began to emphasize these days, along with civic holidays such as New Year's and the Sunday before July 4. Thanksgiving Day, Mother's Day, and Father's Day all found support through the Sunday School, and publishers of church literature provided teachers with examples of opening and closing exercises appropriate to these days.

In the early twentieth century, Marion Lawrance, who for years served as general secretary of the International Sunday School Association, remarked, "There are over two hundred 'Special Days' being observed in the Sunday Schools of North America. . . . At least one hundred of these have come into more or less prominence."[34] Since obviously no Sunday School could acknowledge all of these days, leaders had to choose which were appropriate for their own setting. Lawrance proposed that all Sunday Schools should observe Christmas and Easter ("the two great feasts of our Lord's birth and resurrection") along with Children's Day and Rally Day. Thus, Protestant congregations in traditions that historically rejected the Catholic liturgical year began to adopt a standard rota of special days, which would become a kind of alternative liturgical calendar.[35]

---

34. *Special Days in the Sunday School* (New York, NY: Fleming H. Revell Company, 1916), 7.

35. As Protestants began to reclaim a more expanded liturgical calendar in the second half of the twentieth century, clashes arose as, for example, when Pentecost fell on Mother's Day. Moms usually won out in the battle for attention, even when they competed with the Holy Spirit!

Chapter Four

Contents

10

VII. GOOD FELLOWSHIP DAYS **118**
Birthday Sunday—Visitors' Day—Old Carol Day—Music Day—Song Day—Welcome Day—Pennant Day—Reminiscent Day—Strangers' Day—Church Day—St. Valentine's Day (Heart Day).

VIII. RECREATION DAYS **128**
Picnic (Field Day)—May Day—Swinging Festival—Parade Day (Big Walk Day).

IX. PATRIOTIC DAYS **137**
Patriotic Day (Flag Day, Independence Day, Dominion Day)—Good Citizenship Day—Decoration Day (Memorial Day)—Peace Day—Washington's Birthday—Lincoln's Birthday—Lee's Birthday.

X. FOLK AND FRATERNAL DAYS . . . **144**
Alumni Day—Home-Coming Day—Reunion Day—Sweet Memory Day—Shut-Ins' Day—Farewell Sunday—Pastor's Day—Superintendent's Day—Teachers' Day—Christian Endeavor Day—Epworth League Day—Baptist Young People's Union Day—Young Men's Christian Association Day—Young Women's Christian Association Day—World's Sunday School Day—International Sunday School Association Day (Organized Sunday School Work Day).

XI. EDUCATIONAL DAYS **154**
Education Day—College Day—Day-School Day—Vocation Day—City Institute Day (Community Institute Day, Community Training School Day)—Teacher Training Day—Convention Sunday (Echo Sunday)—Bible Day—Book Day—Exhibit Day—Equipment Day—Honor Day—Inspection Day—Inventory Day—Standard Day—Promotion Day.

A Portion of the Table of Contents of Special Days in the Sunday School[36]

---

36. Lawrance, *Special Days*, 10.

As the more significant special days became standard across the denominational spectrum, exercises associated with the special days, and promoted in Sunday School literature, also became standardized. Rally Day, held the last Sunday in September as students advanced in grade level, typically began with a parade of the children (i.e., a procession) carrying banners. On the Sunday closest to Independence Day in the United States, children would salute both the American flag and the "Christian flag" by raising their hands and reciting a Pledge of Allegiance.

Special day programs could be quite elaborate. As an example of an effective program for Easter, Lawrance described in minute detail an exercise called The Changed Cross, which is worth quoting at length:

> A large cross is made of heavy wire screening, with meshes perhaps a half-inch square. The cross stands six feet high, with front and sides ten or twelve inches wide, and the back open. The members of the school are asked to bring carnations—usually all of one color. The school, also, purchases a quantity, that there may surely be an abundance—seconds, or splits as they are called by the florist, are quite good enough. [Here he describes a procession bringing flowers to the chicken wire cross.] A young man, standing behind the cross, pulls the stems until the flowers are up against the frame. When the cross is covered, it looks as though it were built entirely of carnations. A beautiful Easter lily is inserted in the middle of the cross where the four arms meet, and above the cross, on a wire frame prepared for that purpose, is placed a good-sized teacher's Bible, open, and over this, a small spray of smilax. Reference to the accompanying picture will give some idea of the finished cross. The cross shown was made up of assorted colors. It is much more beautiful when of one solid color. At this point the pastor gives a message, which is intended to be the message of the Easter cross. The lights in the church are all turned off, while the school sings "In the Cross of Christ I Glory." As soon as the singing begins, electric lights are turned on inside the cross. (The wiring has, of course, been done in advance, and the whole electric apparatus, except the bulbs, really forms a part of the cross, but does not show.) At the service last year, referred to above, the carnations were all dark red, and no words can describe the effect upon the audience as this beautiful, blood-red cross shone out in the darkness, while the words, "In the Cross of Christ I Glory," were being sung.

Chapter Four

Changed Cross[37]

---
37. Lawrance, *Special Days*, 28.

Understandably, few churches would follow all of Lawrance's carefully scripted order for "The Changed Cross"; yet many churches did adopt the flower-adorned cross for Easter. To this day, numerous congregations in the southern United States continue to set up a chicken wire cross covered in flowers for Easter Sunday.

Worship as Printed Resources

As the examples above demonstrate, by the early twentieth century, Protestants from the so-called nonliturgical denominations were embracing an increasingly wide variety of ritual practices in the Sunday School. These ad hoc ritual practices were disseminated through books, journals, and magazines in which professional religious educators shared their ideas for engaging children and youth in worship activities that would grab their attention, engage their minds, and shape their habits. The earliest examples of Sunday School worship drew liturgical material primarily from the Bible, historic traditional prayers, and traditional hymns. Yet, with a new awareness of the power of experience to shape piety and behavior, religious educators, such as Powell and Lawrance, began to construct ritual programs with exuberant creativity. Some of the new practices advocated by religious educators were similar to the popular devotions of European Catholics and Lutherans. Lawrance's Changed Cross, for example, was similar to a popular devotion of Hispanic Catholics on the Feast of the Holy Cross, though it is unlikely Lawrance was aware of this similarity. To give a better-known example, the Advent Wreath originated as a family devotional practice in northern Europe, but it gained popularity in public worship among American Protestants through its promotion in religious education publications.

The invention of affordable machines for printing greatly expanded the use of locally printed material in worship.[38] In the early twentieth century, even more humble congregations began to publish bulletins for worship, as well as for use in the Sunday School assembly, and publishers

---

38. On the origins of church bulletins, see David Russell, "A History of Church Bulletins," *Studia Liturgica* 35 (2005): 60–80.

of Sunday School literature supplied liturgical materials that could be duplicated for the assembly. The first publication to employ the phrase "worship resources" is a 1948 collection of materials to use with adolescents.[39] By the 1950s, the *International Journal of Religious Education*, published by the National Council of Churches, had a section entitled Worship Resources, which included orders of worship for various age groups in the Sunday School. Soon the publication of books of worship resources began to expand beyond the domain of the Sunday School, but the concept of producing materials for worship originated among religious educators.

The development of the concept of "worship resources" illustrates the significant shift in the understanding of worship we have already seen in the Revival model. Previous generations of Christians understood public worship as an established group activity to which one submitted oneself. This was the case both for denominations that used prayer books and for nonliturgical churches that avoided printed prayers. Pastors prepared sermons and musicians chose music, but the actual planning of the order and content of Sunday worship required very little attention since it was more or less standard. With the rising emphasis on experience in the early twentieth-century educational methods, worship became a program that leaders had to construct each week to engage the children effectively. The Bible, written prayers, hymns, popular devotional practices, and newly published materials (denominational or otherwise) all became more or less equivalent items in the storehouse of worship resources.

Creative Worship

By the late twentieth century, the direct influence of the Sunday School assembly as an institution had declined, but the character of worship developed in the Sunday School continued to influence congregations. In the 1960s and 1970s, many Protestant leaders embraced with renewed enthusiasm the goal of shaping the hearts and minds of worshipers. The watchword for worship was *relevance*, as seen in the way one congregation described its aspirations for worship:

---

39. David R. Porter, *Worship Resources for Youth* (New York, NY: Association Press, 1948).

> [To c]ompletely divest the service of the nineteenth-century attitudes, customs, and art forms, except selected hymn texts relevant to modern life, with particular emphasis on eliminating the erroneous "sacred music" or "churchy" stereotypes of the early 1900s.[40]

Among mainline congregations this included ethical relevance, typically characterized as a "prophetic voice" that addressed the burning social issues of the day. But it also meant personal relevance, and in the irreverent spirit of the 1960s and 1970s, worship found a new playful spirit—out with the staid forms of tradition and in with worship as "party," using celebrative props such as burlap banners and balloons.[41] Mimes and clowns took their place alongside preachers and acolytes. Worship became "fun" as a way of being socially provocative.

This Creative Worship movement (as it is self-described in numerous worship resource books of the 1970s) is in direct line with the didactic, resource-oriented approach of Sunday School worship. College campus ministries welcomed the Creative Worship movement, as did many mainline theological seminaries, and from the campus, Creative Worship services found their way into local congregations. Creative Worship often used ostensibly traditional forms (call to worship, prayer of confession, etc.) but with decidedly "hip" twists. Here is an example of a call to worship for Christmas, from a widely used collection of resources:

> *Leader:* Good Morning!
> *People:* Good Morning!
> *Leader:* Welcome to another week of life.
> *People:* We have come to celebrate out of gratitude.
> *Leader:* We celebrate not just the past but the present.
> *People:* We celebrate not the day He was born nor the place:
> *Leader:* For that place and time then and there are like nothing
> *People:* Compared with the fact that He is present here and now![42]

---

40. From a description by Kenneth S. Jones of the "Church-O-Theque," a contemporary worship meeting in Washington, DC, in the late 1960s, in David James Randolph, ed., *Ventures in Worship*, vol. 1 (Nashville, TN: Abingdon Press, 1969), 6.

41. See, for example, David James Randolph, *God's Party: A Guide to New Forms of Worship* (Nashville, TN: Abingdon Press, 1975).

42. Randolph, *God's Party*, 12.

Chapter Four

One may immediately notice how "un-churchy" the language sounds, though there are remnants of liturgical vocabulary ("gratitude"). Despite the simple language, however, this call to worship is patently didactic. As worshipers read aloud, they declare they come to celebrate with gratitude, but they also declare they are not celebrating the day or place of Jesus's birth (presumably, though Jesus is not explicitly named) but rather Jesus's presence "here and now." A worshiper might wonder, "Really? I thought I came to celebrate Jesus's birth in Bethlehem." Yet that is part of the didactic method of Creative Worship. Worshipers are made to say things they might find problematic in order to get them to think about what they are saying. The use of exclamation points urges worshipers to recite these statements with enthusiasm. Indeed, the liberal use of exclamation points is a hallmark of Creative Worship, along with use of such banal exchanges as "Good morning!"

The following Congregational Confession illustrates the intensely personal, idiosyncratic tenor of Creative Worship, even as it provokes ethical awareness:

> Lord (slight pause), Lord (pause), Lord, I want you to hear me. I know you do hear me but sometimes when I look around this world, this city, this community, even this church, I fear you must not be listening. Is it a sin to feel this way? . . .
>
> Yes, Father, we know many of your children are in poverty. We know that many of your children are being killed by a war that reflects our own greed, selfishness, and misunderstanding. But we didn't know what to do so we have done nothing. Oh, and about poverty which breeds mistrust and misunderstanding which we sometimes experience right in this neighborhood, we are taking care of that—we are having a meeting, I know it's a long meeting, but it has taken us one hundred years to decide that something needs to be done and even now some appear to be a bit doubtful.
>
> Father (pause), Father (slight pause), I hope you have heard us, Father, for there is so much more to tell, but I'm afraid that this will have to do for now. I know we do not deserve your forgiveness, but please do forgive us. Forgive us, but put heat under our feet and at the ends of our backs, where we insist upon sitting, that we might be free of ourselves to be true instruments for Thee. Amen.[43]

---

43. Randolph, *God's Party*, 21.

The pauses, scripted into the prayer, help the congregation think about what they are saying by slowing down the tempo of reading. The shifts between the first-person singular and plural, the language of deeply personal struggle ("Is it a sin to feel this way?"), and the use of irony ("we are taking care of that—we are having a meeting"), make each reader of the prayer experience the ethical concerns the writer of the prayer obviously felt quite strongly.

Detailed ritual directions for the congregation ("pause . . . long pause . . .") are distinctive features of Creative Worship orders and illustrate worship designers' control over congregational performance. Such instructions are necessary in Creative Worship liturgies to enable a congregation to engage in the unfamiliar ritual. When directions are not printed, leaders of Creative Worship typically give explicit and sometimes lengthy oral directions to the congregations to enable participation.

Another hallmark of the Creative Worship model is the use of freshly composed Statements of Faith in the place of historic creeds or confessions. These statements often combine phrases from historic creeds with phrases that depict mundane aspirations in order to emphasize the immanence of religious faith. Here is an excerpt from a typical example:

> We believe the Holy Spirit works through
> > balloons and ministers
> > daisies and wiggly children
> > clanging cymbals and silence
> > drama and the unexpected
> > choirs and banners
> > touching and praying
> > spontaneity and planning
> > faith and doubt
> > tears and laughter
> > leading and supporting
> > hugging and kneeling
> > dancing and stillness . . .[44]

Unlike the historic creeds or affirmations of faith, which focus on salvation history or the dogmatic content of faith, this statement draws attention to the actions of the local church community as an affirmation of God's

---

44. Ann Weems, *Reaching for Rainbows* (Philadelphia, PA: Westminster Press, 1980), 17–18.

immanence in everything the community does. The congregation is provoked to ask, "I wonder how the Spirit might work through balloons?"

Here is an example of the order printed in a bulletin that shows how Creative Worship works. It is from an actual ecumenical worshiping community near a college campus:

Ecumenical worshiping community, near a college campus
April 20, 1975

THE COMMUNITY GATHERS

Prelude
Greeting
Invocation
Fellowship
Act of Praise
> L. Clap your hands!
> P. Stamp your feet!
> L. Shout your praise to the Lord!
> P. Praise God! Alleluia! Praise God! Amen!

Hymn

TO AFFIRM FAITH

Affirmation of Faith
> L. The Sweet taste of God's grace lingers in our mouths. Let us affirm our faith.
> P. God's love pours out on his people without regard to their merit. He takes us as we are and offers life beyond measure. His love fills us and provides the overflow that we share with others. As we love others, as we are consumed for them, we show our love for God and our thanks for his love for us. This gift of self, this sharing of the wine of life, is our mission.

TO SHARE AND PRAY

Sharing Joys and Sorrows
Pastoral Prayer
Special Music

TO HEAR THE WORD

An Ancient Word: Mark 8:34–38.
A Contemporary Word: Cost of Living (N.B: a devotional reading)
A Comment on the Word: Cost of Loving

TO CONFESS SIN

Confession
> L. We have been angry in our hearts and hurtful in our deeds. Let's confess our sin.
>
> P. Lord God, when the songs of Zion are too hard to sing because of anger and disappointment, forgive us. When in our hearts we harbor bitterness and resentment, forgive us. Teach us that brothers and sisters are to share each other's burdens to become open and honest in thought and deed. Forgive us when we forget and when we prize our hurts rather than discharging them. By the power of Christ Jesus we pray. Amen.

TO DEPART TO SERVE

Announcements
Offering
Circle of Love (N.B.: the congregation forms a large circle, holding hands, as the pastor gives the Benediction)
Benediction
Sharing of Self (N.B.: lots of hugs)

While this order contains several elements of historic Christian worship (invocation, confession, affirmation of faith, benediction, etc.), all of the elements have a creative twist. The "Affirmation of Faith," for example, contains none of the doctrinal statements of a historic creed; rather, the congregation declares a set of religious attitudes: "As we love others, as we are consumed for them." In addition to scripture (An Ancient Word: Mark 8:34–38), the order includes a contemporary reading (A Contemporary Word: Cost of Living—which may have been a poem, though this is not credited in the bulletin). In place of a "sermon" or "message," the preacher offers "A Comment on the Word: Cost of

Chapter Four

Loving."[45] The instructive labeling of each portion of the order ("The Community Gathers," "To Hear the Word," "To Depart to Serve," etc.) is typical of services in the Creative Worship model. The didactic force of this service is to teach the college students in attendance to be kind to each other, to form a close-knit community of support. As in the Sunday School model, this is worship specifically constructed by the leaders for the assessed needs of that particular congregation, just as a "children's sermon" is composed for a group of children. I attended worship with this congregation as a young man, and I can testify that it engaged me thoroughly and formed my expectations of worship. For several years afterward, as I became a pastor, this was the sort of worship I hoped to construct for my congregations.

The Sunday School Macro-Pattern (Typical Example)

Opening Exercises
[Gathering]
Singing
Responsive reading (Matt v. 1–10.)
Prayer
Lord's Prayer
[Apostles' Creed]
Singing
Roll call
Bible Study
Closing
Singing
Memory verse
[Devotional reading]
Benediction

---

45. Creative Worship tends to avoid labels like "sermon," "preaching," or "message." In addition to this example, the preaching is given such tags as "prophetic word," "interpretation," "witness," "response to the reading," and so forth.

Creative Worship Macro-Pattern (Typical Example)

Gathering
Fellowship
Call to Worship
Song
Affirmation of Faith
Opening Prayers
Sharing of Joys and Sorrows
Pastoral Prayer
Special Music
Word Service
Readings
Preaching
Responses to the Word
Confession
Announcements
Offering
Departing to Serve
Benediction
Dismissal
Fellowship

Distinctive Liturgical Units and Character Features of the Sunday School/Creative Worship Pattern

Responsive reading (of scripture, prayers, or other texts)

Printed prayers (thanksgiving, confession, intercession) and other liturgical material composed for a target group, read in unison

Call to worship (responsive)

Affirmation of faith composed for a target group

Children's sermon

Use of readings other than scripture

Written or oral directions for participation in worship

Use of dance or choreographed actions

Use of "props" and object lessons

Thematic worship

Chapter Four

Assessment of the Sunday School/ Creative Worship Macro-Pattern

The character of Sunday School worship, as I have described it, has some similarities to the character of Revival worship. Just as the Revival placed a high priority on novelty as a way of holding attention, the Sunday School model, especially in the early twentieth century, also used novelty to hold attention and to produce fresh experiences in worship. Worship planners of both models construct worship for the effect it has on a congregation. In short, both share a thoroughly anthropological (rather than a theological) understanding of telos of worship; the most important value of worship is its effects on human beings rather than on its ostensible service to God.

Yet the differences between the Revival and the Sunday School forms of worship are significant. Revival worship aims at sudden, emotionally fraught conversion, while Sunday School worship aims for gradual and deliberate Christian formation. Revivals treat the participants as an audience with relatively passive involvement in the conduct of the service. The Sunday School, on the other hand, promotes an active involvement in all of its participants through such actions as responsive readings. Both Revival worship and Sunday School worship depend upon strong leaders to plan and implement worship. However, a Revival is led by "experts," and this professionalism lends mystique and power to Revival preaching and music. The Sunday School began as a lay institution, with leaders chosen from the local setting from among the active members of congregations. Therefore, Sunday School worship, as a model, is much less polished and professional than Revival worship. In short, the Revival is like the theater, with the preacher and musicians putting on a dramatic performance for an audience. The Sunday School is like a classroom or a gymnasium, with the worship planners and leaders putting the congregation through practical exercises, like a teacher or coach.

Sunday School worship recognizes the power of liturgical rituals to form thought and habit, much like Christians understood worship before Charles Finney's "New Measures."[46] Nevertheless, the Sunday School also marks a significant break with earlier Christian understandings of worship, for in the Sunday School virtually all of the ritual of worship is left up to those who plan and construct the service. As noted above, Sunday School leaders in the nineteenth and early twentieth centuries often chose worship resources from books published for the Sunday School market. Before the influence of Sunday School worship, congregations did not ordinarily have to read aloud prayers that changed each week. The churches relied on extemporaneous prayers, which by definition were not printed for congregations to recite together.

The Sunday School changed this by introducing printed prayers and responsive worship to nonliturgical congregations. As children formed in the Sunday School became adults, they brought a desire for printed, responsive forms to the Sunday service. However, with the advent of weekly printed worship bulletins, worship leaders could write their own materials each week and publish them for congregations to recite. Prayers, such as collects and intercessions that formerly had been led by a pastor, were put in mouths of congregations. For churches that adopted the responsive worship of the Sunday School assembly, reading became a required skill for participation in worship.

As the pattern evolved into Creative Worship, such worship meant reading unfamiliar texts rather than participating in a communally and historically shared ritual pattern and prayer forms. The selection of worship materials was entirely at the discretion of the worship leaders. Functionally, Creative Worship maximizes freedom, not for congregations but for the planners of worship who determine virtually every prayer the congregation will utter, every belief they will affirm, and every action they will perform.

This is quite different from the function of liturgy in churches with official prayer books. *The Book of Common Prayer* of the Episcopal Church obviously controls the content of worship for Episcopalians. However,

---

46. See the full discussion of the New Measures in chapter 3 of this book, pp. 54–65.

almost none of what the congregation recites or performs is left entirely to the priest, since the options are stipulated by the book. *The Book of Common Prayer*, therefore, mitigates against clerical domination of worship, for even the priest is part of the social contract that all Episcopalians share in the prayer book. Most of the congregational responses are learned by heart through regular participation in worship, precisely because they do not change week to week. In contrast, the ad hoc content of the Creative Worship model does not allow congregations to learn the liturgy by heart. Ironically, in breaking free from tradition, Creative Worship is arguably the most clerically dominated of the worship patterns we will discuss. No matter how "hip" or "open-ended" or "personally relevant" the language of such liturgy may sound, it is still, at its core, leaders controlling the worship of a congregation, putting their own words into the mouths of each participant. It is one thing to recite regularly a general prayer of confession from historical Anglican liturgy: "Most merciful God, we confess that we have sinned against you in thought, word and deed. . . ." It is quite another to come to worship and read a new confession that begins, "Lord, I fake it a lot. . . ."[47]

Yet many of us do, obviously, "fake it a lot," though the Anglican general confession might allow us to avoid such an admission by hiding behind its stately language and first-person plural pronouns. At its best, this is the strength of Creative Worship: through evocative, personal, ordinary language it provokes us to think about what we are before God. In the tradition of the Sunday School, it educates us about what we believe. It forces us to consider what we say by rote. Above all, it keeps us aware that if worship effects the sanctification of Christian believers, this means it must be supremely relevant to our daily lives.

---

47. Kathryn Rogers Deering, "Prayer of Confession," in David James Randolph, *Ventures in Worship*, vol. 3 (Nashville, TN: Abingdon Press, 1973), 46.

Worship as Education

	Telos (Goal)	***Ethos*** (Qualities of Character)
Nineteenth-century type: Sunday School Assembly	Formation of Christian character Formation for civic duty	Didactic effectiveness Classroom atmosphere Emphasis on active participation Unison, responsive reading Centrality of scripture Use of print material (prayers, readings) Memorization of prayers/responses Adaptation for congregation (children) Strong leadership control Laity-centered leadership
Present form: Creative Worship	Formation for socially relevant Christian witness	Experiential effectiveness Gymnasium atmosphere Emphasis on active participation Unison, responsive reading Use of print material (prayers, readings) Novelty of prayers (ad hoc) Adapted for congregation (relevance) Strong leadership control Use of props Thematic organization

Religious education in the United States has been moving beyond the Sunday School as an institution for some decades. However, where congregations have come to assume that public liturgy is essentially read aloud, printed in a bulletin or projected on a screen, constructed by the worship planners from resources or from their own creative ideas, we still

Chapter Four

see the inchoate influence of the Sunday School pattern of worship. That this connection has largely been forgotten is testimony to how effectively and fundamentally the Sunday School has changed how Protestants practice being church. We will continue to find the influence of the Sunday School as we consider other patterns of worship.

CHAPTER FIVE
Worship, Art, and Social Class

Aesthetic Worship

The bare order of service which characterized the Puritan worship has disappeared with the Puritan Sabbath. Various forms of music, the elaboration of ritual, church decorations and church architecture have been introduced to change the service of worship from its earlier simplicity to one of elaborate aesthetic import. In localities where the concentration of wealth makes it possible, no expense is too great to lavish upon imposing edifices. . . . As one passes from the costly city edifice with its expensive art and luxurious appointments to the country "meeting house" with its aesthetic bareness, the question which appeals with striking force is, What is the significance and value of this modern type of worship?

—John Perham Hylan, 1901[1]

First Church is known for its music program. The pipe organ is a superb instrument, and the church has always hired a skilled organist from the music department of the local university to do it justice. The choir, mostly made up of volunteers from the community, is also quite excellent, due in part to the four professional singers the church pays to lead each section. When choir members in their magnificent cassocks stand in the loft behind the pulpit to perform an offertory from the classical repertoire, the congregation listens with appreciation. They know they have the best church choir in the city.

In the same city, a much smaller congregation also has a choir program but on a humbler scale. A church member who used to teach beginning piano students plays the small electronic organ. The choir, a handful of women and a couple of older men, does its best to sing three-part choral

---

1. *Public Worship: A Study in the Psychology of Religion* (Chicago, IL: Open Court Publishing, 1901), 7.

arrangements, mostly of familiar hymns. When the members of the choir stand in the loft behind the pulpit in their worn choir robes bought years ago through proceeds from a yard sale, the congregation appreciates their commitment, but it knows that First Church has the best church choir in the city.

Why does this small church with minimal resources feel compelled to have a performance choir in worship? This is a result of a pattern that began in the late nineteenth century that I call Aesthetic Worship.

Worship and the Rise of Aesthetic Culture in America

So far, we have examined two major nineteenth-century movements that have made a dramatic impact on Protestant worship in the United States: the Revival and the Sunday School. The Revival sought dramatic Christian conversion of individuals by addressing the affective, emotional part of the human being. The model for the Revival was the professional theater, and the congregation was a passive audience, waiting to be moved to tears. Revival aimed at the gut to arouse passion. The Sunday School, on the other hand, addressed the intellectual aspect of the human being, with conversion being a gradual process of formation. Its model was the school room or gymnasium, using mental and physical activities to shape the character of the individual. It aimed at the head to shape Christian knowledge, attitudes, and habits. If the Revival was thoroughly populist in its aims and methods, the Sunday School sought to raise the intellectual and civic standards of American churches through education. By the middle of the nineteenth century, another movement was brewing in the United States in parallel with the Sunday School's concerns about religious and civic formation. As the nation was becoming more prosperous and settled, educated Americans were increasingly concerned about the standards of the nation's music, art, and literature.

At the rudimentary level, of course, art, music, and literature are part of everyday life and culture; people make things, sing songs, tell stories. The native American peoples had their diverse indigenous arts, African slaves kept the influences of their cultural traditions, and the European colonists brought with them the culture of their home countries. Some of the latter came from the art, music, and literature of European high culture, while other influences came in the form of folk songs and storytelling. However, well into the nineteenth century, European Americans did not seem to draw a line between high art and popular art. Lawrence Levine has shown that in the early nineteenth century the works of Shakespeare were wildly popular, both as literature and as theatrical performance. Shakespeare's plays were performed by amateur and professional troupes all over the United States. Theater companies felt free to abridge Shakespeare's plays to make them more accessible to audiences and sometimes even rewrote the scenes to make them more entertaining for American taste. Shakespeare's *Hamlet* might share a double bill with some melodramatic potboiler or bawdy comedy written by a playwright of less honorable reputation. In other words, in those early years of the nation, Shakespeare was popular culture rather than elite culture. Likewise, European classical music and opera filled the programs of concert halls in most cities and large towns, but musical programs typically combined selections from operas with popular American songs, such as "Home Sweet Home." In short, Americans had a rich culture of musical and theatrical art, but in the early nineteenth century, they did not have a strong sense of "highbrow art" versus "lowbrow art." Rather, art, music, and theater were popular entertainment.[2]

During this early period, the attitudes of American Protestant churches to art ranged from indifference to antipathy. Generally speaking, church art and architecture were austere and functional. Church music was largely congregational hymnody sung a cappella. Few Protestant churches had musical instruments and trained choirs to lead the singing or perform music in worship. Moreover, to the degree that art as a human work could be ostentatious display, religious leaders countered by preaching the value of simplicity. To the degree that art in the form of music and

---

2. See Lawrence W. Levine, *Highbrow Lowbrow: The Emergence of Cultural Hierarchy in America* (Cambridge, MA: Harvard University Press, 1988). I use the terms cautiously due to their racist origins.

theater was entertainment, Protestant leaders urged caution and preached the need for sober, productive living.

The second half of the nineteenth century saw the development of what Levine calls a "cultural hierarchy" in America. Wealthy patrons of the arts no longer tolerated theater or music in halls where audiences felt free to smoke, cheer, boo, and talk back to the actors on stage. They wanted serious Shakespeare and pure classical music, untainted by popularization for the masses. Culturally elite theaters and orchestras in major cities began to distinguish themselves from the rowdy burlesque of popular entertainment. Museums as well were evolving beyond their origins as repositories of curious artifacts to become collections of serious, original art.[3]

As Americans developed a distinction between "highbrow" art and "lowbrow" entertainment, they also began to understand high art as a cultural value akin to religion, as something sacred. Art critics and patrons, under the influence of European romanticism, used the language of religious virtues to describe art as "divine," "spiritual," and "beautiful" and the performer of art as "high priest."[4] High art was a cultural force for social good and spiritual development. From this perspective, to bowdlerize art into popular entertainment was not merely "low class"; it was desecration.[5]

Protestant churches began to respond to the emerging cultural hierarchy and the growing sacralization of art by reconsidering the religious value of music, art, and architecture. Revivalism had already provoked in Protestants an appreciation for the emotional power of musical and dramatic performances as effective "New Measures," and larger congregations were employing capable musicians and singers, not only for their revivals but also for Sunday service. Yet the Finneyite Revival was too much like theatrical entertainment for some influential leaders, who thought

---

3. Levine, *Highbrow Lowbrow*, 146–60.

4. Levine, *Highbrow Lowbrow*, 134–35.

5. Levine calls this nineteenth-century development "The Sacralization of Culture." See *Highbrow Lowbrow*, 132–46.

the emotional excesses of Revivalism cheapened the gospel.[6] The Sunday School, on the other hand, promoted new approaches to music and written prayers by using responsive readings, song books, and other "enrichments" for worship. This gave nonliturgical Protestants a newfound appreciation for church music and printed worship materials. If the Revival provoked Christian leaders to consider the power of music to motivate congregations, the Sunday School movement gave leaders a way to see music and art as respectable Christian practices. Thus, Finneyite Revivalism and the Sunday School movement, in quite different ways, led American churches to incorporate music and art into Sunday worship.

Over the course of the nineteenth century, as frontier settlements evolved into county seat towns, congregations not only began to use choirs, musicians, and other aesthetic enrichments, they also became aware of the artistic quality of church music and art in ways that correspond to Levine's description of the rising cultural hierarchy. Episcopalians tended to embrace "high" art, while Baptists (with some notable exceptions) kept art "lowbrow." Presbyterians, Methodists, and Congregationalists fell between these extremes. Regardless of denomination, however, the preference for "highbrow" art directly corresponded to social class. Wealthy, urban churches showed a preference for high art in architecture and music that was beyond the capacities of rural congregations.[7] This often came down to a competition over which congregations could claim the doctors,

---

6. John Williamson Nevin bemoaned the effects of emotional music used to stimulate men and women on the anxious bench who were "enveloped in the loud tones of some stimulating spiritual song." Of Finneyite Revivals, he comments: "The atmosphere of such a meeting may be exciting, intoxicating, bewildering; but it has no power whatever to dispose the mind to devotion." See *The Anxious Bench* (Chambersburg, PA: Office of the Weekly Messenger, 1843), 47–48.

7. In 1929, H. Richard Niebuhr described the correlation between styles of liturgy in denominations and social class. Middle-class denominations preferred formal ritual, while the "church of the disenfranchised" preferred informal ritual. Of the latter denominations, he comments: "Hence also the formality of ritual is displaced in such groups by an informality which gives opportunity for the express of emotional faith and for a simple, often crude, symbolism. An intellectually trained and liturgically minded clergy is rejected in favor of lay readers who serve the emotional needs of the religion more adequately and who, on the other hand, are not allied by culture and interest with those ruling classes whose superior manner of life is too obviously purchased at the expense of the poor." See *The Social Sources of Denominationalism* (Hamden, CT: Shoe String Press, 1929, reprinted 1954), 30.

lawyers, and successful young businessmen as members.[8] Typical of the growing concern for social class is this letter from a Methodist in New York to the *Zion's Herald*:

> One fact in the history of Methodism in New York, seen and lamented by all who have studied the subject, should have a decisive influence in the settlement of this question: it is the great disparity between the social position and style of living of leading Methodist families in that city, and their style of church architecture and furniture. . . . At first sight, there seems something noble in the spectacle of wealthy merchants leaving their magnificent homes on Sunday, and taking their seats in free and plain churches adapted to the accommodation of the masses, as if perfectly unconscious of any thing uncongenial with their private tastes and habits. But where are those boys and girls? —where but with their young friends, away at the stately churches in Broadway, or up town, sitting in cushioned seats, and beneath Gothic or Grecian arches, delighted with the music of grand organs, and listening to preaching in a style in harmony with the natural beauty of the sanctuary.[9]

This letter to the editor struck a chord with church leaders in both north and south, and excerpts appeared in various publications.[10] Socially privileged Americans were becoming increasingly concerned about cultural refinements, and urban Protestants worried that the wealthy and educated members of the community would be drawn away from their humble buildings to churches that maintained high standards of music and art.[11]

---

8. David R. Bains, "The Liturgical Impulse in Mid-Twentieth-Century American Mainline Protestantism" (Cambridge, MA, Harvard University unpublished dissertation, 1999), 29–30. Bains is quoting Louise F. Bensen, "The Presbyterian Cultus," *The Presbyterian Journal*, vol. 23 (Feb 1882): 2.

9. Letter quoted in L. D. Huston, "Methodist Church Edifices," *The Home Circle* 2 (May 1856): 225.

10. Not without controversy. *The Christian Advocate* called the letter "too truthful and weighty to be neglected by Methodists in any part of the Union." Yet one southern Methodist believed sentiments expressed in the letter were "as light and false as possible." Of ostentatious church buildings, that writer charged: "Who will answer to God in the Great Day for this enormous sacrifice to pride and vanity? Who will render an account for all this worse than wasted money?" (Huston, "Methodist Church Edifices," 226).

11. Bains cites Edwin Whitney Bishop: "Many of our young people, especially the college-bred, turn naturally and easily to the Episcopal Church to satisfy their aesthetic, if not their

Worship with its architectural setting was a venue to display a congregation's self-understanding of its social position.

Music and art in worship, of course, displayed more than social class, and not all Protestant leaders thought music and architecture were merely ways to attract the privileged. Some Protestants began to argue that exposure to good art could play an important role in the formation of good and noble Christians. In an 1856 review of some recently built church buildings, Hiram Mattison, a Methodist pastor and avid abolitionist, praised the attention these buildings gave to aesthetic features. After acknowledging the history of Protestant antipathy to fine art, music, and architecture, he gave a religious justification for good art:

> A religion that renounces the beautiful, and true, and tasteful in nature or art is either mere affectation, or will one day drive its votaries to the hermit's cell or the monastery. True religion, instead of making war upon art and science, is destined to promote and sanctify both, and make them tributary to her own advancement and the glory of God. Science and art are not to melt away and disappear as Christianity advances in the earth, but, on the contrary, will progress as she prevails over ignorance and sin—will reach their acme amid the latter-day glory, and will shine forth as witnesses of the elevating and ennobling tendency of the Gospel of Christ when he shall come to "restore all things," and swallow up death in victory.[12]

For Mattison, if the church were to thrive, it must use art to advance its cause as both "tributary" and "witness" to the "elevating and ennobling tendency of the Gospel of Christ." Obviously, not all uses of art and music could accomplish this. Mattison vehemently opposed theater, opera, dancing, and dance-hall music as "worldly amusements" with their "attendant evils."[13] The church, however, provided the ennobling context in which music and art could be rescued from the music hall and theater and returned to their divinely intended purpose of advancing religion.

---

spiritual, desires" in Bishop's essay "Public Worship," in *Recent Christian Progress*, ed. Lewis Bayles Paton (New York, NY: Macmillan, 1909), 370.

12. "Methodist Architecture," *The National Magazine* (Feb 1, 1856): 124.

13. Hiram Mattison, *An Appeal to Methodists, in Regard to the Evils of Card-Playing, Billiards, Dancing, Theatre-going, etc.* (New York, NY: Carlton & Porter, 1867), 82.

Mattison may be among the first middle-of-the-road Protestants to make such claims, but other prominent ministers, most notably Henry Ward Beecher, were soon adding their voices in support of the religious value of the fine arts.[14] Thus, as large urban Protestant churches gravitated toward ostentatious architecture and music to attract the more privileged social class, Protestant intellectuals were developing theological justifications for the art and music these wealthy urban congregations craved.

Worship as Aesthetic Experience

Like Revivalism and the Sunday School movement, the Aesthetic Worship movement raised concerns about the subjective experience of those who attended services. Prior to the rise of these movements in the nineteenth century, however, Protestant Christians thought about worship primarily through the category of "service," as in the phrase "worship service." Christian worship was a service rendered to God that at the same time allowed Christians to receive God's grace. In other words, worship actually *did something* in real time: it offered service to God. By the end of the nineteenth century, however, Protestant Christians began a shift from thinking about worship primarily as *service* to thinking about worship as *experience*; the chief importance of worship was the effect it had on worshipers rather than on service offered to God. This may be the single most significant conceptual development in modern Christian worship: the move *from worship service to worship experience*.

By the early twentieth century, this experiential conception of worship already had its critics who recognized the danger inherent in over-promoting the psychological effects produced by worship.[15] In 1920, the philosopher James Bissett Pratt published an influential book entitled *The Religious Consciousness* that gave a careful analysis of this problem. Pratt, working with the pragmatist philosophy of William James, accepted that the function of religion was to express and form the subjective experience

---

14. Levine, *Highbrow Lowbrow*, 150.
15. For example, John P. Hylan, *Public Worship*, 88.

of individuals.[16] Yet this did not mean that religious doctrines were irrelevant. On the contrary, "Religion is not so much theology as life; it is to be *lived* rather than reasoned about. In short, religion is not a theory about reality; it *is* reality."[17] According to Pratt, the problem with approaching religion as an experience alone was that this ignored the fact that sincere adherents also wanted to know that their experiences were grounded in true, objectively "factual" understandings of God and the world:

> Religion is not merely a feeling; it is, as Professor James says, "a postulator of new facts as well." The religious consciousness inevitably considers its religion objective as well as subjective. And if it be said that the *value* of religion at any rate is subjective only [a position Pratt identifies with modern Protestantism] then at least religion must not know that this is the case; for if it learned the secret[,] both its value and it would cease to be even subjective.[18]

In other words, Pratt argued that in order for modern Protestant Christianity to do that on which it places the highest value—shape the subjective faith and moral values of the modern person—it must not lose what he calls its "objective validity." Pratt saw this is a danger of modern Protestantism:

> The attempt to produce merely subjective religious effects is always in danger of defeating itself. For religion, as we have seen, involves a belief which means to have objective validity. . . . The worshiper in the Protestant Church must be made to feel, as the Catholic feels at the mass, that *something is really being done*—something in addition to the subjective change in his own consciousness. . . . In other words, what the Protestant service needs more than anything else is the development of the objective side of its worship.[19]

Does Protestant worship have anything to do with objective reality, or is it merely manipulative effects? This is the serious question posed by Pratt's analysis.

---

16. James Bissett Pratt, *The Religious Consciousness* (New York, NY: Macmillan, 1920), 6.
17. Pratt, *The Religious Consciousness*, 7.
18. Pratt, *The Religious Consciousness*.
19. Pratt, *The Religious Consciousness*, 307.

By suggesting that Protestant worship needed to reclaim "objective validity," Pratt was not calling for a return to an understanding of worship as divine appeasement or some miracle, such as of transubstantiation as in the Roman Catholic Church. He considered such crudely objective views of worship impossible for modern, scientifically minded individuals. Nevertheless, he argued that authentic modern worship must involve the sincere belief that it is genuine communion with the living God through prayer and praise, that it actually does something objectively real. Otherwise, worship was merely emotional manipulation, and emotional manipulation worked only so long as people did not know they were being manipulated. In short, Pratt challenged not only the "New Measure" methods of revivalism, which put so much stress on the emotional effects, but also the arbitrary "enrichments" of worship being promoted via the Sunday School.

Not a few Christian leaders began to take notice of the problem raised by Pratt.[20] Among them, Von Ogden Vogt, a prominent minister in Chicago, and William Sperry, dean of Harvard Divinity School, wrote books that attempted to reclaim an objective core to Protestant worship without abandoning the modern turn toward experience. For these writers, aesthetic experience was key.

Vogt led the way with his widely read *Art and Religion*, a book that, despite the title, is actually about worship as art: "The art of worship is the all-comprehending art. No other art can satisfy the demand of human nature for an all-inclusive experience. Nor can the conditions favorable to that experience be ever freshly reproduced without the aid of all the arts."[21] So closely is art connected to religion and the expression of religion in worship, Vogt claimed, that the origin of art and religion in human

---

20. While Pratt and his book, *The Religious Consciousness*, have largely been forgotten, his work was very influential well into the twentieth century for pastors and scholars who wrote about worship. Moreover, his book appeared on the required reading list (the "Course of Study") for Methodist pastors, starting with The Methodist Episcopal Church, South in 1934 and continuing with The Methodist Church until 1944.

21. Von Ogden Vogt, *Art and Religion* (New Haven, CT: Yale University Press, 1921), 4.

history is virtually the same: "Religion has been historically the great fountain source of art, and the art of worship the mother of all arts."[22]

The connection between art and religion is not merely historical; it is also experiential. "To perceive beauty [the expression of art] is to be moved by something of the same emotional course as attends on the perception of Divinity. And to create beauty is in some sense to participate in the character of Divinity."[23] Just as religion grasps the reality of God through the feelings of awe, gratitude, and dependence, art grasps "the *feel* of reality, the *taste* of existence, the *texture* of the world."[24] Thus, the artist seeks essentially the same end as the teacher of religion, "a more nearly immediate experience of reality" than can be achieved by the rational mind alone.[25]

Willard Sperry likewise stressed the need for Protestant worship to reclaim aesthetics as a way to denote its objective core. For Sperry, the end of worship is to seek God, to recognize oneself in the presence of God. While worship would always have an effect on the moral lives of individuals, this is an *indirect* effect of seeking God as the proper end. In the same way, art is not a means toward some other ends other than beauty and truth. Here, Sperry argued, is a serious flaw in Protestant worship: "Protestant worship is failing everywhere to-day because it unconsciously suggests that it is not an end in itself. . . . Its reference is to man and not to God. It is a means for self-help rather than for self-expression, thanksgiving, dedication."[26]

---

22. Vogt, *Art and Religion*, 18.

23. Vogt, *Art and Religion*, 23. Philosophically, Vogt understood beauty, along with truth and goodness, as transcendental predicates of Supreme Being and of God and the fount of being: "Beauty is one of the three supreme categories of value. It follows that religion is directly concerned with beauty, for religion is the experience of the highest value. The three values are constantly interwoven in human experience. The true and the good are beautiful. The beautiful, most highly speaking, is both true and good. That which is false is not beautiful; it is an ugly lie. That which is bad is not beautiful; it comes of an ugly temper. Whether you are aware of it or not, there is a pleasure in the truth and a satisfaction in the contemplation of the good which are in some measure aesthetic feelings" (23). In this way, Vogt implicitly addresses the connection between worship and ethics. Beauty, truth, and goodness are different facets of the unity of reality. Each facet always fully implicates the others.

24. Vogt, *Art and Religion*, 25.

25. Vogt, *Art and Religion*, 26. Vogt does not credit the romantic theology of Frederick Schleiermacher, but he is undoubtedly indebted to him.

26. Willard R. Sperry, *Reality in Worship* (New York, NY: MacMillan, 1925), 248–89.

In this context, Sperry makes his case for art: "Here the artist sets us right, when he tells us that things which are ends in themselves move us far more profoundly than things which are simply means to other ends."[27] This is why, Sperry claimed, art is so important for worship. Good art gives access to reality in a way that addresses Pratt's concern for objective worship. It renders an experience of a reality outside the mind of the individual worshiper. Worship as a form of aesthetic experience is the experience of the reality of God who is good, true, and beautiful.

If worship is art, however, it must be *good* art if it is to serve its proper end—the glory of God who is good, true, and beautiful. Unfortunately, in the estimation of Sperry, Vogt, and a host of Protestant liturgists who followed them, much Protestant worship was aesthetically trivial. Something had to change if the church were to continue to be a cultural force for good.

Aesthetic Form in Worship

In 1936, Henry Sloane Coffin (the famous preacher and President of Union Theological Seminary in New York) commented on Protestant worship at the turn of the century:

> In the non-liturgical churches the ritual took on a formal informality. It had a pattern of praise and prayer and instruction; but many ministers, in order to be at ease and friendly, fell into a "chatty" manner. . . . Churches with an architecture and ritual of this sort and a home-like atmosphere were designed to foster an impression of the "humanness" of God. The element of awe was absent from worship. The attitude towards Deity was familiar. Here was a family gathering of the children of an unseen Father. At its best the service mediated the friendliness of God, and no one dare disparage the genuinely Christian characters which were nurtured and the influential Christian movements inspired by it. But it always ran the risk of becoming so human that it ceased to suggest the Divine.[28]

---

27. Sperry, *Reality in Worship*, 249.

28. Henry Sloane Coffin, "Public Worship, in Samuel McCrea Cavert and Henry Pitney Van Dusen, eds., *The Church through Half a Century: Essays in Honor of William Adams Brown* (New York, NY: Charles Scribner's Son, 1936), 187–88.

As Coffin penned these words, he and many other leaders were increasingly of the opinion that a casual approach to worship would not continue to be effective as the cultural standards of North Americans continued to rise.[29]

Through the influence of the Sunday School, Protestant churches had already begun to use various historical, largely Anglican, liturgical pieces as "enrichments" for worship: the Lord's Prayer, the Apostles' Creed, responsive readings, chants such as the *Gloria Patri*, or *Te Deum Laudamus*. Adding a *Te Deum* to a "chatty" service, however, could not address both the desire for better aesthetics and the profound need for an objective core to worship. Vogt was particularly harsh in his criticism of Protestant orders of worship:

> Recently there have been many attempts at improvement, some of them significant and successful. For the most part, however, they are spoken of as "enrichment of the service," "the use of forms," "an elaborate order of worship." None of these phrases explains much, or indicates any genuinely artistic achievement. They do evidence a dissatisfaction with something sadly in need of improvement. But the need is not more formalism nor enrichment nor elaboration. The need is for unity, simplicity, and beauty. There are many "enriched" services composed simply of the typical, ugly, average American order with additions of musical numbers, choir responses, vestments, or read prayers, *a kind of glorified city edition of the common town order*. All these things jumbled together, however elaborate, or however beautiful in detail, do not make a noble liturgy. Nothing is beautiful that does not have unity, harmony, wholeness.[30]

Both Vogt and Sperry proposed a need for an organizational principle for Protestant worship that could supply an aesthetically beautiful form displaying "unity, harmony, wholeness." They found their principle in the biblical account of the call of the prophet Isaiah (Isaiah 6:1-8). Vogt identified five stages that he identified in Isaiah's call:

---

29. Coffin remarked, "The swift spread of culture could not fail to affect the forms of public worship" ("Public Worship," 185).

30. Vogt, *Art and Religion*, 42. My emphasis.

Chapter Five

> **ORDER OF WORSHIP BASED ON CALL OF ISAIAH 6:1–8**
>
> | | |
> |---|---|
> | Vision | "I saw the Lord high and lifted up…" |
> | Humility | "Woe is me. I am lost, a man of unclean lips…" |
> | Exaltation | "…yet my eyes have seen the Lord of hosts." |
> | Illumination | "Now that this (live coal) has touched your lips…" |
> | Dedication | "Here am I, send me…" |
>
> Von Ogden Vogt, *Art and Religion*, 1921

The first stage, Vision, should both inspire and make an impression on worshipers of the glory of God. A processional hymn would lead into a responsive call to worship, or even better (because more sophisticated-sounding), Introit with the minister reading scripture verses interspersed with choral responses proclaiming "the reality and nature of God." This leads naturally into the next stage, Humility, which corresponds to a confession of sin, followed by a hymn of praise (Exaltation). Scripture readings, collects, pastoral prayers, a creed, and responsive materials constituted Illumination. Finally, the order concludes with Dedication, which basically means the offering. This five-stage outline formed the first half of a service, which was followed by the sermon and closing hymn.[31]

Sperry took a slightly different tack. He analyzed the Isaiah passage as displaying a sequence of thesis, antithesis, and synthesis:

> **ORDER OF WORSHIP BASED ON CALL OF ISAIAH 6:1–8**
>
> | | |
> |---|---|
> | Thesis | "I saw the Lord high and lifted up…" |
> | Antithesis | "Woe is me. I am lost, a man of unclean lips…" |
> | Synthesis a. | "Now that this (live coal) has touched your lips…" |
> | Synthesis b. | "Here am I, send me…" |
>
> Willard Sperry, *Reality in Worship*, 1925

---

31. Vogt, *Art and Religion*, 161–62. While Vogt would hate the comparison, I suggest these five stages take the place of the Preliminaries in the Revival pattern. Be that as it may, well into the twentieth century teachers of preaching and worship used Vogt's model for Protestant liturgical orders. I myself was introduced to this pattern in a Christian education course during my studies as a theology student at Candler School of Theology in 1979.

Indeed, Sperry saw this "thesis, antithesis, synthesis" structure as the form of all historical acts of worship, such as prayers, psalms, and hymns. "Why should not a religious service definitely follow this order? What other order can it follow?" he asked his readers.[32]

Neither Sperry nor Vogt believed the call of Isaiah was the historical *origin* of the Judeo-Christian pattern of worship as such. Rather, it was a prime example of the "significant form" of all human encounters with the divine, Judeo-Christian or otherwise. Worship was parallel to the form of the human encounter with an aesthetic object. If the church were to pay sufficient attention to the aesthetic form of worship, as illustrated by the call of Isaiah, it could provide "higher and better enjoyments than any of the arts."[33]

Thus, Vogt and Sperry led the way in providing nonliturgical Protestants justification for the theological and practical importance of aesthetics in the form, content, and character of public worship. For example, Albert Palmer, president of Chicago Theological Seminary, wrote a book on worship whose first chapter was entitled bluntly, "Where Worship Fails Today."[34] Chiefly, Palmer listed lack of solemnity, reverence, and good art, and a consequent lack of meaningful congregational participation.[35] He and many others thought that good aesthetics was the way to reclaim and to present to congregations the objective reality of God, "good aesthetics" meaning specifically the highbrow sensibility and character of the aspiring upper-middle class.

Aesthetic Worship and Architecture

What sort of architecture would be appropriate for such worship? Under the influence of the Revival, church architecture had taken on the utilitarian form of the auditorium or even the theater.[36] Churches built

---

32. Sperry, *Reality in Worship*, 293.

33. Vogt, *Art and Religion*, 164.

34. Albert W. Palmer, *The Art of Conducting Public Worship* (New York, NY: Macmillan, 1939), 4–16.

35. By 1944, Palmer's book was recommended for the Methodist Course of Study.

36. See Jeanne Halgren Kilde, *When Church Became Theatre: The Transformation of Evangelical Architecture and Worship in Nineteenth-Century America* (New York, NY: Oxford University Press, 2002).

on the Revival plan typically had pews across the center of the auditorium with side aisles, similar to a theater. Stages were large, with a central podium and a large, visible, elevated space for musicians and choir behind the podium stage. On the other hand, under the influence of the Sunday School, some congregations also began to construct their worship environments more like a comfortable home or a child's nursery, with muted colors, drapes on windows, and carpets.

Aesthetic Worship, however, required architecture that could elicit awe and reverence, and for that designers turned to the architecture of medieval Europe, especially Gothic styles. Gothic church buildings had been widely employed by wealthy, urban American congregations since at least the middle of the nineteenth century. While Episcopalians were the first to copy Gothic interiors as well as structures, the Aesthetic Worship movement now recommended Gothic interiors for all Protestant denominations. Vogt in particular praised the beauty and reverence of Gothic churches, but he also offered some practical reasons for recommending Gothic chancels:

> The religious and ecclesiastical reasons are more important to some than the artistic. The pulpit at the center certainly tends to throw the chief dependence of the service upon the sermon, and in such a manner as greatly to minimize the possibilities and values of other exercises of worship. A successful chancel far better creates an atmosphere of worship before ever the service begins. And after the service has begun, it fosters reverence through all the parts. . . . Strangely enough, it accomplishes all this without losing the vitality or function of the pulpit. Leaving the chancel and ascending the pulpit, the minister thus selects it as the appointed station for his own free utterance and whatever prophetic word has been given him to speak. The sermon is not minimized, while other parts of the service may be greatly improved by the greater significance of the objects of visual attention and by the greater variety of movement in the conduct of the service rendered possible by the central chancel plan.[37]

Not only would such an arrangement evoke awe and reverence before God, it would also impress upon clergy the importance of proper liturgi-

---

37. Vogt, *Art and Religion*, 216.

cal leadership and indeed move them toward it: "It is harder for any man to conduct a loose, flippant, or formless service in such a building."[38]

Large urban congregations embraced Gothic style for their interiors, but so did many small and rural congregations. The Bureau of Architecture for The Methodist Episcopal Church, for example, strongly advocated Gothic chancels and offered affordable plans for Gothic interiors to encourage modest congregations to build this way:[39]

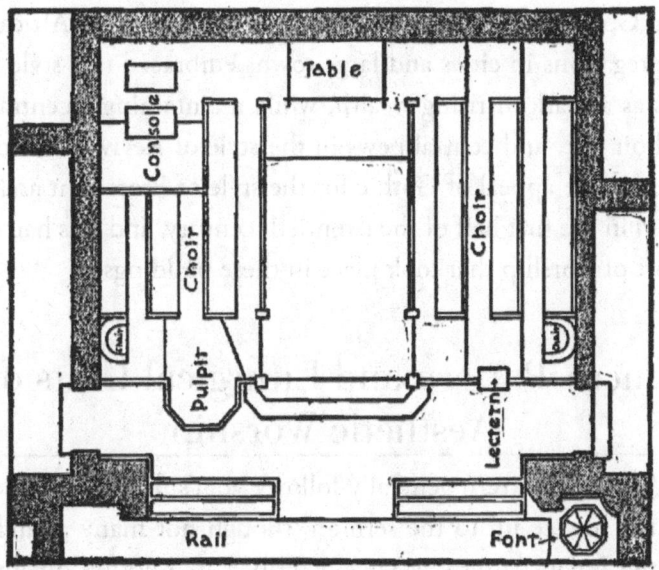

Thus, in the twentieth century, Protestant meeting houses and worship auditoriums gave way to Gothic chancels and naves. Even the new language of "chancel" and "nave" among Protestants illustrated this new liturgical aesthetic. Central pews were replaced with central aisles to accommodate processions. Choirs and musicians were located to the sides of divided chancels. The pulpit was moved to one side of the chancel stage, with a lectern placed on the opposite side. Small communion tables were replaced by larger, more substantial "altar" tables, elevated from the floor and placed in a central

---

38. Vogt, *Art and Religion*, 216.

39. J. Hastie Odgers and Edward G. Schutz, *The Technique of Public Worship* (New York, NY: The Methodist Book Concern, 1928), 61.

location at the back wall of the chancel. Ostentatious, exposed organ pipes in the theatrical style framed a reredos, which could be a commanding piece of art (such as the magnificent carved reredos of First United Methodist Church in Evanston, Illinois), or a suspended cross in front of a drape.

While Gothic buildings and chancels were especially prominent in many affluent Protestant churches (Methodist buildings in particular were influenced by the Architecture Bureau), the central pulpit was simply too established in some denominations to be easily overcome by appeal to a consistent Gothic sensibility. Both European American and African American congregations in cities and large towns embraced this style for their buildings as a mark of rising wealth, while maintaining a central pulpit, central choir loft, and central pews in the style of Revival auditoriums.[40] Nevertheless, the appeal of Gothic for the style of Protestant architecture dominated in the first half of the twentieth century, and this had an effect on the sort of worship that took place in these buildings.

Macro-Pattern and Liturgical Units of Aesthetic Worship

The Aesthetic pattern generally follows Vogt's fivefold outline for the order of the service up to the sermon, though not many churches fully adopted the Isaiah pattern as Vogt described it. Another obvious influence for the Aesthetic pattern is the Order of Daily Morning Prayer of the Episcopal *Book of Common Prayer*. In some Episcopal congregations, a collection of money, a sermon, and a closing benediction were appended to Morning Prayer to serve as a complete morning service. The placement of the sermon at the end of the order and the separation of the scripture readings from the sermon by various liturgical units such as the creed, prayers, and offertory is typical of the Aesthetic model. Perhaps the most

---

40. W. E. B. DuBois, *The Negro Church*, report of a social study made under the direction of Atlanta University, together with the proceedings of the eighth Conference for the Study of the Negro Problems, held at Atlanta University, May 26, 1903 (Google eBook), 72. For a description and diagram illustrating a more recent example of this style of architecture of an African American congregation, see Brenda Eatman Aghahowa, *Praising in Black and White: Unity and Diversity in Christian Worship* (Cleveland, OH: United Church Press, 1996), 50–54.

notable feature of the printed orders is the use of historic, technical titles (especially Latin) of various elements of the service: introit, doxology, *Gloria Patri*, psalter, offertory, sermon, and so forth. Other features of the macro-pattern include the use of vestments by the ministers and choir, most derived from the academic style: black robes with stoles for clergy, gowns with stoles for the choir. Indeed, a performance choir is an essential component of Aesthetic Worship, as is the use of hymnbooks and a preference for classical music or hymn tunes arranged in a chorale style.

The pattern developed several distinctive liturgical units. While none of these units are unique to the pattern, nonetheless, they are hallmarks of it.

Aesthetic Worship typically begins with either a call to worship or a processional of the choir and liturgical ministers during the singing of a hymn. The practice of beginning with a call to worship comes from the Puritan tradition, which, of course, did not have a procession. The purpose of an opening processional hymn, historically, has been to get the choir and clergy into their places with appropriate dignity. It is not uncommon for Aesthetic Worship to begin with a call to worship led by the pastor, who then hurries down a side aisle in order to join in the procession of the choir during the first hymn; this conflates practices from the Westminster Directory for Worship with Anglo-Catholic ritual.

The use of an acolyte to "bring in the light" for the altar candles during the procession and to "carry out the light" during the closing hymn became a regular practice in many churches, even those that did not have a formal procession of the choir. This is a twentieth-century innovation. In fact, before the late nineteenth century, nonliturgical American Protestants did not have candles on their communion tables.[41]

The confession follows the opening procession in keeping with Vogt's pattern but also, not coincidentally, with the sequence of actions in the service of Morning Prayer in the 1928 *Book of Common Prayer*. Apart from Episcopalians and Lutherans, a formal general confession was not

---

41. As late as 1927, prominent Methodist Hugh D. Atchison, pastor of St. Luke's Methodist Episcopal Church in Dubuque, Iowa, commenting on recent developments in worship, noted, "Altars and even candles are being introduced, often with banal and sometimes quite grotesque results." "A More Adequate Service of Worship in Methodist Episcopal Churches," *The Methodist Review* (May 1927): 360.

part of worship in Protestant churches until the Aesthetic movement in the twentieth century.

Responsive readings entered into many Protestant services via the influence of the Sunday School. However, this form of reading psalms was embraced by the Aesthetic movement.

The Apostles' Creed (or a more contemporary affirmation of faith) followed by the *Gloria Patri* is another Aesthetic development that can still be found in southern congregations in particular. A substantial prayer led by the pastor (the pastoral prayer) also falls in this part of the order.

The development of an elaborate ritual sequence around the collection of money is, perhaps, the most important innovation to come from Aesthetic Worship. Most Protestant churches in the United States did not regularly take a collection of money during worship until the late nineteenth century. Rather, church operating funds were collected primarily through pew rentals or through other means such as regular personal visits from church stewards. By the 1880s, Presbyterians and Methodists began to include collections of money during Sunday worship.[42] Gradually, the word *offering*, with its explicit religious connotations, replaced the more generic *collection* as the preferred name for the rite. Once churches referred to collections as an offering, the amount of ritual attention given to the collection of money increased dramatically.

The development of the offertory in the official order of The Methodist Episcopal Church illustrates this evolution. At the 1888 General Conference, the Committee on Revision of the Ritual proposed a new Order for Public Worship on the Lord's Day worship that, like previous Methodist orders, did not include a collection of money. However, during discussion, a delegate to the conference successfully proposed an amendment to add a collection of money to the new order. The next major revision came in 1905 with the *Methodist Hymnal*, and an order that shows numerous Aesthetic Worship features. Following the "Lesson from the New Testament" were "Notices, followed by Collection; during or after which an Offertory may be rendered." The word *offertory* here connoted a musical piece rather than the presentation of the money, which was still

---

42. James Hudnut-Beumler, *In Pursuit of the Almighty's Dollar: A History of Money and American Protestantism* (Chapel Hill: University of North Carolina Press, 2007).

called *collection*.[43] In 1920, the Methodists made a few more revisions; they dropped the word *collection* and replaced it with "Worship in the presentation of tithes and offerings, during or after which an Offertory may be rendered."[44] In 1932, the Methodists again revised the order, adding a lengthy rubric to the taking of an offering: "Here, when convenient, may be sung an anthem: the offering also being received and reverently brought to the Minister, the congregation meantime rising; and it should be placed upon the Table with singing or prayer."[45] There is no missing the ritual importance of rubrics that go so far as to comment on the reverence of the ushers! This is quite a shift from 1888.[46]

The amount of space the offering sequence took up in a typical worship bulletin illustrates the significance of this liturgical unit. It is not uncommon to find four or more subtitled lines in a bulletin given over to the offering:

> Offering [The minister announces the offering with a standard line such as "Let us present our tithes and offerings to the Lord."]
>
> Offertory [This may be a choral anthem. During the music, ushers come forward to receive the plates from the minister. They pass plates down pews, moving toward the rear of the auditorium.]
>
> Doxology [Congregation stands to sing as ushers process the plates to the front of the church and give the plates to the minister at the altar table.]
>
> Prayer of Dedication [The minister turns to the table, lifts the plates, and says a prayer.]

In the Aesthetic Worship model, therefore, the offering grew to be the most highly ritualized portion of the order. Here congregations found the answer to Pratt's concern about objectivity in worship. In the giving of money, "something is actually being done." In short, the development

---

43. *The Doctrines and Disciplines of the Methodist Episcopal Church, 1904*, par. 70, *The Doctrines and Disciplines of the Methodist Episcopal Church, South, 1910*, par. 224.

44. *The Doctrines and Disciplines of the Methodist Episcopal Church, 1920*, par. 72.

45. *The Doctrines and Disciplines of the Methodist Episcopal Church, 1932*, par. 511.

46. For a longer treatment of the history of the money collection, see L. Edward Phillips, "Eucharist and Money," in *A Wesleyan Theology of the Eucharist: The Presence of God for Christian Life and Ministry*, ed. Jason Vickers (Nashville, TN: General Board of Ordained Ministry of The United Methodist Church, 2016), 223–28.

of a money offering provided a core reality to worship and filled the role of the offering of the Eucharist in the Catholic worship. By the middle of the twentieth century, churches urban and rural, small and large ritualized money with a regimen of ushers bringing plates of cash and personal checks to be "offered" to God with all the pomp of a medieval high mass.

Typically, the sermon follows the offertory sequence. One hallmark of the Aesthetic model is the separation of the reading of scripture from the sermon by several liturgical units.

The "Invitation to Christian Discipleship," which comes before a final "Hymn of Invitation" or "Hymn of Dedication" is the final liturgical unit found in many Aesthetic Worship orders. This unit is an aestheticization of the altar call of the Revival model.

Today, congregations that still embrace Aesthetic Worship advertise themselves as Traditional churches. Not many congregations maintain the full Gothic style advocated by Vogt and Sperry, and those that do tend to be large (but often shrinking) historically wealthy urban churches. At the very least, Traditional Worship means the use of hymns, robed choirs, classical-style anthems, an organ, printed responsive reading, call to worship, confession, Lord's Prayer, elaborate offertory, and academic vestments on the clergy. In some orders, the pastoral prayer and offertory follow the sermon, rather than precede it, illustrating the influence of the Word and Table model that will be discussed in chapter 8. Finally, Traditional Worship almost always includes a children's sermon, showing the continuing influence of the Sunday School model.

ORDER OF SERVICE
A Typical Aesthetic Order
Order of Worship II, *Methodist Hymnal* 1935

ORDER OF WORSHIP II

Let the People Kneel or Bow in Silent Prayer upon Entering the Sanctuary

THE PRELUDE. The people in devout meditation.

THE CALL TO WORSHIP, which may be said or sung.

HYMN. If a Processional, the hymn shall precede the Call to Worship, and the people shall then rise at the second stanza and join in singing.

THE INVOCATION, concluded with the Lord's Prayer. The people seated and bowed.

THE ANTHEM; OR CHANT, such as the Venite or the Te Deum, or the Lord's Prayer.

RESPONSIVE READING.

THE APOSTLES' CREED.

> I believe in God the Father Almighty, Maker of heaven and earth; and in Jesus Christ his only Son our Lord; who was conceived by the Holy Ghost, born of the Virgin Mary, suffered under Pontius Pilate, was crucified, dead, and buried; the third day he rose again from the dead, he ascended into heaven, and sitteth at the right hand of God the Father Almighty; from thence he shall come to judge the quick and the dead. I believe in the Holy Ghost; the holy catholic Church; the communion of saints; the forgiveness of sins; the resurrection of the body; and the life everlasting. Amen.

THE GLORIA PATRI.

> Glory be to the Father, and to the Son, and to the Holy Ghost; as it was in the beginning, is now, and ever shall be, world without end. Amen.

LESSON FROM THE HOLY SCRIPTURES.

THE PASTORAL PRAYER. The people seated and bowed.

THE OFFERING.

THE OFFERTORY. (This should accompany the offering.)

THE PRESENTATION OF OFFERINGS, with Prayer or Offertory Sentence.

HYMN. The people standing.

THE SERMON.

PRAYER. The people seated and bowed.

THE INVITATION TO CHRISTIAN DISCIPLESHIP.

HYMN OR DOXOLOGY. The people standing.

SILENT PRAYER—BENEDICTION. The people seated and bowed.

THE POSTLUDE.

Chapter Five

Traditional Order, Typical[47]

PRELUDE
The prelude marks the beginning of our worship service. Please use this time for reflection and prayer.

INTROIT "The Lord Is in His Holy Temple" Chancel Choir

CALL TO WORSHIP (responsive reading)

* HYMN OF PRAISE

* PRAYER OF CONFESSION (unison)
    (a moment for silent confession)

* DECLARATION OF PARDON AND GLORIA PATRI

WELCOMING OUR NEW MEMBERS

CHILDREN'S TIME

NEW TESTAMENT READING

ANTHEM "WONDROUS LOVE" CHANCEL CHOIR

SCRIPTURE READING

SERMON

* HYMN OF RESPONSE

PRAYERS OF THE PEOPLE & LORD'S PRAYER

OFFERTORY SENTENCE

PRESENTATION OF TITHES AND OFFERINGS

OFFERTORY (organ solo)

* DOXOLOGY AND PRAYER OF DEDICATION

* HYMN OF DEDICATION

* BENEDICTION

* CHORAL RESPONSE "Amen" Chancel Choir

* POSTLUDE

    *THOSE ABLE, PLEASE STAND.[48]

---

47. The lines in ALL CAPS are taken as they appear in the bulletin. My more descriptive comments are in brackets. An asterisk indicates congregation standing.

48. This is the standard order posted as an example of the traditional service of New Providence Presbyterian Church, Maryville, Tennessee, http://www.newprovidencepres.org/traditionalbulletin1, accessed March 14, 2012. Used by permission.

Distinctive Liturgical Units and Character Features of the Aesthetic/Traditional Worship Pattern

Vested choir and ministers

Choral anthems using a performance choir

Gothic chancel, altar, pulpit, and lectern

Use of traditional ecclesiastical language for elements of service (e.g., *Gloria Patri*, introit)

Order of worship printed in weekly bulletin

Use of printed prayer rather than extempore prayer

Responsive reading (of scripture, prayers, or other texts)

Printed prayers (thanksgiving, confession, intercession) and other liturgical material

Procession of choir and ministers

Call to worship (responsive)

Choral introit

General confession, read in unison

Elaborate offering sequence

Invitation to Christian discipleship

Chapter Five

Assessment of the Aesthetic/Traditional Worship Pattern

Aesthetic Worship began as a response to the rising cultural hierarchy in nineteenth-century America. More refined worship, many Protestants believed, would attract more educated and socially advantaged worshipers, and Levine's account of the rise of a cultural hierarchy in America demonstrates that this belief was sociologically justifiable.[49] The cultural hierarchy, indeed, spread across the cultural divide of white and black American Protestants. As wealthy European American congregations were leaving behind the exuberant styles of frontier religion, African American leaders in the early twentieth century were also calling for less emotionally manipulative preaching and more "intelligent worship." Some black intellectuals believed that newer black denominations were filling this need among the rising and increasingly educated black middle class.[50] African American congregations affiliated with predominately Anglo-American mainline denominations gravitated toward the Aesthetic Worship model.[51]

Yet Aesthetic Worship has always had its critics who worried that, whatever religious effect Gothic styles might create, American congregations would not be able to understand them. Henry Sloane Coffin complained:

> Gothic architecture has been responsible for the introduction into Protestantism of the incongruous elements. Stained-glass windows have been imported or copied with figures which have no meaning whatsoever for American congregations. Much of the symbolism in these churches is unintelligible to those who worship in them.[52]

---

49. Also, as noted in chapter 1, Mark Chavez has shown that socioeconomic class continues to be a very strong marker of preferences in worship. The higher the social class (indicated by education and wealth), the stronger the preference for highbrow art, architecture, and music in worship.

50. See various reports in DuBois, *The Negro Church*, 62, 123, 162.

51. Aghahaowa, *Praising God in Black and White*, 4–6, 60–68.

52. Henry Sloane Coffin, *Public Worship: The Church through Half a Century: Essays in Honor of William Adams Brown* (New York, NY: Charles Scribner's Sons, 1936), 183–206. Trinity Methodist Episcopal Church in Springfield, Massachusetts, tried to solve this problem by putting an image of Charles Lindbergh in a stained-glass window!

Furthermore, despite attempts to find an essential form for worship in Isaiah 6, pastors continued to treat the various liturgical units of historic worship as "enrichments," arbitrary liturgical pieces to be used in ways that disconnected them from their historic meaning. In short, as popular as it became for large urban and county-seat towns, Aesthetic Worship continued to display a *nouveau riche* style of aesthetics. A harsh critic might conclude that worship that aimed at a more cultured and refined character (which Aesthetic Worship literature meant by "reverent") is merely classism thinly veiled. Indeed, Vogt's disparaging remark about "the common town order" of service revealed his social class bias.

The leaders of the Aesthetic movement in the twentieth century, however, wanted more for worship than to pander to the tastes of the wealthy. They longed for worship that exhibited more substance than the enrichments of the Sunday School or the new measures of the Revival. They yearned for worship that had the feeling of objective reality in the way that the ecstatic prayer meetings did in frontier days for Protestants, or that the mass did for Catholics, but without insulting their modern sensibility. If Protestant worship could only have a more intelligent form, if its art were only of a higher caliber, if its prayers were less trivial, if its architecture better fit the awe-full reality of God, they believed, modern Protestants would be able to experience the objective reality of the transcendent God. They raided the storehouse of the church's tradition to find their models, and since the history of the Western church was so deeply connected to the development of European aesthetic culture, Aesthetic Worship privileged the European cultural tradition. That, too, is part of its character.

As the model was promoted by its intellectually serious apologists, the focus was on the experience of "awe" in the presence of a holy God, as this paralleled the experience of encountering a work of art. This was not the ecstatic experience of the camp meeting or Revival but a cool, sophisticated experience of contemplation. The awe-inspiring art of Gothic architecture and ceremonial were particularly suited for this. In the end, however, Aesthetic Worship promoted the effects of Gothic art without the substance of Gothic art, that is, without the Catholic theological worldview that gave it context. This led to the incongruity of Protestants using ritual, art, and architecture that did not fit their theology of church and sacrament. As one Methodist critic of Aesthetic Worship remarked in 1927, "But surely in our worship there must be something better than outright imitation of methods and symbols whose doctrinal associations are frankly repudiated."[53] Yet, without the "doctrinal associations" of the methods, all that was left was their emotional effects—more artistically refined, perhaps, but effects nonetheless.

Throughout the twentieth century, wealthy Protestant congregations employed the effects of Aesthetic Worship as a sign of their social status. Moreover, as we have seen with other models, less wealthy and rural congregations imitated the worship of large city churches. Small congregations took on elaborate offertory rituals, printed bulletins with "churchy" language, robed choirs (even if some continued to resist vested ministers), and anthems. They did this despite the strain placed on the financial and personnel resources of their congregations. Yet for one important reason these congregations rarely achieved the experience of "awe" that was so important to the apologists of Aesthetic Worship: Aesthetic Worship done well takes tremendous financial resources and skill. Just as an excellent performance of a Beethoven sonata yields a qualitatively different experience than a mediocre performance, Aesthetic Worship requires virtuosos of music, art, architecture, and oratory for its effective execution. Few congregations have the means to do it well enough to evoke awe. This is a significant problem with Aesthetic Worship as a model.

When Protestant congregations advertise worship services as Traditional, they mean some remnant of the very recent tradition of Aesthetic Worship with its hymnbooks, robed choirs, printed prayers, and vested clergy. They may be trying to evoke nostalgia for the mid-twentieth century when such worship was the hallmark of tall steeple churches in every county-seat town. American Protestants of the middle class, however, have grown increasingly disaffected with the ostentatious style of Aesthetic Worship. For reasons much too complicated to try to dissect in this brief account, Americans in general no longer revere the elitism of highbrow art in the ways they did in the early twentieth century. As cultural aspirations have changed, Protestants have grown wary of the implicit classism of the Aesthetic Worship model. Few congregations maintain a strict adherence

---

53. James A. Beebe, "Some Reflections on Public Worship," *The Methodist Review*, vol. 43, no. 3 (May 1927): 346.

to the elevated language of Aesthetic Worship or exclusively embrace European choral music or organ repertoire. Aesthetic Worship is a social occasion "you get dressed up for," and white, middle-class Americans today do not get dressed up for much of anything.

But perhaps that is not all this style of worship means. Traditional Worship as it is practiced in most congregations may not produce awe, but it can communicate a sense of reverence. Since reverence is not much in vogue in contemporary American life, Traditional Worship has become for some congregations not classism but rather a form of resistance to the casual religion of contemporary middle-class Protestantism.

	Telos (Goal)	*Ethos* (Qualities of Character)
Late nineteenth- to early twentieth-century type: Aesthetic Worship	Sophisticated spirituality for sophisticated congregations Awe in the presence of God	Highbrow art Gothic architectural effects Hymns and prayers stress transcendence of God Elevated language Ostentation Print-oriented prayer and ritual Academic-style vestments Classical music (primarily organ) Performance choir
Present form: Traditional Worship	Reverent spirituality Reverence for God	Emphasis on art Gothic architectural effects Use of hymnbooks Somewhat elevated language Nostalgia Print-oriented prayer and ritual Vested choir and ministers Classical-style music (primarily organ) Performance choir

Chapter Five

For almost fifty years now, Aesthetic Worship as it took shape in the early twentieth century has been gradually waning in influence, though this may be more the result of an evolution in aesthetic taste than in the rejection of an aesthetic approach to worship altogether. Nevertheless, many American Protestants continue to embrace Aesthetic Worship as Traditional Worship, unaware of the irony that this "tradition" is barely a century old.

CHAPTER SIX

Spiritual Power and Carnal Ecstasy

Pentecostal Worship

Lord, as of old, at Pentecost,
Thou didst Thy pow'r display—
With cleansing, purifying flame,
Descend on us today.
Refrain:
Lord, send the old-time power, the Pentecostal power!
Thy floodgates of blessing, on us throw open wide!
Lord, send the old-time power, the Pentecostal power!
That sinners be converted and Thy Name glorified!

—"Pentecostal Power," Charles H. Gabriel, 1912[1]

I arrive at the church almost thirty minutes before the appointed time for worship. As I enter the mostly empty room, I see a small group of women and men on their knees in front of the stage. They are praying—or rather, singing and weeping before the Lord, out loud and at the same time. Some are waving their arms over their heads, others have their hands palm up in front of their chests. One is laying her hands on the shoulders of another.

As other worshipers arrive and find their seats, musicians gradually take the stage. The drummer hits a few shots on her drums, and a guitarist strums a few chords on his very loud electric guitar. It feels almost as if a garage band rehearsal is about to begin, but soon the musicians

---

1. Public domain at http://library.timelesstruths.org/music/Pentecostal_Power/, accessed December 23, 2017.

start singing a very rhythmic, very repetitive song, "Praise you, Jesus, I just want to praise you." The music is so loud, I feel it in my bones. The congregation joins in without being invited. They stand, they sing, some begin to sway, others to jump, others to wave their arms and dance. Not a few have brought tambourines. I can hardly tell when this song ends and the next begins. Nor do I notice when the appointed time to begin the service had passed; worship is already well underway, "Praise Jesus!"

This is Pentecostal Worship.

Pentecostal Worship: Embodying the Reality of God

The previous chapter proposed that Aesthetic Worship developed as American cultural tastes became more refined. Many urban Protestants wanted dignified worship to attract and keep more sophisticated members. If the Aesthetic Worship movement pushed the didactic practices of Sunday School toward the refinement of cultural taste, the modern Pentecostal movement took the emotional power of the Revival and developed it in an opposite direction toward a fully embodied, more exuberant form of worship.

Like the Revival and Sunday School patterns, Pentecostal Worship focuses on experience, and like Aesthetic Worship, it seeks experience as an *encounter* with something *real*. While Aesthetic Worship looks to art as a way to encounter the "something real" of worship, the Pentecostal pattern looks to embodied, visceral manifestations of spiritual power, in charismata and intense spiritual experience, as that "something real." This is not experience as a mental activity or as mere awareness of the presence of the numinous, as in the other patterns. For Pentecostals, worship is a full-bodied, participatory engagement with the power of God. The hallmarks of Pentecostalism (speaking in tongues, spiritual healing, divine prophecy, miraculous signs) manifest intense awareness of God's presence, and the characteristic response to this presence is to surrender to it.[2] This

---

2. Gerardo Marti, "*Maranatha* (O Lord, Come): The Power/Surrender Dynamic of Pentecostal Worship," *Liturgy* 33, no. 3 (2018): 20–28.

is the objective core and the *telos* for worship for the Pentecostal model: an embodied, participatory, ecstatic encounter with the Holy Spirit of God.

Pentecostalism as a global movement began to mushroom in the twentieth century, but as Grant Wacker's sympathetic history of Pentecostalism identifies, numerous streams flowed together to birth the movement. The emphasis on heartfelt conversion coming out of the Great Awakening, Methodist concern with personal holiness, and Finneyite Revivalism's reiteration of these themes in the nineteenth century are all precursors to Pentecostalism.[3] Likewise, manifestations of Pentecostal-like phenomena appear in accounts of early Methodist prayer meetings, where participants sang, prayed, and shouted, and some worshipers fell on the ground in an apparent faint (which Pentecostals would call "being slain in the spirit") and some had visions of God.[4] Frontier camp meetings of the early nineteenth century also anticipated Pentecostal Worship, as described in the eyewitness account by Barton Stone, one of the founders of the Disciples of Christ. Stone was present at the Cane Ridge camp meeting of 1801, which took place near Lexington, Kentucky, and he recounts:

> The bodily agitations or exercise, attending the excitement in the beginning of this century, were various, and called by various names. The falling exercise was very common among all classes, the saints and sinners of every age and of every grade, from the philosopher to the clown. The subject of this exercise would, generally, with a piercing scream, fall like a log on the floor, earth, or mud, and appear as dead. . . .
>
> The jerks cannot be so easily described. Sometimes the subject of the jerks would be affected in some one member of the body, and sometimes the whole system. When the head alone was affected, it would be jerked backward and forward, or from side to side, so quickly that the features of the face could not be distinguished. When the whole system was affected, I have seen the person stand in one place, and jerk backward and forward in quick succession, their head nearly touching the floor. . . .

---

3. *Heaven Below: Early Pentecostals and American Culture* (Cambridge, MA: Harvard University Press, 2001), 1–3.

4. Henry D. Rack, *Reasonable Enthusiast: John Wesley and the Rise of Methodism* (Nashville, TN: Abingdon Press, 1989), 194–97.

Chapter Six

The dancing exercise. This generally began with the jerks, and was peculiar to professors of religion. The subject, after jerking awhile, began to dance, and then the jerks would cease. Such dancing was indeed heavenly to the spectators; there was nothing in it like levity, nor calculated to excite levity in the beholders. The smile of heaven shone on the countenance of the subject, and assimilated to angels appeared the whole person. Sometimes the motion was quick and sometimes slow. Thus they continued to move forward and backward in the same track or alley till nature seemed exhausted, and they would fall prostrate on the floor or earth, unless caught by those standing by. While thus exercised, I have heard their solemn praises and prayers ascending to God.

The barking exercise, (as opposers contemptuously called it,) was nothing but the jerks. A person affected with the jerks, especially in his head, would often make a grunt, or bark, if you please, from the suddenness of the jerk. . . .

The laughing exercise was frequent, confined solely with the religious. It was a loud, hearty laughter, but one sui generis; it excited laughter in none else. The subject appeared rapturously solemn, and his laughter excited solemnity in saints and sinners. It is truly indescribable.

The running exercise was nothing more than that persons, feeling something of these bodily agitations, through fear, attempted to run away, and thus escape from them; but it commonly happened that they ran not far before they fell, or became so greatly agitated that they could proceed no farther.

I shall close this chapter with the singing exercise. This is more unaccountable than anything else I ever saw. The subject in a very happy state of mind would sing most melodiously, not from the mouth or nose, but entirely in the breast, the sounds issuing thence. Such music silenced everything, and attracted the attention of all. It was most heavenly. None could ever be tired of hearing it. Dr. J. P. Campbell and myself were together at a meeting, and were attending to a pious lady thus exercised, and concluded it to be something surpassing anything we had known in nature.[5]

---

5. James R. Rogers, *The Cane Ridge Meeting-house*; to which is appended the autobiography of B. W. Stone, and a sketch of David Purviance by William Rogers (Cincinnati, OH: The Standard Publishing Company, 1910), 159–62.

Stone's observations of the Cane Ridge camp meeting parallel the physical manifestation that would become staples of Pentecostal meetings. Even Stone's depiction of "the singing exercise" is similar to the Pentecostal practice of "singing in the Spirit," and it may even be a veiled reference to glossolalia, since he claims it was "something surpassing anything we had known in nature."

African American Christian experience and practice is another extremely significant source of modern Pentecostalism, and predominantly black Pentecostal denominations today constitute a major segment of Pentecostalism in America. It was not uncommon for African slaves to attend camp meetings, and it well may be that the phenomena witnessed by Stone developed under the influence of these African attendees. Many African slaves were forced to become Christians as a fact of their enslavement by white Christian masters, though they had formerly been Muslims or practitioners of African traditional religions. They kept many exuberant liturgical practices of their homeland, as far as their circumstances allowed, adapting the practices of White Christians to the practices they already knew by heart. Some masters permitted or even required their slaves to attend the worship services of their Euro-American congregations, but some also allowed (or in some cases did not know about) gatherings where slaves engaged in worship in their own communities. These services were filled with vigorous singing, praying, dancing, and shouting. Preachers, often illiterate but inspired by the power of the Holy Spirit, preached (and shouted and chanted) the stories of scripture from memory, and their congregations joined in these sermons through call and response.[6] Thus, a distinctively non-European form of Christian worship evolved in America, a form untethered to the disembodied spiritual worldview of the European Enlightenment. For these African American worshipers, mental and spiritual experience simply *was* physical experience, which is to say their worship practices show that they did not adopt the mind-body dualism of the European Americans.

---

6. For a concise account, see Marva Wilson Costen, *African American Christian Worship* (Nashville, TN: Abingdon Press, 1993), especially chapter 6, "Worship in the Invisible Institution," 36–49.

Chapter Six

Whatever its roots, conventional histories of the modern Pentecostal movement trace its sprouting to the entwined story of two men, Charles F. Parham and William J. Seymour. Parham was a white preacher and faith healer from Kansas (at one time, an itinerant Methodist), who had long been intrigued with the accounts of glossolalia, healing, and other miraculous experiences of the early church in the Book of Acts and 1 Corinthians. Parham organized a small group of followers in Topeka to begin earnestly seeking the full gifts of the Holy Spirit, and in 1901, he and other members of the group began to experience the gift of speaking in tongues.[7] After moderate success in Kansas, in 1905 Parham moved to Houston where he established a Bible school to teach the Pentecost revival. His followers soon took the movement to Chicago, New York City, and other major urban areas.[8]

His most notable student was William J. Seymour, an African American holiness preacher who attended Parham's lectures before starting a ministry in Los Angeles, California, at what he called the Azusa Street Mission.

Worship at the Azusa Street Mission was not a series of discrete meetings but more like a single, undulating event that happened every day of the week. According to Frank Bartleman, one of the few members of the Azusa Street congregation who wrote about his experience:

> The services ran almost continuously. Seeking souls could be found under the power almost any hour, night and day. The place was never closed nor empty. The people came to meet God. He was always there. Hence a continuous meeting.[9]

---

7. T. P. Thigpen, "Parham, Charles Fox," in *Dictionary of Christianity in America* (Downers Grove, IL: InterVarsity, 1990).

8. Wacker, *Heaven Below*, 6. While Parham was initially supportive of Seymour, they had a parting of the ways over the racial mixing at the Azusa Street revival. Parham was prone to the white racism of the day. For accounts of the interracial origins of Pentecostalism, see Gastón Espinosa, *William Seymour and the Origins of Global Pentecostalism* (Durham, NC: Duke University Press, 2014), 96–108; Wacker, *Heaven Below*, 228–35.

9. Frank Bartleman, *Azusa Street* (Plainville, NJ: Logos International, 1980), 58.

More people would attend on Sunday mornings, and the meeting would swell during posted daily meeting times. Yet, no one, it seems, ever pronounced a benediction and sent the crowd on its way.

Seymour, who founded the mission, was the leader, and he would preach at many of the meetings. However, preaching did not dominate the service, and anyone moved by the Spirit could testify or preach. Indeed, in the early days of the Azusa meeting, the worship space did not have a platform or pulpit. The only rule for the meeting was to respond to the Spirit of God. "We had no human programme," Bartleman claimed. "All was spontaneous, ordered by the Spirit. We wanted to hear from God, through whoever he might speak."[10] Bartleman provides a moving description of how such a meeting unfolded:

> When we first reached the meeting we avoided as much as possible human contact and greeting. We wanted to meet God first. We got our head under some bench in the corner in prayer, and met men only in the Spirit, knowing them "after the flesh" no more. The meetings started themselves, spontaneously, in testimony, praise and worship. . . . We had no prearranged programme to be jammed through on time. Our time was the Lord's. We had real testimonies, from fresh heart-experience. Otherwise, the shorter the testimonies, the better. A dozen might be on their feet at one time, trembling under the mighty power of God. We did not have to get our cue from some leader. And we were free from lawlessness. We were shut up to God in prayer in the meetings, our minds on Him. . . . The Lord was liable to burst through any one. We prayed for this continually. Some one would finally get up anointed for the message. All seemed to recognize this and gave way. It might be a child, a woman, or a man. It might be from the back seat, or from the front. It made no difference. . . . Some one might be speaking. Suddenly the Spirit would fall upon the congregation. God himself would give the altar call. Men would fall all over the house, like the slain in battle, or rush for the altar en masse, to seek God. . . . I never saw an altar call given in those early days. God himself would call them. And the preacher knew when to quit. When He spoke we all obeyed. . . . The presence of God was so real.[11]

---

10. Bartleman, *Azusa Street*, 57–58.
11. Bartleman, *Azusa Street*, 59–60.

Clearly, spontaneous obedience to the Spirit was the character of such a meeting, but this did not mean that it did not have some recognizable pattern. Indeed, several features of Bartleman's description are stereotypical of Pentecost services even today: beginning with "praise and worship," followed by an extended period of testimony, preaching, and finally an extended "altar call" during which worshipers responded to the voice of God in fervent prayers for redemption, healing, or baptism in the Spirit all accompanied by physical manifestations in the bodies of the worshipers.[12]

The *telos* of Pentecostal Worship at Azusa Street, and in large measure the goal of Pentecostalism today, is "baptism in the Holy Spirit," which initiates a lifelong experience of the power of the Spirit in one's life. This was both intensely personal and highly communal. The evidence that one had received baptism in the Holy Spirit was, chiefly, speaking in tongues. Other evidence included holy laughter, being slain in the spirit, shouting, dancing, divine healing, prophecy—all these were concrete evidence of an encounter with the Holy Spirit. The community of worshipers encouraged these manifestations and verified them. If someone gave a "message in tongues," someone else rose "to interpret the message," or else it was determined not to be genuine. If someone were "slain in the Spirit," a fellow worshiper would help as they fell to the floor. Worshipers would touch each other by laying hands on the head, shoulders, or back of someone needing "deliverance" from a problem or seeking baptism in the Holy Ghost. Testifying and preaching could be a sort of tag-team action, with one person beginning a message that was finished by another who felt a strong "anointing" to give a word to the church. Singing in Pentecostal Worship is a vigorous communal event, typically done from memory and, in the early days of Pentecostalism, rarely planned out in advance. Song leaders or other members of the congregation would begin songs as they felt led by the Spirit, and one song would lead into another without any break until the congregation spontaneously moved from singing to prayer and testimony. One of the most notable musical practices at Azusa Street

---

12. For a similar description of a Pentecostal meeting in Chicago, only three years later than Bartleman's account but written for a scholarly journal, see Frederick G. Henke, "The Gift of Tongues and Related Phenomena at the Present Day," *The American Journal of Theology* vol. 13, no. 2 (1909): 196–99.

was what Bartleman called "singing in the Spirit," which seems to parallel the "singing exercise" in the camp meetings a century earlier:

> It [singing in the Spirit] was a spontaneous manifestation and rapture no earthly tongue can describe. . . . It was sometimes without words, other times in "tongues." The effect was wonderful on the people. It brought a heavenly atmosphere, as though the angels themselves were present and joining with us. . . . The spirit of song given from God in the beginning was like the Aeolian harp, in its spontaneity and sweetness. In fact it was the very breath of God, playing on human heartstrings, or human vocal cords. The notes were wonderful in sweetness, volume and duration. It was "singing in the Spirit."[13]

While many of the worship practices at Azusa Street were boisterous or even cacophonous, singing in the Spirit was more restrained and entailed the highly communal practice of ad lib harmony.

> The Azusa Street Mission itself attracted the attention of the local press, and with this came skeptics along with the merely curious. One of the most telling criticisms concerned the promiscuous attitude of participants toward gender and race, for in its origin Pentecostalism eagerly affirmed the spirit-led ministry of women and ignored the race and ethnic barriers of American culture. As the movement evolved into various Pentecostal denominations, not all groups maintained the astonishing egalitarianism of Azusa Street in its heyday, and many Pentecostal groups and denominations promoted a strong patriarchal theology that promoted the clear superiority of men as leaders (the language often used is "headship") over women, even down to the level of the family. Yet, even in the present day, many Pentecostal congregations are more open to the ministries of women than some historic denominations, and some urban Pentecostal congregations are more racially diverse than many mainline Protestant urban congregations.[14]

Beyond the egalitarianism, however, the wide and rapid expansion of the movement suggests that many American Christians at the beginning

---

13. Bartleman, *Azusa Street*, 56–57. While there are surprisingly few examples of this sort of singing on the World Wide Web, an example can be found at http://wn.com/Singing_in_Tongues, accessed April 5, 2016.

14. Kevin D. Dougherty, "How Monochromatic Is Church Membership? Racial-Ethnic Diversity in Religious Community," *Sociology of Religion* vol. 64, no. 1 (Spring 2003): 65–85.

of the twentieth century were hungry for the exuberant style of worship that Pentecostalism offered.[15] I suggest that the more sensationalist aspects of this movement are really only a part of a broader cultural reaction against the impersonal and disembodied forms of official religion developing in the major Protestant denominations. By the late nineteenth century, Finneyite Revivalism had waned as a way of giving people the experience of something that felt "really real," and people were longing for something to fill the gap. The Sunday School and the Aesthetic forms of worship, on the other hand, were pushing a more intellectual style of faith with a "cooler" emotional content, a form of worship that appealed to educated, sophisticated believers. What these forms of worship promoted as an imaginative simulation of religious feeling, the Pentecostal movement sought as an actual, physical experience of the power of God.

Pentecostalism Goes Mainline: The Charismatic Movement

Today, in the United States, Pentecostalism is much broader than the free-church and holiness type of churches in which it began.[16] Indeed, by the middle of the twentieth century, Pentecostal forms of spirituality spread to mainline denominations. In the 1960s, Dennis Bennett, an Episcopal priest, began writing about his experiences of speaking in tongues. This spurred the beginning of what began to be called the Charismatic Renewal that soon spread among Methodists, Presbyterians, Lutherans, and many other mainline Protestants. By the late 1970s a vigorous Catholic Charismatic movement received cautious but genuine support from the Vatican. The University of Notre Dame had begun hosting yearly meetings for Catholic Pentecostals in 1967, and with this Vatican support, by

---

15. Similar movements were also underway in Europe and other parts of the world. See Henke, "The Gift of Tongues and Related Phenomena at the Present Day," 193–95.

16. On the history of Pentecostal Worship, see Swee Hong Lim and Lester Ruth, *Lovin' on Jesus: A Concise History of Contemporary Worship* (Nashville, TN: Abingdon Press, 2017).

1974 over 25,000 were attending the gathering.[17] John Wimber, a rock musician who founded the Vineyard movement, represents what now is called the Third Wave of the Pentecostal/Charismatic Renewal. The worship music of the Vineyard, and particularly its stress on spiritual intimacy, has grown to be extremely influential in churches throughout the world, not only for Pentecostals but also among Protestants and Catholics.[18]

Mainline Protestant and Catholic Charismatics share with Protestant Pentecostals experience of a direct encounter with the Holy Spirit that provokes in the believer a relationship with God that is palpably real. Furthermore, Charismatics and Pentecostals share a belief that the presence of God is manifest through gifts of the Holy Spirit. The free church Pentecostals tend to be biblical literalists. Pentecostal/Charismatic spirituality can make Catholics and Episcopalians more intensely committed to the sacraments, to the rites of anointing with oil, and to the rituals of healing. Charismatics and Free Church Pentecostals have a great deal in common, so much so that it would not be far off the mark to say that the Pentecostal/Charismatic movement is the remaining serious manifestation of an ecumenical movement. Catholic and Protestant Charismatics and Free Church Pentecostals often find it remarkably easy to worship together.[19]

The Character of the Pentecostal/Charismatic Worship

Pentecostal/Charismatic Worship is an *event* in which the worshipers expect to have an encounter with God that directly engages their bodies and emotions. I therefore characterize the *telos* of this form of worship as uninhibited divine (group) encounter. This encounter is initiated for individuals through "baptism in the Holy Spirit," a singular event in which

---

17. Thomas J. Csordas, *Language, Charisma and Creativity: The Ritual Life of a Religious Movement* (Berkeley and Los Angeles: University of California Press, 1997), xiv. Note, at its beginning the Catholic Charismatics tended to refer to themselves as "Catholic Pentecostals."

18. Brian Spinks, *The Worship Mall: Contemporary Responses to Contemporary Culture* (New York, NY: Church Publishing, 2010), 95ff.

19. See Daniel E. Albrecht, *Rites in the Spirit: A Ritual Approach to Pentecostal/Charismatic Spirituality* (Sheffield, UK: Sheffield Academic Press, 1999), 36–41.

persons experience the unmediated power of the Holy Spirit, and which, typically, bestows on them the "gift of tongues," that is, the ability to pray in a "language" that they do not speak naturally.[20] Though this spiritual experience is very personal, it is also intensely communal, for the full exercise of spiritual gifts belongs within the gathered body of believers. Indeed, Pentecostal Worship does not so much *express* the meaning of the church as it *creates* the church as a living, complex, but unified body. The *ethos* of Pentecostal Worship stresses physical gestures and movement, emotional exuberance, egalitarian participation, intimacy with God, and expressions of ecstasy among the leaders and congregation. The visual ritual symbols of Pentecostal Worship tend to be minimal: Bible, pulpit, preacher, praise band. The altar, for example, is not a distinctive piece of furniture but the open area between the congregation and the stage. However, the ritual symbols are not primarily expressed through visual art and architecture (which tends to be functional and austere), but through auditory and kinesthetic "icons," which are the stereotypical sounds of Pentecostal Worship (praise music, shouts of Halleluiah, glossolalia, etc.) and movements (dancing, swaying, lifting hands, etc.). As Albrecht shows, these auditory/kinesthetic icons of Pentecostal Worship functionally envelop the participants in the spiritual world in much the same way that icons in Eastern Orthodox churches mediate the divine world for its congregations.[21]

There is a definite erotic aspect to this intensely personal and physical encounter with God, as we see in Brenda Eatman Aghahowa's description of worship in a Pentecostal congregation:

> Often, I am struck by the sensual, almost sexual, nature of much of the audience participation and of the overall worship at Fire Baptized and other black churches with similar worship. The bodily swaying, the flailing on the

---

20. There are many anecdotal reports of persons "praying in tongues" in a language that someone else hears as an actual language, particularly in missionary contexts. However, "tongues" is usually not an actual language but a collection of "non-sense" syllables (from the speaker's perspective) that has the flow of language. Speaking in tongues can be exercised by individuals in public worship as part of praying together in worship, but it can just as well be used devotionally. In the Pentecostal tradition, if a person is led by the Spirit to offer a "message in tongues" to a congregation, then someone else must also receive the "gift of interpretation" to provide the meaning. However, this "interpretation" is not a translation in the linguistic sense.

21. Albrecht, *Rites in the Spirit*, 143–48.

floor, the crying out, the rising of music (and response to it) to fever pitch, the general frenzy, and the resultant "high" or sense of spiritual intoxication derived from this worship all seem, for lack of a better term, almost orgasmic.

Like the best intercourse, the worship experience at Fire Baptized and other churches like it is at once totally exhausting and totally exhilarating—a totally satisfying experience.[22]

While Aghahowa describes an African American Pentecostal congregation, this account could just as well describe any number of predominantly Anglo or Hispanic Pentecostal/Charismatic congregations. Pentecostal Worship is an encounter to which one submits fully, willing to lose control to the experience itself. This is worship with gyrating bodies and lots of sweat, with pumping, rhythmic music and songs that crescendo to soaring climaxes. Unlike other patterns we have examined, Pentecostal Worship involves a great deal of physical touching: holding hands, laying-on of hands, and embraces. In short, it has the erotically charged atmosphere of a dance club or a rock concert, where the vocal participation and bodily engagements of the audience are essential to the event itself.[23]

In addition to the sexual dynamic, moreover, Pentecostal Worship provides an alcohol-free, drug-free way of feeling wonderfully out of control, of breaking out of the ordinary realm of the senses and analytical thinking. Being "drunk in the spirit" is a common description of Pentecostal experience and reflects the lack of inhibition and joy a person feels when worshiping this way.

Wolfgang Vondey offers an alternative metaphor to describe the overall character of Pentecostal Worship: that of "play" that is expressed in improvisational jazz:

Play, in its essence, is not a performative construct of reason but an unfolding of the imagination based on the collective activity of a community

---

22. Brenda Eatman Aghahowa, *Praising in Black and White: Unity and Diversity in Christian Worship* (Cleveland, OH: United Church Press, 1996), 99.

23. When I was an undergraduate student in the mid-1970s, a friend observed how much attending a rock concert was like going to his Pentecostal church, and how much Mick Jagger acted like a Pentecostal preacher.

> characterized by a broad spectrum of improvisation. The structure of jazz, with its creative, interpretative, and extemporaneous character, illustrates how complex this spectrum can be without necessitating fixed structures. . . . Jazz play cultivates an "aesthetic of surrender" that invites openness not by negating the predictable but by affirming the creative engagement of one another.[24]

The "play" of Pentecostal Worship, thus, accomplishes spontaneity within its stereotypical patterns, just as the playing of jazz works within the musical conventions of scales, notes, instruments, and rhythms. It is both structured and spontaneous. The jazz metaphor, however, suggests a certain technical skill that overlooks the egalitarian *ethos* of Pentecostal Worship. Rather, I suggest, such worship is more like the loosely structured, imaginative play of children on a playground.[25] Such play has no self-conscious objective other than to engage its participants, though it accomplishes many indirect objectives such as physical exercise, creative mental development, and learning problem-solving skills. Children's games are not performed for an audience. Likewise, Pentecostal Worship is not performed for an audience, nor is it even performed *for* God. Rather, Pentecostal Worship understands God the Holy Spirit to be a fully engaged participant in the play of worship.

Order in Pentecostal Worship

Pentecostal Worship values spontaneity, and without question it is less formally constructed than the patterns we have so far examined. Yet, as I have already noted, the overall structure of a Pentecostal Worship service is similar to the threefold outline of the Revival pattern. Albrecht, who has done a careful ritual analysis of hundreds of Pentecostal Worship services, identifies what he calls the "foundational/processual structure" with three

---

24. Wolfgang Vondey, *Beyond Pentecostalism: The Crisis of Global Christianity and the Renewal of the Theological Agenda* (Grand Rapids, MI: Eerdmans, 2010), 139.

25. Lim and Ruth, "The Music of Contemporary Worship: Origins through the 1980s," in *Lovin' on Jesus*, 58–66.

primary building blocks of Pentecostal Worship: the Rite of Worship and Praise,[26] the Rite of Pastoral Message, and the Rite of Altar/Response. Around these building blocks are the gathering/dispersing rites, and in between come transitional rites. Each of the foundational/processual rites is made up of what Albrecht calls "microrituals," a wide range of communally acknowledged ritual actions from which the congregation or leaders may draw spontaneously (raising hands, speaking in tongues, kneeling, dancing, and so forth).

Foundational and Processual Rites in Pentecostal Ritual

Gathering and Greeting Rites

> RITE OF WORSHIP AND PRAISE
>
> Transitional rites
>
> RITE OF PASTORAL MESSAGE
>
> Transition (brief)
>
> RITE OF ALTAR/RESPONSE
>
> Transition (brief)

Farewells and Dispersing[27]

Gathering and Greeting

Albrecht notes that there is typically a genuine friendliness in Pentecostal congregations, and this is part of what makes them successful. For example, they almost always have designated greeters who shake hands and speak with both regular attendees and visitors.

---

26. It is more common to find the term "praise and worship" today, with a conscientious order to this: praise (a more boisterous communal action) gives rise to worship (a more intimate communal action). I will discuss this below.

27. Albrecht, *Rites in the Spirit*, 153–54.

Chapter Six

Rite of Worship and Praise

The Pentecostal Pattern often has no obvious beginning. Rather, as the congregation gathers and greets one another, music will begin, and, as in the opening illustration, people already gathered at the front of the church for prayer will gradually filter out into the congregational seating area to join in singing. For most Pentecostals, this first unit of the service is made up almost exclusively of singing and primarily of singing *praise* songs. Indeed, Pentecostals tend to call the opening praise segment of the service "worship," for in this model "worship" equals praise. The identification of worship with praise is a significant marker of this pattern.[28] Usually there will be several songs without dead time between each piece; music will flow from song to song over the course of twenty or thirty minutes (or sometimes longer). Often this will be led by a worship team (rather than a choir), but almost always the congregation will join in right away. The instruments tend to be guitar, bass, drums, or other instruments we typically see in a rock band rather than a traditional church organ; if there is an organ, it tends to be an electronic organ or synthesizer. As Albrecht says, music functions as an auditory icon for Pentecostals. The congregation will spontaneously (but invariably) stand, clap, or raise their hands.

The Rite of Worship and Praise is a distinctive liturgical unit of the Pentecostal pattern and is quite distinct from the use of hymns in historic Protestant worship. Hymns in historic Protestant churches place strong emphasis on the meaning of text set to music, and the structure of the music is strongly influenced by the poetic lines of the hymn text. They tend to be rather brief (three to four minutes), and they have a definite beginning and conclusion. The Rite of Worship and Praise, on the other hand, places less emphasis on the poetic and cognitive depth of the text and more emphasis on the music, especially the degree to which the tune can engage the congregation in vigorous singing. Moreover, the Rite of Praise and Worship strings songs together without interruption as a way

---

28. Lim and Ruth trace the influence of Psalm 22:3 in the King James Version: "But thou art holy, thou that inhabitest the praises of Israel," beginning with the writing of influential Pentecostal leader of the Latter Rain movement, Reg Layzell, and further popularized by the writings of Judson Cornwall. See *Lovin' on Jesus*, 124–31.

to establish a mood conducive to the surrender of one's heart and mind to worship.

In the Rite of Praise and Worship, there is little or no downtime between songs, and transitions that do occur are filled with ejaculations such as "Praise the Lord," "Thank you, Jesus," and "Hallelujah," often modeled by the worship team. Sometimes, when it has elicited a great deal of response among worshipers, the song will end with the congregation engaged in "concert" prayer during which each individual voice is in simultaneous prayer and praise, talking with God, a sort of continuation of the music itself.

Typically, the loud and rhythmic opening praise songs that come in the first minutes of the rite will transition to more meditative songs of praise near the end of the set, which Albrecht says, "help to move worshipers into a more 'intimate communion.'"[29] Here we also see gestures and hear prayer but softer, less demonstrative—whispered or murmured praise rather than shouts. At this point in a service we might find a prophetic word or message in tongues and interpretation. Here is where "singing in the Spirit" occurs.

There can be a variety of actions in the Rite of Praise and Worship, but as Albrecht observes:

> At the center of the variety exists the belief among the congregants that they are actually experiencing the presence of God in an intimate, immediate, mystical way. . . . The salient belief that God by God's Spirit *acts*, *involves* and *concerns* God's self with the contemporary world and its people both within the church and in the workaday world underlies all the ritual expressions.[30]

That said, there is almost always a definite shape to the intensity of the Rite of Praise and Worship. The first song will begin at a fast tempo and focus the energy of the congregation for active engagement. The next one or two songs will increase the level of energy, but the last song will almost

---

29. Albrecht, *Rites in the Spirit*, 159.
30. Albrecht, *Rites in the Spirit*, 159–60.

always slow the tempo to allow the congregation to begin to settle in the Spirit for what will follow.

Transition Rites

The tension is relaxed after the Rite of Praise and Worship. This is a time to prepare for the message, and this typically occurs via more relaxed prayer, asking for concerns from the congregation, along with announcements, greeting of visitors, and, notably in the black churches, introductions of special guests.[31] During the transition, the collection is taken, with plates passed among the rows of worshipers, or in black Pentecostal churches, the congregation may process to the front of the church to place their offering in plates on the communion table or in baskets held by ushers.[32] Singing, led by the praise band or choir, accompanies the collection and functions as the last preparation for the message.

The order of the various actions here described can differ from congregation to congregation, and even from service to service in the same congregation. Many Pentecostal congregations also include another musical piece led by the praise band or choir. As a juncture between the two main components of the service ("worship and praise" and "message"), the transition exhibits more flexibility in overall structure than what precedes and follows.[33]

Rite of Pastoral Message

The Rite of Pastoral Message will usually begin with the reading of scripture, and, in some congregations, the first part is essentially a Bible

---

31. Cheryl J. Sanders, *Saints in Exile: The Holiness-Pentecostal Experience in African American Religion and Culture* (New York, NY: Oxford University Press, 1996), 51. Sanders proposes that the significance of welcoming visitors "by name" in the black church "can be a countercultural act that affirms the oneness of all humanity before God. During the aftermath of slavery, the public announcement of one's name, hometown, home church, and pastor in black church services was not only an important means of establishing personal and social identity but also a vital networking function . . . for the reunion of individuals and families who had been sold away from each other as slaves" (69).

32. Sanders, *Saints in Exile*, 69.

33. We will also see the same sort of flexibility in the transition between the "Word" service and "Table" service in the "Word and Table" pattern.

study.[34] Gradually, however, the Rite of Pastoral Message will become more participatory, with the congregation making spontaneous verbal shouts of "Amen" and so forth. By the conclusion of the message, the congregation will have returned to the emotional intensity of the Rite of Praise and Worship. The Rite of Pastoral Message concludes with another transition, which is the altar call, during which the pastor will ask people to come to the front of the worship space to make a response to the Spirit that has moved the congregation through the message.

Rite of Altar/Response

The Rite of Altar/Response of Pentecostal Worship follows the shape of the altar call in the Revival pattern. However, while the altar call of the Revival aimed at bringing people to a conversion experience, or to recommitment for "backsliders," the Pentecostal altar call includes this and much more. People may be asked to come forward to receive baptism in the Spirit or healing or anointing for some special purpose, or to support those who are coming forward or to pray or simply to join in an unspecified response to the Spirit. It is not uncommon for most of the congregation to come forward. This is a time when congregational participation in singing may not be quite so comprehensive, and often the praise band or choir will sing as the rest of the congregation processes to the front of the church.[35] This rite can take fifteen minutes or even longer, especially if the congregation feels the Spirit moving in their midst. This comprehensive form of altar call is a distinctive liturgical unit of the Pentecostal pattern.

Farewells and Dispersing

The Rite of Altar/Response may conclude with a closing prayer (rather than a benediction) led by the pastor. Sometimes this closing prayer takes place even as the congregation continues to participate in the altar call. This prayer functions as a conclusion to the service for persons who want

---

34. Sanders, *Saints in Exile*, 47.
35. Sanders, *Saints in Exile*, 45.

to leave, while not requiring a strict dismissal of those who are still "receiving ministry" through the altar call. Just as the service began with a gradual convening of the congregation, the service ends with a gradual dispersal. There is symmetrical shape to this pattern: a "soft" beginning as people gather and a "soft" conclusion as they disperse. Likewise, just at the energy of the Rite of Praise and Worship begins at a high level before settling down as the service transitions to prayer and announcements, the message begins at a lower energy level and peaks at the altar call.

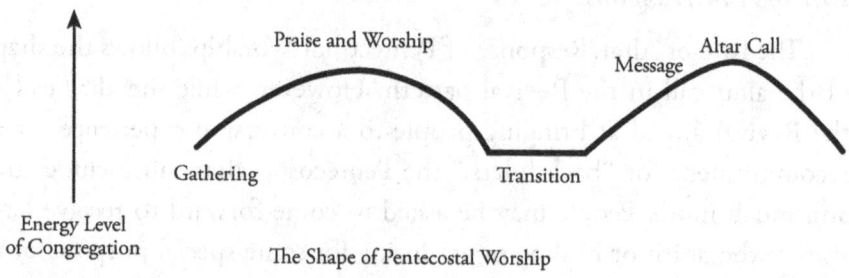

The Shape of Pentecostal Worship

Contemporary Praise Worship

The contemporary worship of many Pentecostal churches that are becoming more mainstream and among Charismatic congregations of mainline denominations is what is often called Praise and Worship. This is also the standard pattern of midweek worship for some non-Pentecostal megachurches that have Seeker Services on Sunday and Saturday evenings. While a Seeker Service aims to introduce the unchurched to the Christian message, the Praise and Worship service engages Christians in more uninhibited experiences of worship and also in deeper, more theologically and ethically challenging preaching. In the early 1980s, Bill Hybels, senior pastor of the Willow Creek Community Church in Barrington, Illinois, introduced his congregation to the midweek Praise and Worship service after he experienced worship in a Charismatic congregation. Hybels was deeply moved by the personal intimacy and intensity of singing and prayer in the Charismatic service, and he believed his growing congregation of dedicated believers would become closer to God by learning to worship in the uninhibited style of the Charismatics.[36] Throughout the 1980s and 1990s, Willow Creek called the midweek service the church's worship service, and distinguished it from the Seeker Service, which was aimed at the unchurched who were not yet ready for the more intense style of Praise and Worship. Just as the Willow Creek Seeker Service has reintroduced American Protestant churches to a less intense but highly effective form of the Revival pattern, likewise their midweek service has introduced Protestants to a less intense form of Pentecostal worship.[37] The widely used term "contemporary worship" conventionally refers to both the Seeker Service and the Praise and Worship model, though it is important to distinguish the distinctive goal and character of each of these two patterns: the Seeker Service develops out of the Revival tradition, while Praise and Worship emerges out of the Pentecostal tradition.

In outline, a Praise and Worship order follows the same pattern as Pentecostal Worship—that is, it has a clear bipartite structure of singing and message. Singing constitutes the bulk of the first portion of the service, which music planners call the worship set, following the Pentecostal/Charismatic precedent where the singing and prayer constitute "worship." The message constitutes the bulk of the second half.[38]

The purpose of the worship set is to lead the congregation into intimacy with God. Worship begins with a call to worship, during which the worship leader invites the congregation to enter into God's presence. This may but need not be preceded by a song to "warm up" the gathering. After the call to worship, the standard order will move from songs of praise and adoration, with a fast or medium tempo, during which the congregation (standing!) will sway, bounce in time, or even dance. Gradually, the fast-tempo praise songs transition to songs of prayer, confession, and intimacy,

---

36. Joe Horness, "Contemporary Music-Driven Worship," in *Exploring the Worship Spectrum*, ed. Paul E. Engle (Grand Rapids, MI: Zondervan, 2004), 108.

37. In 2007, following the "Reveal" self-study, Willow Creek began to introduce more participatory worship elements into its weekend services, which are now less narrowly focused on seekers.

38. Spinks, *The Worship Mall*, 96.

which employ a slower tempo. During the final song, the congregants often raise their hands above their heads and lift their faces upward (often with eyes tightly shut). The worship set concludes with the entire congregation softly praying concurrently. For Charismatic congregations, this prayer may include glossolalia, or singing in the Spirit.

Andy Park, a worship leader connected to the Vineyard church, provides an example of the "classic progression" of a worship set, with suggested "beats per minute" indicating the tempo and energy of the songs:[39]

"We Want to See Jesus Lifted High"	"Lord, I Lift Your Name on High"	"In the Secret"	"Who Is Like Our God"	"How Great Thou Art"	"Holy and Anointed One"	"This Is Love"
132 bpm	88 bpm	126 bpm	82 bpm	80 bpm	70 bpm	66 bpm

With the exception of the second song in this list ("Lord, I Lift Your Name on High"), the songs show a gradual decrease in tempo. However, Park notes that beats-per-minute is less important than the "energy" of the song. His point is to move from high energy to a gentler level of energy as the set transitions from praise and adoration to intimacy. We may also note a thematic progression in the songs Park has selected. "We Want to See Jesus Lifted High" suggests a call to worship and expresses the goal of the entire worship set. The songs that follow express praise and adoration. "Holy and Anointed One" is a tender love song to Jesus, and "This Is Love" expresses complete surrender to God.

The congregation sings by following words projected on screens and also from memory. Since tunes are not printed out (as in a hymnbook), congregants learn the music by actively participating in the singing, and

---

39. Andy Park, *To Know You More: Cultivating the Heart of the Worship Leader* (Downers Grove, IL: InterVarsity Press, 2002), 164. See Brian Spinks's analysis of Park's description of worship sets in *The Worship Mall*, 105–6.

like hymns, the tunes tend be repetitive to allow quick learning of the melodies. Furthermore, Praise and Worship leaders often employ songs that are receiving airplay on contemporary Christian radio stations, which means that new songs may already be familiar to members of the congregations. Even so, too much new music hinders active engagement of the congregation, and preparers of worship sets are careful to mix songs that the congregation knows well with one or at most two new songs per set.

A period of transition follows the worship set during which come announcements and the collection. Other actions that may come during this transition are the learning of a new song or a testimony or the performance of a dance ensemble or a dramatic skit related to the message that will follow.

The message in the Worship and Praise order begins with teaching drawn from scripture (with the text projected). However, from there, it tends to be much less dramatic than the preaching found in Pentecostal and Holiness congregations. There will be fewer verbal congregation responses (not many "Amens"). Rather, the style of preaching usually takes its cue from the intimacy of the songs at the end of the worship set. The preacher may sit on a stool next to an unimposing stand to hold any notes. The message has the form of expository reflections on the scripture passage combined with observations from the pastor's spiritual journal. Typically, the message will stress the authenticity of the pastor and will relate the pastor's personal struggles with faithful living. Unlike Pentecostal preaching, a Praise and Worship message does not build to a fever pitch; rather, it ends with an invitation to go deeper into an intimate relationship with God.

A prayer and a song follow the message, along with an altar call inviting people to come forward for prayer, personal healing, or some other personal need. The music and singing that follow the message return to the slower, more intimate style of the song at the conclusion of the worship set. While there may be a final prayer and dismissal, often some members of the congregation will continue to pray at the front of the church as others depart.

Chapter Six

> **Distinctive Liturgical Units and Features of the Pentecostal Pattern**
> A sequence of congregational songs that "flow" into each other without interruption
> Communal "Singing in the Spirit"
> Speaking/praying in "tongues"
> Prophetic messages from members of congregation
> A message (sermon) that gradually increases in tempo, volume, and emotional intensity
> Expressive, spontaneous verbal responses of congregation during preaching
> Altar call for conversion, healing, "Baptism in the Spirit," and other needs
> Indefinite beginning and conclusion of worship service
> Use of electrified instruments and drums
> Expressive, spontaneous gestures and movements (lifting hands, kneeling, dancing)
> Emphasis on sincerity of congregational participation

The Praise and Worship service continues to exhibit many of these features of Pentecostal Worship, especially the participatory aspects.

> **Distinctive Liturgical Units and Features of the Praise and Worship Pattern**
> A sequence of congregational songs that "flow" into each other without interruption
> [Communal "Singing in the Spirit"]
> A message (sermon) that is similar to the Seeker model
> Altar call for conversion, healing, "Baptism in the Spirit," and other needs
> Indefinite beginning and conclusion of worship service
> Use of electrified instruments and drums
> Expressive, spontaneous gestures and movements (lifting hands, kneeling, dancing)
> Emphasis on sincerity of congregational participation

Assessment of the Pentecostal Macro-Pattern

Over the course of the twentieth century, liturgical reform in the Western churches searched for a profoundly real encounter with God in worship that neither the Revival or the Sunday School could offer. Mainline Protestants in North America sought this reality through the transcendent power of aesthetic form and art.[40] Pentecostal believers seek to experience God's divine power as the core reality of worship. This experience is not mere awareness of the presence of the numinous, as in some other patterns of liturgical reform. For Pentecostals, worship is a full-body, participatory, and ecstatic encounter with the Holy Spirit. This is worship that transcends nationality and ethnicity and that allows Pentecostals to feel at home in worship settings regardless of geographic location. This distinctive Pentecostal character somewhat parallels the experience of Catholics who intuitively recognize the order of the mass across national boundaries.[41] It also transcends racial and ethnic boundaries in ways that historically mainline churches still find difficult.[42]

That said, Pentecostal worship certainly has liabilities. I have not stressed these liabilities in this chapter because criticism of the Pentecostal movement so easily tends toward caricature. But I would be remiss not to recognize that Pentecostal Worship is especially vulnerable to the charlatan. Preachers of the so-called prosperity gospel and underground communities of serpent handlers are part of the larger Pentecostal tradition.

In the twenty-first century we are finding less radical forms of Pentecostalism. If we think of the Seeker Service as "Revivalism lite," the Praise and Worship model of service is a sort of "Pentecostalism lite." Although many large mainline congregations have adopted Praise and Worship styles for one of their contemporary offerings, these services rarely include the more intense ritual expressions of healing, anointing, pouring out one's heart before the community, or glossolalia.

Following on Eatman Aghahowa's sexual metaphor noted above, the Praise and Worship model can become an easy spiritual promiscuity, producing a quick thrill of spiritual intimacy but without the lifelong commitment and rigor of spiritual disciplines. In many ways, the Praise and Worship model reflects the more casual and open approach to intimacy that is so

---

40. See, for example, Willard L. Sperry, *Reality in Worship* (New York, NY: Macmillan, 1925).

41. See Mark Porter, "Charismatic Worship and Cosmopolitan Movement(s)," *Liturgy* vol. 33, no. 3 (2018): 4–11.

42. Birgitta J. Johnson, "Singing Down Walls of Race, Ethnicity and Tradition in an African American Megachurch," *Liturgy* vol. 33, no. 3 (2018): 37–45.

prevalent in modern America. That is, it can be a sort of spiritual "hookup" without the rigor and long-term commitment of marriage and family life.

Yet, setting aside for a moment these liabilities, the growth of Pentecostal/Charismatic styles of worship does demonstrate a healthy resistance to the overly intellectual worship practices of many mainline congregations. And it does demonstrate a hunger for worship that is really about God and which therefore absolutely should feel real and yield palpable joy in the life of believers.

	Telos (Goal)	*Ethos* (Qualities of Character)
Early twentieth-century type: Pentecostalism	Spiritual union through baptism in the Holy Spirit	Cultivation of feelings of ecstasy Exuberant praise Effusive body participation Patterns learned by heart Extemporaneous prayer Congregational egalitarianism Rhythmic music
Present form: Praise and Worship	Deep personal experience of intimacy with God and spiritual power	Feelings of spiritual intimacy Highly repetitive music Active body participation Extemporaneous prayer Congregational egalitarianism Non-elevated forms of ritual language

Many forms of worship and prayer can be simulated in an academic classroom or in a church worship setting. However, I cannot imagine saying to my students, "OK, let's all speak in tongues to get a feel for that." Or "Let's try out being slain in the spirit." Such ritual actions may be faked or lampooned, but they resist simulation. This is because believers who have experienced such practices know they are profoundly real.

CHAPTER SEVEN

Democratic Worship

The Prayer Meeting

> *If possible, get every one to take some part. If the experienced ones are brief, there will be time for all, and the timid ones will not feel that in offering a few simple words of prayer they are laying down a copper coin beside the golden contribution of another. We shall never have the ideal prayer-meeting till all participate in it, as really as the whole family, from oldest to youngest, have part in the social celebration of Thanksgiving day. No Christian can come with the purpose of being a mere spectator, without doing a wrong to the Church and to himself. That each one should give according as God hath prospered him is the true rule for the prayer-meeting no less than for the contribution-box. Are you self-distrustful and shrinking? Do not think you must say some great thing; say some little thing that you believe and feel.*
>
> —"Everybody Should Contribute to the Prayer-Meeting," Rev. A. D.[1]

The worship leader of his small congregation has opened the service with a call to worship and a familiar hymn. "Now, before our morning prayer," he says, "it is time for the joys and concerns. Who has a joy they would like to share?" A woman speaks, "Our son came to visit with his family. It is such a joy to have them, and especially our two grandchildren. As you can see, they are here with us this morning." The pastor responds, "Yes, good to see that beautiful family here sharing a pew. Others?" Another woman speaks, "My father is home from the hospital. Thanks for all the prayers for his recovery. He is doing just fine, considering." Whispers of "Wonderful" and "Amen" fill the room. A six-year-old boy raises his hand. "I have a big mosquito bite." The pastor smiles and

---

1. *The Treasury: An Evangelical Monthly for Pastors, Christian Workers, and Families*, vol. 1, no. 9 (Jan 1884): 569.

asks, "Is that a joy or concern?" He answers, "A joy. It feels so good when I scratch." People chuckle as the pastor shifts, continuing to gather material for the pastoral prayer that follows.

Prayer as Interactive, Extemporaneous Social Activity

As we saw in the previous chapter, the Pentecostal model understands worship as a highly interactive and even intense group activity. In terms of participation, Pentecostal Worship is very egalitarian, as the opening quotation to that chapter makes clear. Ideally, every person in the congregation participates robustly. Such participation aims to stimulate an authentic, unhindered intimacy with God. I have proposed that Pentecostal Worship arose in part as a reaction against the perceived artificiality of Revival worship and Sunday School worship, and against the elitism of Aesthetic Worship.

The Prayer Meeting is another distinctive model of worship that was a nineteenth-century precursor to Pentecostalism. Like Pentecostalism, the Prayer Meeting is both egalitarian and strives for intimacy—but with a different emphasis. Whereas Pentecostal Worship promotes intimacy with God, the Prayer Meeting promotes interpersonal intimacy among the participants, sharing extemporaneous prayers, testimonies, joys, and concerns.

Historically, prayer has had such a central place in worship that it may seem strange to describe the Prayer Meeting as a distinctive model. To cite a notable example, the Anglican Church tradition has referred to its essential worship text as the *Book of Common Prayer*. This title indicates an important aspect of prayer that it promotes: *common* prayer, that is to say, *communal* prayer and *public* worship. These prayers are contained within an official publication of the Anglican Church, and the content is formal and fixed.

Prayer and worship, however, are not always formal and fixed. They can also be extemporaneous to a greater or lesser extent. Of course, according to principle 1 for understanding the character of worship ("All worship follows patterns"), completely spontaneous worship and prayer are not sustainable.[2] For, inevitably, worshipers will incorporate some es-

---

2. See chapter 1, p. 8–9.

tablished, learned patterns and vocabulary. For many Christians, "Lord Jesus, I just wanna say, Lord" is an established form for opening a prayer, just as "The Lord be with you" is for others. That said, the Prayer Meeting model of worship of the early nineteenth century promotes more extemporaneous styles of prayer and speaking, resisting not only formal printed prayers (as many Puritan-influenced traditions already did) but even prayers written down by the pastor right before worship.

Foundational to the Prayer Meeting model is the recognition that Christians need to gather for communal prayer in addition to the standard, required Sunday service. In the eighteenth and nineteenth centuries, the Sunday service—even in the Free Church, Congregationalist traditions—was inevitably dominated by the pastor, who preached the sermon and led the prayers.[3] In contrast, the Prayer Meeting, which typically took place at a different time or even on a different day of the week, encouraged everyone who attended, young and old, men and women, to offer prayers and testimonies.

In 1870, Presbyterian minister J. B. Johnson defended the need for these less-formal services by appealing to the precedent of Israel in the Old Testament, noting that, "The prayer-meeting formed a part of the divinely appointed worship during the whole period of the Levitical economy, distinct from Tabernacle or Temple, and from the synagogue worship."[4] Likewise, Johnson notes, the New Testament includes numerous accounts of Christians gathering for prayer. Hebrews 10:23–25 provides a key to the form of these gatherings: "And let us consider one another to provoke unto love and to good works: Not forsaking the assembling of ourselves together, as the manner of some is; but exhorting one another: and so much the more, as ye see the day approaching." As Johnson explains this biblical text, the author of Hebrews could not be talking about regular family prayers because families would not need to assemble, as they are already together in one place. Furthermore, the author cannot be describing an assembly for public worship because in public worship "there cannot be, consistently,

---

3. Quaker worship offered a notable exception.

4. J. B. Johnson, *The Prayer-Meeting, and Its History, as Identified with the Life and Power of Godliness, and the Revival of Religion* (Philadelphia, PA: S. A. George and Co., 1870), 35.

a reciprocal exhortation. . . . [T]he authorized ministry officially exhorts; but never submits to formal exhortation—one exhorting, then another, in turn."[5] In contrast to public worship, the Prayer Meeting of the New Testament was a gathering in which "prayer and conference" were the chief activities. As such it occupied a middle ground between formal public worship led by a pastor exercising strict order and authority, and informal family prayer, where even women and children actively gave voice to prayers and exhortations.

As Johnson recounts the history, such meetings for prayer among laity became rare during the long medieval reign of the oppressive Roman Catholic Church, but they were rediscovered in the Protestant Reformation. He demonstrates the periodic recovery of the Prayer Meeting throughout the history of the church, notably the Scottish Church in the seventeenth century, the Methodist movement in the eighteenth, and contemporaneously with Johnson, the businessmen's prayer meeting revival of 1857–1859.[6] In Johnson's first example, lay-led meetings arose among seventeenth-century Scottish Presbyterians as a reaction against the order of King Charles I and the Archbishop of Canterbury William Laud that the Scots must accept a modified version of the Anglican *Book of Common Prayer* and an episcopal form of church order.[7] Lay-led prayer meetings were a key to the success of the Presbyterian resistance. These meetings would become known among Presbyterians as "Fellowship Prayer Meetings," distinct from the regular Lord's Day preaching service.

For his second example, Johnson points to John Wesley's Methodist class meetings, which were "the secret of the unparalleled success of the Methodist Church, in its first organization, in all the early settlements of the colonies, and in the new Territories of the West. They were always organized into prayer-meetings, or class-meetings."[8]

---

5. Johnson, *The Prayer-Meeting*, 50.

6. See John D. Hannah, "The Layman's Prayer Revival of 1858," *Bibliotheca Sacra* vol. 134, no. 533 (1977): 59–73.

7. Johnson, *The Prayer-Meeting*, 42–43. For details see, for example, W. M. Hetherinton, *History of the Church of Scotland* (New York, NY: Robert Carter and Brothers, 1856), 180–82.

8. Johnson, *The Prayer-Meeting*, 155–56.

Finally, he points to the prayer revival of 1858, which began in response to the Wall Street crash of 1857 with a gathering of New York businessmen for prayer and soon spread to other cities around the country. Johnson credits this revival as a key to the success of the Union army and the triumph of the Abolitionists: "Had there been no revival in 1858, the church would still have remained, to such an extent, under the leadings of the South, that the war for the Union and for the cause of liberty would have ended in the triumph of slavery, and fall of American liberty, personal, civil and religious."[9] In each of these cases, Johnson describes the close connection of lay-led prayer and mutual exhortation to the vitality of religious and social life.

This vitality of the Prayer Meeting, according to Johnson, is grounded in the democratic principle of social equality:

> A chapter of thrilling interest might be written here, showing, from unquestioned history, that the prayer-meeting has ever been the nursery of civil and religious liberty. It is an institution thoroughly democratic—an institution of the people, for the people, and administered by the people; an institution that recognizes the perfect equality of every one admitted to its privileges—and to these all have a right. It knows no aristocracy—no caste—no class. Here the Prince and the beggar sit down together—here the Pastor and the layman officiate alike—here the male and the female, the old and the young—all that pray, may mingle together in the enjoyment of equal rights and equal powers.[10]

In Johnson's telling, the Prayer Meeting embodied the quintessential ideals of the American revolution: "Trace back American liberty—all that is noble and Christian in it—along whatever line of history we may, to English Puritans, to Holland or Scotch Presbyterians, we will find its cradle is the prayer-meeting."[11]

---

9. Johnson, *The Prayer-Meeting*, 194.

10. Johnson, *The Prayer-Meeting*, 138.

11. Johnson, *The Prayer-Meeting*, 137. As Karen Westerfield Tucker notes: "The ideals of democracy undergirded the prayer meeting in its early years and contributed to its success" (*American Methodist Worship* [New York, NY: Oxford University Press, 2001], 231).

Chapter Seven

The Format of the Prayer Meeting

As it developed in the United States, the *telos* of the nineteenth-century Prayer Meeting was to embody and enact full human equality before God. This *telos* suggests an *ethos* that emphasized interpersonal engagement, sharing of prayers and needs, and giving mutual advice and encouragement both as the participants offer prayer and as they give personal testimony. As one commentator noted: "The prayer-meeting is designed mutually to encourage and aid each other in practical Christian life."[12] This *ethos* downplays professional, ordained clergy in favor of the untrained, unaffected layperson. As far as it was practical, leadership rotated among the participants in order to demonstrate the equality of each person in the congregation.

The empowering democratic character of the Prayer Meeting made it attractive to African American congregations, and limited evidence suggests that it formed a central place in the religious experience of black American Christians, both before and after the Civil War.[13] In his description of three antebellum black Baptist congregations in Savannah, black pastor James M. Simms notes that the Prayer Meeting was held at sunrise on each Sunday, the first of three morning services. Simms also provides descriptions of the oppressive regulation of attendance by slave holders.[14] The majority of Prayer Meetings in the antebellum years, however, took place not in authorized church buildings but in clandestine, outdoor "hush harbors," where slaves met to worship free from the supervision of white masters and white clergy, and at great personal risk.[15]

The structure of the Prayer Meeting was not rigid, but it did exhibit some stereotypical patterns.[16] In the late eighteenth century, Methodist

---

12. Wooster Parker, "Death by Edification," *Household Reading: Selections from the Congregationalist* (Boston, MA: Galen James & Co., 1867), 32.

13. A few examples can be found in Eileen Southern, *African-American Traditions in Song, Sermon, Tale, and Dance, 1600s–1920: An Annotated Bibliography of Literature, Collections, and Artworks* (New York, NY: Greenwood Press, 1990).

14. *The First Colored Baptist Church in North America Constituted at Savannah, Georgia, January 20, A.D. 1788* (Philadelphia, PA: L. B. Lippencot, 1888), 63.

15. Albert J. Raboteau, *Slave Religion: The "Invisible Institution" in the Antebellum South*, updated edition (Oxford, UK: Oxford University Press, 2004), 212, 333.

16. See Lester Ruth, *A Little Heaven Below: Worship at Early Methodist Quarterly Meetings* (Nashville, TN: Kingswood, 2000), 84–85.

meetings in England and Scotland seemed to focus on extempore prayer and a cappella singing. At least, that is how the well-known bookdealer James Lackington remembered the meetings from his brief sojourn with the Methodists in the mid-1770s. In his 1791 memoir, Lackington notes that the British Methodists had different types of "private meetings," of which the "prayer-meeting is the least private of any of them." He continues: "To the prayer-meetings they often invited people who were not of their society; an hymn was first sung, and then they all knelt, and the first person that felt a motion made an extempore prayer; when he had done another began; and so on for about two hours."[17] Some forty years later, Jonathan Crowther provides a description of British Methodist Prayer Meetings circa 1814 that exhibit some expansion of those contents. These meetings, Crowther says,

> Are in much esteem, and well attended by the Methodists, especially on Sunday evenings. These are usually held in private houses, both in cities, towns, and villages in the country; they generally continue about an hour, and are very useful to many persons, who from want of decent clothes, or unavoidable confinement, do not attend any place of worship during the day. Religious impressions have been made upon many minds at these meetings. They are very useful also, in affording young men, of piety and promising abilities, an opportunity of exercising their gifts in prayer and exhortation. Three or four persons exercise at a prayer meeting, each giving out a hymn, and then offering up an extemporary prayer.[18]

From this description we catch a glimpse of a typical meeting in the early nineteenth century in Britain. It lasted about an hour. Dress was casual, making it popular among people who did not want to dress for church or did not have the means to do so. Leadership rotated. People suggested songs during the service. Various persons offered extemporaneous prayer. As an aside, I note here that this pretty well describes various small prayer groups I've attended over the years.

---

17. James Lackington, *Memoirs of the First Forty-Five Years of Life* (London: printed for the author, 1791), 109.

18. Jonathan Crowther, *A True and Complete Portraiture of Methodism or the History of the Wesleyan Methodists*, second revised ed. (London: Richard Edwards, 1814), 260.

Methodists in the United States adopted the practice of the British, and the 1792 *Discipline of The Methodist Episcopal Church* required such: "The preacher who has the charge of a circuit, shall appoint prayer meetings wherever he can, in his circuit."[19] In their notes on the 1796 *Discipline*, the first Methodist Episcopal bishops, Thomas Coke and Francis Asbury, attached this justification: "The authority of appointing prayer meetings will not, we think, be disputed by any. Many of our greatest revivals have been begun and chiefly carried on in our prayer meetings. We wish that the utmost zeal might be manifested by those who have the charge of circuits in the execution of this direction."[20]

Early Methodists made frequent mention of the power of the Prayer Meeting to energize congregations as well as to convert sinners. In his autobiography, frontier Methodist preacher Peter Cartwright commented that "Prayer-meetings have accomplished great good, as practised [sic] in the Methodist Episcopal Church." He further commented on the egalitarian nature of these meetings: "Some of my earliest recollections are those Methodist prayer-meetings, where men and women, young and old, prayed in public." He especially singled out the power of women's prayers: "We know there have been fashionable objections to females praying in public, but I am sure I do not exaggerate when I say I have often seen our dull and stupid prayer-meetings suddenly changed from a dead dog to a heavenly enjoyment, when a sister has been called on to pray. . . ." Yet he wondered, "Are [prayer-meetings] not growing into disuse among us?"[21]

While Cartwright extols the virtues of the Methodist Prayer Meeting, he also indicates that at least sometimes they were "dull and stupid"! When the Prayer Meeting worked well, it was a powerful motivator for Christian living and an attractive venue for generating conversions. However, the Prayer Meeting often fell short of its potential. By the time Johnson published his history of the Prayer Meeting in 1870, other writers

---

19. Robert Emory and W. P. Strickland, *History of the Discipline of The Methodist Episcopal Church* (revised) (New York, NY: Carlton & Porter, 1857), 151.

20. Emory and Strickland, *History of the Discipline of The Methodist Episcopal Church*, 363.

21. Peter Cartwright, *The Autobiography of Peter Cartwright, the Backwoods Preacher* (New York, NY: Phillips & Hunt, 1856), 517.

were beginning to ask what was going wrong with how the Prayer Meeting was being practiced in local congregations.

Fixing the Perfunctory Old-Fashioned Prayer Meeting

Beginning in 1872, the celebrated (and controversial) Congregationalist preacher Henry Ward Beecher published his monumental *Yale Lectures on Preaching*, a work that goes far beyond instructions in how to construct and deliver a sermon. A substantial part of the second year series of lectures covered the significant role of the Prayer Meeting in the ecology of a Protestant congregation. Yet he began his discussion with a surprisingly harsh critique:

> I suppose there is hardly any other part of church service that is regarded with so little estimation in the community at large as the prayer-meeting. And I think facts will bear me out in saying that this feeling is participated in by the Church, on the part of the greatest number of its members, nine out of ten of whom look upon it as perhaps a duty, but almost never a pleasure.... In most churches I think that is the feeling in regard to the prayer-meeting: that it is dull; that it is for the most part without edification; that in some mysterious way it may be blessed to the soul's good,—but how, they do not know. Persons resort to it when they cannot very well help it.[22]

Beecher confessed that as a child he had considered the Prayer Meeting a chore to be tolerated, and he claimed that children generally still have negative feelings about the Prayer Meeting: "There is another bad side to it,—children do not like it; and anything that children dislike in religious service, habitually and universally, has reason to suspect itself."[23]

Beecher, nevertheless, believed that the Prayer Meeting had the potential to be the core gathering of a successful congregation: "Now, it is notorious that the prayer-meeting is 'below par,' and therefore it may be the more striking to say that, for my part, I regard it as the very centre and heart of

---

22. Henry Ward Beecher, *Yale Lectures on Preaching*, 3 vols. (New York, NY: Ford, Howard & Hulbert, 1881), second series, 53.

23. Beecher, *Lectures on Preaching*, second series, 54.

church life." Moreover, according to Beecher, the Prayer Meeting embodied the "democratic theory" of worship that pastors of his day were embracing:

> We have thrown off hierarchical methods of worship; we have advanced—I mean the Presbyterian and Congregational Churches and their confreres have advanced—the theory of the equality of the church in its members; the idea that it is a family and body of believers; that it has in itself inherently the gifts through any ministerial channel except reason and the ordinary methods of communication. This is our theory.[24]

At its best, Beecher asserted, the Prayer Meeting demonstrates "the power of individual experiences," "promotes fellowship," "discourages censorious judgement," "cherishes mutual helpfulness," "discovers mutual needs," and "makes truth personal."[25] Yet he warned his students that to maintain such a meeting over time "is about the hardest work you will ever know. It will tax your ingenuity the most."[26]

Beecher proposed several reasons for the perceived failure of prayer meetings: a "poverty of material" for use in preparing focus topics, the overbearing deacon or elder who "smothers meetings through too much control," and "stale speakers and speeches."[27] He also discussed some practical issues that hinder the meetings, such as failure to start or end at the announced times or using a room that is too large to enable intimacy. But the biggest problem, Beecher suggested, is a lack of emotional fervor, and, indeed, his list of the hindrances to an effective meeting are problems precisely because they dampen fervor.[28] Religious feelings, however, cannot be produced by mere exhortation. Beecher warned, "You can never make people feel by scolding them because they don't feel. You can never move anybody by saying, 'Feel!'"[29] And a little later, he added, "Nothing is so

---

24. Beecher, *Lectures on Preaching*, second series, 54–55.

25. Beecher, *Lectures on Preaching*, second series, 55–69.

26. Beecher, *Lectures on Preaching*, second series, 82.

27. Beecher, *Lectures on Preaching*, second series, 86–87.

28. Beecher describes how a good Prayer Meeting generates what sociologist Randall Collins calls "emotional energy," a social power effecting group solidarity. See *Interaction Ritual Chains* (Princeton, NJ: Princeton University Press, 2004), 47–101.

29. Beecher, *Lectures on Preaching*, second series, 94.

barren, nothing so unprofitable, as urging men to feel, when the shorter way is to make them feel."[30] Instead of exhortations, the leader of the Prayer Meeting, like the preacher at a Revival, should employ techniques aimed to provoke feelings:

> In general, feeling results from the presentation of some fact or truth that has a relation to the particular feeling you wish to produce. If I wanted to make you weep, I would not tell you an amusing story; I would, if I wanted to make you laugh, and that story had a relation to laughing. If I wished to make you weep, I would tell you some pathetic incident, the truth embodied in which had some sympathetic relation to feeling. Charge yourself with this: "If these people are to feel, I, as the minister of the Holy Ghost, am to be the cause of it by applying to their minds such treatment, such thoughts, as stand connected with the production of feeling."

"The human soul is like a harp," Beecher asserted, and the leader is the harpist. "If they [the participants in the Prayer Meeting] do not feel, it is because you do not play well. If they do feel, it is because you are a master of your business."[31]

Beecher's appeal to the affective dimensions of the meeting is quite similar to Charles Finney's New Measures approach to the Revival.[32] Good leaders would lead by example, offering their own fervor and emotional openness as a model to draw (and develop) kindred spirits: "Be yourself fervent; and fervency creates fervor, as sparks lead to sparks."[33] But whereas Finney compared the Revival preacher to an actor emoting for effect, Beecher appealed to the interior life of the leader:

---

30. Beecher, *Lectures on Preaching*, second series, 96.

31. Beecher, *Lectures on Preaching*, second series, 95.

32. See chapter 3, p. 44–47.

33. Beecher proposed the same sorts of appeal to personality in his approach to preaching. According to E. Brooks Holifield, Beecher represents the turn to a distinctively American populism in clergy leadership: "Some of the most eminent preachers, from Henry Ward Beecher to Phillips Brooks, practiced a style of pulpit oratory that conveyed, in Brooks's phrase, 'truth through personality.' The preacher was to 'be natural' and even 'buoyant,' to avoid the rigid forms of earlier doctrinal sermons, and to engage the audience through stories and illustrations" (*God's Ambassadors: A History of the Christian Clergy in America* [Grand Rapids, MI: Eerdmans, 2007], 161).

> Men are so many instruments, and you are a skillful player; and you will have success just as the Spirit of God dwelling in you kindles your soul to that power, to that perception of truth, to that sympathy with it, to that knowledge of men; for the sense of God brings the sense of human nature. They both lie in the same plane, and he that has one will be very apt to have the other. They train together.[34]

Good leaders connect sympathetically with the members in order to evoke social solidarity. The ideal here is not the Lord's Day peaching service, or the church business meeting, or the Sunday School class discussion but a small, spontaneous gathering of friends:

> You will notice that, after a prayer-meeting, which has been very dull and very stiff and very proper, has been closed, and the brethren gather around the stove, they commence talking socially among themselves, and then it is that the real conference-meeting begins. One deacon says, "Brother So-and-so, when you were speaking on such a topic you said so and so." He goes on and makes quite an effective little talk, but you could not have dragged it out of him with an ox-team during the meeting; and so one and another will speak up and join in, and they will get warmly interested in their discussion. Around the stove was the real meeting. The other was the mere *simulacrum* of a meeting.[35]

In short, a good Prayer Meeting pursued a *telos* of social equality through the *ethos* of social intimacy. If the Prayer Meetings of a congregation had lost the power to attract willing participants, Beecher thought the meeting needed to recapture this fundamental goal and corresponding character.

The Prayer Meeting in the Early Twentieth Century

Keeping the Prayer Meeting fresh continued to be a pastoral concern at the turn of the century for both white and black congregations. And attendance continued to be smaller than pastors hoped. In 1890, black pastor (and poet) George Marion McClellan published a story of a Prayer

---

34. Beecher, *Lectures on Preaching*, second series, 96.
35. Beecher, *Lectures on Preaching*, first series, 75.

Meeting in his small church in Louisville, Kentucky. McClellan confessed, "It was prayer-meeting evening; but I was not in the best spirit, nor in a very prayerful state of mind." He went on to complain that "three deacons and five good sisters came in for prayer meeting. There were no others."[36]

Twenty years later, in his "Research into the Conditions of the Negro Race in Southern Towns"[37] white sociologist Howard W. Odum conducted field observations about church life. His published results include this description of the Prayer Meetings in black congregations:

> The weekly prayer-meetings are held on Tuesday, Wednesday, Thursday or Friday night; the effort is made not to have the meetings of the different churches conflict. Church services begin at eight or eight-thirty o'clock in summer—earlier in winter; the hour is placed late in order that any whose duties keep them may attend. However, the attendance at prayer-meeting is not large, varying in the different churches, the average being from five to twenty-five. This attendance is smaller than formerly, owing partly to the fact that some of the lodges meet at the same time. As a rule, men are in the majority at the mid-week meetings; most of the older men attend. The pastor is not always present at the prayer-meeting, though it is his custom to attend. Sometimes he conducts the service or makes a talk. More generally the service is conducted by an appointed leader; the hour is spent in singing and praying and talks from the members present; the service is an impressive one. The leader "lines" each song and all respond in the singing; at those services where only a few are present, the leader calls on each one for prayer, and it often happens that every person present, man and woman, has led in prayer before the service is concluded; some have prayed more than once. Their prayers are very appropriate for the occasion. There is no hurry, and the meeting extends to a late hour; often a group of five or ten remain singing, praying, and talking until eleven o'clock; after service they ask after each other's "folks."[38]

---

36. "A Wednesday Night Prayer Meeting Episode," *The Christian Union*, vol. 41 (June 5, 1890): 810–11.

37. The full title of his published dissertation is *Social and Mental Traits of the Negro: Research into the Conditions of the Negro Race in Southern Towns. A Study in Race Traits, Tendencies and Prospects* (New York, NY: Columbia University, 1910).

38. Odum, *Social and Mental Traits of the Negro*, 59–60.

Chapter Seven

Odum's scientific-observer account of the Prayer Meeting illustrated practices distinctive of black congregations, notably the lining out of songs by the leader and the extension of the ending-time to "a late hour." However, Odum also indicated similarities in the Prayer Meeting with the practices (and problems) of white congregations Johnson and Beecher described. First of all, the meetings took place during a weeknight. Second, attendance was less than at the principal Sunday services that focused on preaching. Third, while the pastor typically attended (and might lead), the leader could be a layperson. Fourth, the service contained sharing of personal and family information. Fifth, everyone participated in prayer, talks, and singing, which is to say that the meeting enacted democratic participation.

Not far into the twentieth century, however, many larger Methodist and Baptist congregations in towns and cities were becoming more educated and consequently more concerned to raise the social class of their worship practices. A transition toward the Aesthetic model of worship, described in chapter 5, also began to affect the practices of the Prayer Meeting, particularly in white congregations. But while African American Christians continued to embrace more enthusiastic forms of singing, prayer, ritual, and preaching, even some large black congregations were beginning to rein in the exuberance, notably in cities with a college-educated elite.

In a detailed study of religious education in black colleges in the early twentieth century, David H. Sims surveyed twelve "Negro Colleges." His survey included some fascinating information about the various religious services that were part of the required extracurricular formation of students: "Church preaching service, Sunday School, Young People's meetings, Week-day Prayer meetings," and so on. Sims found that students were appreciative of most of these religious services, except for the midweek Prayer Meeting, which they almost uniformly found to be a waste of time. The structure of these meetings followed a typical format of "sentence prayers," singing, personal testimony, and in most cases, topics for discussion. And Sims wryly adds a fifth element: "sleeping."[39] Overall, he found,

---

39. David H. Sims, "Religious Education in Negro Colleges," *Journal of Negro History* V (1920): 185.

"In the great majority of instances the opinion is that the prayer meeting is a bore and should be abandoned."[40] Meetings that were the most successful (relatively speaking) were those that were "the least traditional," which Sims implied were meetings that introduced topics for discussion relevant to contemporary life. Sims's own assessment of student attitudes is telling: "The prayer meetings in all except four institutions follow a program which was effective for those who lived in another civilization. The traditional Negro prayer meeting does not function religiously in the life of the Negro college student."[41] As these young, educated black men and women became leaders in congregations across the United States, they would bring these attitudes into their local churches.

White congregations were experiencing similar problems with the Prayer Meeting. Pastors began to publish books with titles such as *The Redemption of the Prayer-Meeting* and *New Life in the Old Prayer-Meeting*.[42] Baptist minister Kerr Boyce Tupper captured a wide diagnosis of the problem:

> Go into the ordinary prayer meeting and you will find just this the order: two hymns, a prayer, a hymn, scripture reading, the same brother called on to pray that prayed last week, another hymn, too long an address by the pastor, another hymn, an urging of the brethren to say something, a long pause, then a long speech or a long prayer by some good brother, another pause, benediction—and intelligent people going home sometimes disgusted instead of inspired.[43]

Boyce Tupper's solution? "What a need there is in our midweek services of less monotony, more variety." Indeed, increased variety of speakers, exercises, orders, music, and theme is the main solution proposed by virtually

---

40. Sims, "Religious Education in Negro Colleges," 188.

41. Sims, "Religious Education in Negro Colleges," 205.

42. J. George Laller, *The Redemption of the Prayer-Meeting* (Nashville, TN: Smith and Lamar, 1911); John Franklin Cowan, *New Life in the Old Prayer-Meeting* (New York, NY: Fleming H. Revell, 1906).

43. Kerr Boyce Tupper, "Response: What Change, if Any, Is Demanded in the Prayer Meeting?" in *Twenty-First Annual Baptist Autumnal Conference for the Discussion of Current Questions* (New York, NY: Baptist Congress Publishing, 1904), 93.

all of the critics who want to re-energize what all of them deemed to be an important ministry of Christian congregations.

Underneath each critical diagnosis we find a commitment to the democratic ideals that a vibrant Prayer Meeting should manifest, along with the recognition that such ideals were difficult to maintain. Indeed, the democratic Prayer Meeting is much more difficult to achieve than the hierarchical model of the Sunday preaching service or pastor-led Bible study, as this anecdote of Baptist Curtis Lee Laws illustrates:

> A few days ago a dear friend, the minister of one of our ritualistic churches, was visiting me in my study. . . . He said to me candidly and unhesitatingly, "I am utterly opposed to the open and democratic idea of the prayer meeting. The minister is the only authorized and authoritative teacher of Christianity. Change your testimony and prayer service into a service of instruction. Lecture to your people on the doctrines of Christ, making your addresses simpler and more personal than your sermons, and conduct the worship yourself. You will find that the meeting will be more satisfactory and more delightful in every way."

Laws concedes the point that the democratic Prayer Meeting was fraught with abuse:

> No one of us would challenge the statement that testimonies are sometimes perilously near to the ridiculous in their psychology, their scripture interpretation and their theology, and no one would question the fact that the minister is generally the best qualified to teach and to exhort; but in granting these contentions the theory of the democracy of the prayer meeting has not been abandoned.[44]

Nevertheless, for Laws, this democratic principle continues to be the ideal toward which the Prayer Meeting must aim, as impossible as it may be in actual execution:

> Such is the ideal toward which I am trying to bring the prayer meeting of my own church, but like many others I have failed. There is a vast differ-

---

44. Curtis Lee Laws, "What Change, if Any, Is Demanded in the Prayer Meeting?" in *Twenty-First Annual Baptist Autumnal Conference for the Discussion of Current Questions* (New York, NY: Baptist Congress Publishing, 1904), 69–70.

ence between the real and the ideal. Yet in the ideal I find inspiration for constantly renewed efforts. The democratic theory of the prayer meeting is the right theory. Let us hold to this plan.[45]

Contemporary Prayer Meetings: Share Group, Covenant Group, the House Church

While some congregations still hold Prayer Meetings similar to those described in the previous centuries, today the distinctive practice of democratic meetings has evolved into various "small group ministries" known by assorted catchphrases. For example, in the late 1960s United Methodists promoted the Lay Witness Mission, a program that brought a team of laity for a weekend of intense sharing of stories of religious conversion and personal renewal in both church-wide meetings and small group venues. The genius of the mission was intentional use of the visiting lay missioners as models of personal sharing, religious testimony, and heartfelt prayer by the lay missioners. The Lay Witness Mission concluded with the Sunday morning service, but the actual high point of the mission took place on Saturday night, when members of the host congregation were encouraged to offer their own personal testimony, to pray for renewed faith, and in not a few instances, "to give their hearts to Jesus" in a conscious decision to seek personal conversion. Follow-up to these intense small group sessions included the organization of ongoing "share groups," small gatherings of laity that met weekly in homes or other convenient, private venues to continue the format of sharing personal experiences and prayer. That is to say, it took the form of a Prayer Meeting.[46]

---

45. Laws, "What Change?" 77. Laws does not provide the name or denomination of his "ritualistic" acquaintance, but there was a long debate in the Episcopal Church between low church evangelicals and Anglo-Catholics over the legitimacy of Prayer Meetings. See Albert Barnes, *The Position of the Evangelical Party in the Episcopal Church*, fifth edition (Philadelphia, PA: James A. Moore, 1875), 36–37, 62.

46. See Ben C. Johnson, *A Road to Renewal: A Manual for a Lay Witness Mission* (Atlanta, GA: Lay Renewal Publications, 1967?). This is the standard description of the program.

Small group ministry continues to be promoted by countless books and articles on church revitalization as the key to growing a successful, vibrant congregation. In some churches, laity are organized into "covenant groups" or "discipleship groups" or "small groups." As the paradigmatic megachurch of Willow Creek explains on its website: "At Willow, we believe life transformation happens best in community—and we live that out through small groups."[47] For the sake of simplicity, I will refer to all the current small group forms of the Prayer Meeting, such as those described above, as the House Church.[48]

Research by the Barna Group gathered data on the rise of House Churches in the United States in 2006.[49] While the House Church exhibits a variety of formats, Barna found that some practices are widely shared:

- 93 percent have spoken prayer during their meetings
- 90 percent read from the Bible
- 89 percent spend time serving people outside of their group
- 87 percent devote time to sharing personal needs or experiences

With the possible exception of "serving people outside of their group," these practices are hallmarks of the old-fashioned Prayer Meeting model, as is the focus on intimacy and democratic participation. Indeed, Barna notes that "the intimacy and shared responsibility found in most house churches requires each participant to be more serious about their faith development."[50] The House Church is, therefore, a powerful method of encouraging Christian personal growth.

---

47. https://www.willowcreek.org/en/connect/ministries/small-groups-and-section-communities/south-barrington, accessed July 8, 2019.

48. However, some researchers distinguish the House Church from other types of small groups connected to conventional congregations. See "Who Is Active in 'Group' Expressions of Faith? Barna Study Examines Small Groups, Sunday School, and House Churches," June 28, 2010, https://www.barna.com/research/who-is-active-in-group-expressions-of-faith-barna-study-examines-small-groups-sunday-school-and-house-churches/, accessed July 9, 2019.

49. "House Churches Are More Satisfying to Attenders Than Conventional Churches" (January 8, 2007), https://www.barna.com/research/house-churches-are-more-satisfying-to-attenders-than-are-conventional-churches/, accessed July 9, 2019.

50. "House Churches Are More Satisfying to Attenders."

Democratic Worship

Parenthetically, a key catchphrase in the House Church model that expresses the "personal needs and or experiences" is the "sharing of joys and concerns." This may be the most distinctive liturgical unit to develop in this model.[51]

Popular writer Frank Viola, who has collaborated with Barna, argues that in the early days of Christianity, such small house church gatherings were the core of the church rather than large, public meetings. Viola quotes a lecture by Howard Snyder to describe the mutuality embodied in the House Church model:

> The New Testament teaches us that the church is a community in which all are gifted and all have a ministry. The church as taught in Scripture is a new social reality that models and incarnates the respect and concern for people that we see in Jesus Himself. This is our high calling. And yet the church, in fact, often betrays this calling. House churches are a big part of the way out of this betrayal and this paradox. Face-to-face community breeds mutual respect, mutual responsibility, mutual submission, and mutual ministry. The sociology of the house church fosters a sense of equality and mutual worth, though it doesn't guarantee it.... House churches are revolutionary because they incarnate this radical teaching that all are gifted and all are ministers.[52]

Viola contends that this is not a practice of democracy as majority rule (as in American-style democracy) but a practice of mutuality in a consensus-building community. Furthermore, Viola and Barna (and other proponents of small groups) recognize that the intimacy of the House Church fulfills a very different purpose than large worship gatherings that simply cannot provide for such intimate sharing and rotation of leadership. In short, like the Prayer Meeting model, the House Church model fulfills a distinctive goal and character: to manifest the equality of Christian believers through interactive group participation.

---

51. See, for example, the description of a local house church gathering at http://events.r20.constantcontact.com/register/event?oeidk=a07efo4k67vf8dd2400&llr=l6qbvhcab, accessed July 9, 2019. Other examples abound. The first examples I have been able to locate of the phrase "sharing of joys and concerns" date to the mid-1970s in descriptions of small group worship venues.

52. Frank Viola, *Reimagining Church: Pursuing the Dream of Organic Christianity* (Colorado Springs, CO: David C. Cook, 2008), 93–94.

Chapter Seven

There is not enough space in this chapter to examine all of the various permutations of the Prayer Meeting format, but below are two examples:

The Prayer Meeting Macro-Pattern (typical example)

Gathering (casual)
Singing of several well-known songs or hymns
Scripture lesson (on a theme)
Reflection on the lesson by a leader
Responses to the lesson by the group
Personal sharing
Sentence prayers (or longer) rotating among group
[Final hymn or song]
Closing prayer by an individual
[Additional fellowship time]

House Church Macro-Pattern (typical example)

Gathering (in a home or small venue)
[The gathering may begin with a meal and a table blessing]
[Singing, if the group has musical leadership available]
Scripture reading or devotional lesson
Personal reflection on lesson
Sharing of joys and concerns
Sentence prayers rotated among group
[Singing]
Closing prayer, led by a leader in the group
*Some groups may include a Lord's Supper rite at the beginning or conclusion of the meeting

Distinctive Liturgical Units of the Prayer Meeting/House Church Pattern

Sentence prayers
Sharing of joys and concerns
Group reflection on lesson/theme

Assessment of the Prayer Meeting/ House Church Worship Macro-Pattern

In 1 Corinthians 12, the Apostle Paul compares the church to a body made up of many parts, and he asserts that each individual Christian is an essential part of that body. Every Christian has a valuable contribution for the whole; no one is insignificant; we bear each other's burdens; we share each other's joys. Paul's analogy is the rationale for the Prayer Meeting.

If Acts of the Apostles and several of the epistles portray the church as the fellowship of a priesthood of all believers (to reference a concept the great reformer Martin Luther recovered from scripture), then the Prayer Meeting puts that concept into practice. As a counterweight to church hierarchies (and abuses of power that hierarchies inevitably commit), the Prayer Meeting may be the quintessential Protestant form of worship.

Today, studies of thriving congregations point to the importance of small groups for vibrant ministries—and this would seem to be the case for congregations of all sizes.[53] If the Prayer Meeting pattern of worship has waxed and waned over the last two hundred years, it is blossoming again in the present through various small group ministries. I would suggest that this format of intimate community forms the basis of such varied social organizations as Alcoholics Anonymous, Marriage Encounter, and even nonreligious therapeutic emotional support groups, group therapy, New Age encounter groups, or even book groups.

History also shows that the Prayer Meeting format has some distinctive liabilities. Egalitarian forms of community are difficult to maintain over time. Concrete evidence for the stability of small groups is insufficient to make a definitive assessment, but even Frank Viola, who is a

---

53. "No matter the size of the congregation, individuals involved in small, relational groups that meet for prayer, discussion, and Bible study are more likely to express a sense of belonging, attend religious services more often, and give financially at a higher rate than are persons not involved in such groups." Kevin D. Dougherty and Andrew L. Whitehead, "A Place to Belong: Small Group Involvement in Religious Congregations," in *Sociology of Religion* vol. 72, no. 1 (2011): 107.

strong advocate, has acknowledged that the typical House Church lasts between six months and two years.[54] In other words, Viola confirms what Beecher had learned during his ministry in the late nineteenth century: "The most difficult thing that you will have to do in your ministry is to maintain a live prayer-meeting. It is about the hardest work you will ever know."[55]

Indeed, small groups of any sort tend to go through phases beginning with what Viola calls the honeymoon period. But once the initial excitement of newly formed friends evolves, the honeymoon gives way to what Viola calls the "crisis period," when the group almost inevitably experiences "conflicts, disagreements, or problems with difficult people." If the group survives this phase, Viola suggests it will be because "people in the group are able and willing to take their life and issues to the cross and die to self in the area that is being challenged." Finally, if the group continues, it might reach a phase Viola calls Tested Body Life, during which "real community is experienced," but he adds parenthetically, "at least for a while." In short, even for the mature House Church, genuine community can be fleeting. And here I can add an "Amen" based on my own experience with small group ministries.[56]

Not only is the intimacy of the House Church model difficult to maintain over time, the model also can suffer from one of its most effective features: egalitarian participation, which tends to become boring. Once members of a group have shared personal stories and confessed their most significant struggles and hopes, the group meetings often become more routine. Equal time for every member is an admirable goal, but in reality, some people will simply strike others as more or less interesting. Not everyone is good at offering prayer or leading a song. Some people are, frankly, more profound in their theological reflections.

---

54. "Frank Viola Answers Questions," *Simple Church Journal* (Sept 3, 2006), https://sojourner.typepad.com/house_church_blog/2006/09/frank_viola_ans.html, accessed July 9, 2019.

55. Beecher, *Lectures on Preaching*, second series, 92.

56. "Frank Viola Answers Questions."

Furthermore, even egalitarian groups will inevitably develop leaders, and some leaders are more skilled than others. And some leaders can become toxic. The literature on small groups frequently admits that a danger of the House Church is the problem of the teacher who promotes outright heretical theological viewpoints, and there is ample anecdotal evidence of damage done to impressionable members of such groups. If small groups can lead to deeper congregational participation and personal growth, in some bad cases such groups have fomented division and split congregations.

Despite these liabilities, there is no reason to deny that the Prayer Meeting and the House Church forms of worship can play a productive role in the ecology of congregations if counterbalanced with forms of worship that decenter the individual. Proof texts for the Prayer Meeting/House Church model that center church in small groups come from the New Testament Epistles. However, passages from the Revelation of John suggest a more transcendent model of church and worship. I investigate this Catholic model in the next chapter.

	Telos (Goal)	*Ethos* (Qualities of Character)
Nineteenth-century type: The Prayer Meeting	To manifest the democratic ideal of Christian equality	Family atmosphere
		Informal dress
		Gender-inclusive participation
		Emotional intimacy
		Open sharing of personal concerns
		Laity voicing short prayers in turn
		Religious testimony
		Brevity of didactic addresses
		Open discussion of scripture and/or topic
		Singing of emotionally rich hymns
		Laity exercising leadership (at least in part)

	Telos (Goal)	*Ethos* (Qualities of Character)
Present form: House Church	To embody the egalitarian ideal of Christian community	Meeting in homes
		Family atmosphere
		Informal dress
		Shared/rotating leadership
		Full group participation (gender-inclusive)
		Open sharing of joys and concerns
		Interpersonal intimacy
		Brevity in teaching/ scripture reading
		Open discussion
		[Group singing]
		[Shared meal]

Regardless of which model of church is at the center of ecclesiology—the small gathering or the larger meeting (and the debate between congregationalism and episcopalism rages on)—the proponents of the Prayer Meeting worship model all agree that it is distinct from the larger gatherings for worship and preaching, the "Sunday service." Yet as the opening vignette of this chapter illustrates, this has not prevented elements of the Prayer Meeting *ethos* from slipping into the Sunday preaching service, especially in smaller congregations. Before the nineteenth century, Christians did not, as far as I can tell, expect the Sunday service to fulfill their need for interpersonal intimacy. By the end of the twentieth century, the "sharing of joys and concerns" had come to be an expected liturgical unit of the worship of small congregations. I examine such conflation of patterns in some detail in chapter 9.

Nevertheless, while intimacy is a distinctive character trait of this model, perhaps the most important ideal characteristic of the Prayer Meeting is the full and active engagement of every member of the group in all aspects of the gathering. As the late nineteenth-century essay quoted at the head of this chapter states succinctly: "No Christian can come with the purpose of being a mere spectator, without doing a wrong to the Church and to himself. That *each one* should give according as God hath prospered him is the true rule for the prayer-meeting no less than for the contribution-box."[57] An exhortation to which I add my own hearty "Amen!"

---

57. Rev. A. D., "Everybody Should Contribute to the Prayer-Meeting," 569.

CHAPTER EIGHT

The Catholic Model

Liturgical Ordo and Deep Traditions

And so, with your people on earth and all the company of heaven we praise your name and join their unending hymn:
Holy, holy, holy Lord, God of power and might,
heaven and earth are full of your glory.
Hosanna in the highest.
Blessed is he who comes in the name of the Lord.
Hosanna in the highest.

—"The Great Thanksgiving," *The United Methodist Hymnal*[1]

The Methodist pastor is with her husband on a trip to Rome. On Sunday morning they decide to attend the 9 a.m. mass at St. Peter's Basilica in the Vatican. The Pope does not preside at these weekly Sunday masses, but that really does not matter; she is more interested in seeing a more typical Sunday service in Rome with a priest and congregation.

This morning mass is for local parishioners, and the language of the service will mostly be Italian. The Methodist pastor does not speak Italian, and neither does her husband. She wonders, "Will I be able to understand any of this?"

After an opening processional hymn, the priest addresses the congregation:

"Nel nome del Padre e del Figlio e dello Spirito Santo."

---

1. *The United Methodist Hymnal*, "Word and Table: Service I" (Nashville, TN: The United Methodist Publishing House, 1989), 9.

Chapter Eight

The Methodist pastor finds herself reflexively responding with the congregation: "Amen!" as if she couldn't really help herself. The priest continues, "*La grazia del Signore nostro Gesù Cristo, l'amore di Dio Padre e la comunione dello Spirito Santo sia con tutti voi,*" and the congregation responds in unison, "*E con il tuo spirito.*" The pastor follows along quietly, "And with your spirit (*I think I'm getting this.*)"

When the liturgy comes to the Great Thanksgiving, the priest declares, "*Signore sia con voi,*" and the Methodist pastor joins in the entire opening exchange, whispering the familiar words in English: "And also with you," "We lift them up to the Lord," "It is right to give our thanks and praise."

Afterward, the pastor says to her husband, "Who would have thought we Methodists from Illinois would be so connected to this Roman Catholic service in Italian at St. Peter's Basilica?"

This anecdote is from a trip I took with my wife in 2004. At that time, Sara was the associate pastor of First United Methodist Church in Evanston, Illinois. We were both reared in small churches deeply influenced by Revival, Sunday School, and Prayer Meeting models of worship. Evanston First UMC, on the other hand, mostly followed the United Methodist ritual for Holy Communion as found in *The United Methodist Hymnal* (1989) and *Book of Worship* (1992). These two liturgical books were deeply formed by ecumenical liturgical scholarship of the twentieth century that provides our final paradigm of *telos* and *ethos*. I call this pattern the Catholic Liturgical Renewal model.

The term *Catholic Liturgical Renewal* requires some clarification. By *catholic*, I do not mean the Roman Catholic Church, though *catholic* does include the Roman liturgy as it has been practiced in history. Rather, I use this word for its more basic meaning, "the church universal." This is the use of the term in the Apostles' Creed, and of our declaration, "I believe in the holy catholic church." In the ancient creed, and in its modern meaning, *catholic* denotes geographic universality (the church everywhere), temporal universality (throughout all time), and cosmic universality (both on earth and in heaven). Applied to worship, this means that in some profound way the worship of Christians in any time and place is essentially what Christians always and everywhere have done. Of course, in actual practice Christians have varied in how they have worshiped and in how they have understood the meaning of worship. Nevertheless, the Catholic Liturgical Renewal model has attempted to uncover the fundamental, historical order of Christian worship against which any particular practice or theology may be evaluated. Just as the Revival model evaluates worship according to its emotional power or the Sunday School model evaluates worship according to its capacity to educate, and so forth, the Catholic Liturgical Renewal model evaluates worship according to a fundamental order that encompasses all time, place, and space.

The scholars of the Catholic Liturgical Renewal turned especially to the earliest historical patterns of Christian worship as a primary source for determining the basic order of Christian worship. The discovery of previously lost or unknown patristic texts in the late nineteenth and early twentieth centuries, such as the so-called *Apostolic Tradition of Hippolytus*, gave liturgical scholars what they believed was a tantalizingly clear window into the worship practices of the church in its infancy. This historical reconstruction of early Christian practice deeply influenced the reforms of the Vatican Council II of the Catholic Church in the early 1960s and the subsequent revisions of Roman Catholic liturgical books. It also dramatically influenced the official liturgical revisions of many mainline Protestant denominations in the United States. Since the 1970s, Episcopalians, Presbyterians, Lutherans, United Methodists, and the United Church of Christ have all revised their official hymnals and worship books, drawing deeply upon the Catholic Liturgical Renewal model. Notice that I specifically say "official hymnals and worship books." Many local congregations of these Protestant denominations have resisted the Catholic Liturgical Renewal model, and we will consider some reasons for this at the conclusion of this chapter.

Precursors to the Catholic Liturgical Renewal Model

In the turn to historical precedents, the Catholic Liturgical Renewal was similar to earlier reform movements. As the critical principle for criticizing and reforming the church, many churches in the Protestant Reformation and after looked to what they believed was the practice of the apostles in the New Testament. But by the nineteenth century, not all Christians were so enamored with historical precedent. As I showed in chapter 3, Charles Finney and his followers radically questioned the significance even of New Testament practices for setting precedents for how Christians should worship. Given his New Measures approach to worship, Finney was sure God did not care how we worshiped so long as the church was able to produce converts. Historical precedent simply did not matter to Finney. Converts did.

The Restorationist Movement

Finney persuaded many Protestant leaders. But not all were willing to adopt his radical anti-traditionalist stance. The Restorationist movement in the early nineteenth century, which gave rise to the Church of Christ and the Disciples of Christ, made the practice of the New Testament church the central principle for reform. Alexander Campbell, a leader of the movement, wrote a series of essays on church order that argued for an essential uniformity to Christian worship:

> It follows then that there is a divinely authorized order of christian [sic] worship in christian assemblies, and that this worship is uniformly the same, which was to be demonstrated on principles of reason. These positions are capable of rational demonstration on other grounds than those adopted; but this plan was preferred because it was the shortest, and, as we supposed, the most convincing. This is only preparative or introductory to the essays which are to follow upon the ancient worship of the christian church. We are hastening through the outlines and shall fill up the interior after we have given an essay on each of the following topics. They continued stedfastly [sic] in the apostles' doctrine—in breaking of bread—in fellowship—in prayers—praising God.[2]

Campbell's proof text for the Christian order of worship was Acts 2:42–47. From this passage (and a few others) Campbell and others in the Restorationist movement initiated one of their most significant features: the

---

2. Alexander Campbell, "A Restoration of the Divine Order of Things. V. The Order of Worship," in *The Christian Baptist*, vols. 1–7 (Revised by D. S. Burnet, with Mr. Campbell's last Corrections) (Cincinnati, OH: D. S. Burnet, 1835), 166.

The Catholic Model

establishment of a weekly service of the Lord's Supper. Indeed, a weekly Lord's Supper continues to be a hallmark of the Church of Christ and the Disciples of Christ.

When Campbell wrote his essay on worship, Episcopalians were more than a century away from recovering a weekly practice of Holy Communion. And while most Catholic churches in the nineteenth century held daily masses, as a rule most laity did not commune more than a few times a year. Campbell was recovering the practice of weekly communion at a time when virtually no other Protestant or even Catholic congregation practiced weekly communion. However, Campbell argued that anything less than a weekly commemoration of the supper was patently unbiblical:

> While Romanists, Episcopalians, Presbyterians of every grade, Independents, Methodists, Baptists &c., acknowledge the breaking of bread to be a divine institution, an act of religious worship in christian assemblies, they all differ in their views of the import of the institution, the manner and times in which it is to be observed, and in the appendages thereto belonging. In one idea they all agree, that it is an *extraordinary* and not an ordinary act of christian worship; and consequently, does not belong to the ordinary worship of the christian church. For this opinion they have custom and tradition to show, but not one argument worthy of a moment's reflection, not even one text to adduce as a confirmation of their practice. Who ever heard a text adduced to prove a monthly, a quarterly, a semi-annual, or an annual breaking of bread?[3]

For Campbell, the weekly Lord's Supper was a biblical mandate, but it was also more than merely an act of obedience to biblical precedent. Rather, he argued:

> [The Lord's Supper] is acknowledged to be a blissful privilege, and this acknowledgment, whether sincere or feigned, accords with fact. It was the design of the Saviour that his disciples should not be deprived of this joyful festival when they meet in one place to worship God. It will appear, if it does not already to the candid reader of these numbers, that the New Testament teaches that every time they met in honor of the resurrection of the

---

3. Campbell, "A Restoration of the Divine Order of Things. V. On the Breaking of Bread, no. 1," 175.

Prince of life, or when they assembled in one place, it was a principal part of their entertainment, in his liberal house, to eat and drink with him. He keeps no dry lodgings for the saints; no empty house for his friends. He never bade his house assemble but to eat and drink with him. His generous and philanthropic heart never sent his disciples hungry away. He did not assemble them to weep and wail, and starve with him. No: he commands them to rejoice always, and bids them eat and drink abundantly.[4]

This is a startlingly beautiful exposition of the supper in harmony with the historic practices of the church in the New Testament.[5]

Campbell and the Restorationists are not typically placed in the line of reforms leading up to the Catholic Liturgical Renewal movement. They were steadfastly against any sort of fixed liturgy of the sort found in the Episcopalian *Book of Common Prayer*. Nevertheless, this frontier movement embraced a fundamental, universal order for Christian worship that transcended local congregations. While Campbell did not directly challenge Charles Finney's New Measures approach to worship (see pp. 44–47 above), his theology implicitly rejected the sort of novelties advocated by Finney.

The Mercersburg Movement

In the mid-nineteenth century, a group of theologians in the Reformed Church in the United States on the faculty of the denominational seminary in Mercersburg, Pennsylvania, marshaled a direct challenge to the emotionalism and novelty of New Measures revivalism. The Mercersburg movement developed a theology and liturgical practice that recovered some key insights of John Calvin, especially as these insights were grounded in patristic sources. Mercersburg theologian John Williamson Nevin's scathing critique of the New Measures, a treatise entitled *The Anxious Bench*, was the first salvo.[6] Nevin argued, "Religion must have forms, as well as an inward living

---

4. Campbell, "A Restoration of the Divine Order of Things. V. On the Breaking of Bread, no. 1," 175.

5. Unfortunately, not all followers of Campbell would adopt his rich understanding of the Lord's Supper, even if they did continue to practice weekly communion. See Keith Watkins, "Worship in the Christian Church (Disciples of Christ)," *Worship* vol. 51, no. 6 (1977): 486–96.

6. Chambersburg, PA, *The Weekly Messenger*, 1843.

force. But these can have no value, no proper reality, except as they spring perpetually from the presence of that living force itself. The inward must be the bearer of the outward."[7] The proponents of the New Measures, however, trivialized the very purpose of the forms themselves:

> They propose to rouse the Church from its dead formalism. And to do this effectually, they strike off from the old ways of worship, and bring in new and strange practices, that are adapted to excite attention. These naturally produce a theatrical effect, and this is taken at once for an evidence of waking life in the congregation. One measure, losing its power in proportion as it becomes familiar, leads to the introduction of another. . . . And yet they are measures, when all is done; and it is only by losing sight of the inward power of truth, that any can be led to attach to them any such importance.[8]

For Nevin, the problem with New Measures was that they are all effect and no substance, "quackery in the garb of religion, without its inward life and power."[9]

In a later historical study of the Eucharist, Nevin did not deny that traditional forms of church were also vulnerable to abuse: "The actual may indeed fall short immeasurably of the idea it represents; the visible Church may be imperfect, corrupt, false to its own conception and calling."[10] However, this did not diminish the reality they are meant to convey:

> But still an actual, continuously visible Church there must always be in the world, if Christianity is to have either truth or reality in the form of a new creation. . . . An outward Church is the necessary form of the new creation in Christ Jesus, in its very nature; and must continue to be so, not only through all time, but through all eternity likewise. Outward social worship, which implies, of course, forms for the purpose, is to be regarded as something essential to piety itself.[11]

---

7. John Williamson Nevin, *The Anxious Bench* (Chambersburg, PA: Office of the Weekly Messenger, 1843), 51–52.

8. Nevin, *The Anxious Bench*, 52–53.

9. Nevin, *The Anxious Bench*, 52.

10. John Williamson Nevin, *The Mystical Presence: A Vindication of the Reformed or Calvinistic Doctrine of Holy Eucharist* (Philadelphia, PA: J. B. Lippincott & Co., 1846), 5.

11. Nevin, *The Mystical Presence*, 5.

The foundational principle undergirding Nevin's theology of the historic, visible church was the incarnation of Jesus Christ: "The incarnation of the Son of God, as it is the principle, forms also the true measure and test, of all sound Christianity, in this view. . . . This is the proper, deep sense of all liturgical services in religion."[12] If the incarnation was the principle from which the forms of church life drew their meaning, Nevin argued, the Eucharist was the core practice of the church that manifested this principle. Thus, according to Nevin, the Eucharist is the central, visible practice of the incarnation of Jesus that, by extension, grounds all genuine liturgical practices. As he wrote in his evaluation of a newly proposed liturgy of the German Reformed Church:

> No liturgy, then, can be worthy of its name, which is not framed in such a way as to make the sacrament of the Lord's Supper its cardinal office, while all its other offices and parts are so order as, silently at least, to come under some inward relation to this, and to take from it their key note and reigning tone.

Such worship was not a "means to something else."[13] Such worship was the visible realization of the Christ in the world. In short, the Mercersburg portrayed Christian worship as real, concrete participation in the universal and eternal body of Christ. This concept of worship as participation in the universal body of Christ is the *telos* of what would become the Catholic Liturgical Renewal model.[14]

The Anglo-Catholic Movement

The rise of Anglo-Catholicism in the Anglican Church in the nineteenth century is a third precursor to the Catholic Liturgical Renewal. The Oxford movement in England, with its embrace of a catholic ecclesiology that drew upon patristic sources, was the major theological impetus

---

12. Nevin, *The Mystical Presence*, 5.

13. Nevin, *The Mystical Presence*, 6.

14. Surprisingly, given the centrality of the Eucharist Mercersburg theology, the movement did not explicitly advocate for weekly communion. As one study of the movement notes regarding the Mercersburg understanding of eucharistic practice, "Virtually nothing was written regarding either the matter of frequency or balance." See Jack Martin Maxwell, *Worship and Reformed Theology: The Liturgical Lessons of Mercersburg* (Eugene, OR: Pickwick, 2009), 388.

of Anglo-Catholicism. Intellectual leaders of the movement (John Henry Newman, Edward Pusey, and John Keble, among others) began the publication of a series of ninety Tracts of the Times that argued for the continuity of the Church of England with the "holy, catholic, apostolic Church." Indeed, they claimed that the Church of England was essentially a third branch of the church catholic, the other two branches being the Roman Church and the Orthodox Church.

The Tractarians, as they were called, promoted a very high theology of the sacraments and ordination: real presence of Christ in the Eucharist, baptismal regeneration through the rite itself, and apostolic succession in the ordination of bishops. These doctrines, Newman argued in *Tract 34: Rites and Customs of the Church*, may not be explicitly called for within the scriptures, but they were part of a tradition going back to the first few centuries of Christianity. Beginning with 1 Corinthians 11, Newman showed that Paul considered such established customs of the church to be of binding importance, even on matters that may seem trivial, such as hairstyle:

> Let us consider that remarkable passage, (1 Cor. xi. 2–16) which, I am persuaded, most readers pass over as if they could get little instruction from it. St. Paul is therein blaming the Corinthians for not adhering to the custom of the Church, which prescribed that men should wear their hair short, and that women should have their head covered during divine service; a custom apparently most unimportant, if any one ever was, but in his view strictly binding on Christians. He begins by implying that it is one out of many rules or traditions (παραδόσεις) which he had given them, and they were bound to keep. . . . Here then at once a view is opened to us which is quite sufficient to remove the surprise we might otherwise feel at the multitude of rites, which were in use in the Primitive Church, but about which the New Testament is silent; and further, to command our obedience to such as come down to us from the first ages, and are agreeable to Scripture.[15]

---

15. "The reader of ecclesiastical history is sometimes surprised at finding observances and customs generally received in the Church at an early date, which have not express warrant in the Apostolic writings; e.g. the use of the cross in baptism." Newman, *Rites and Customs of the Church, Tracts for the Times 34.1.* https://en.wikisource.org/wiki/Tracts_for_the_Times/Tract_34, accessed August 20, 2019.

The point, Newman argued, is that the New Testament writers could not possibly have mentioned every ritual custom of the primitive church, but this did not mean that these customs were no less important for being unrecorded by scripture. Some important customs are merely inferred:

> [At t]he original institution of the Eucharist, as recorded in the Gospels, there is no mention of consecrating the elements; but in 1 Cor. x. 16, St. Paul calls it "the cup of blessing, which we bless." This incidental information, vouchsafed to us in Scripture, should lead us to be very cautious how we put aside other usages of the early Church concerning this sacrament, which do not happen to be clearly mentioned in Scripture . . . which seems to have been universal in the Church.[16]

To buttress his argument, Newman cited evidence of this unwritten, binding tradition in the patristic authors such as Basil, who in the fourth century would claim: "For, should we attempt to supersede the usages which are not enjoined in Scripture as if unimportant, we should do most serious injury to Evangelical truth; nay, reduce it to a bare name."[17] In the end, Newman concludes, "that rites and ordinances . . . far from being superstitious, are expressly sanctioned in Scripture as to their principle and delivered to the Church in their form by tradition."[18]

Newman's apology for the customs of the church illustrated the Oxford movement's concern to find the universal practices that united the three great branches of the catholic church: Roman, Orthodox, and Anglican. But while the Tractarians reclaimed the shared traditions of the early church, they were more interested in ecclesiology and theology than in the fine points of ritual practice. The recovery of Anglo-Catholic architecture, art, and ceremonial must be credited to a parallel movement centered in Cambridge: the Camden Cambridge Society. Just as the Oxford movement turned to patristic sources, the Camden Cambridge Society found inspiration in the Gothic architecture as the pinnacle of Christian art.[19]

---

16. Newman, *Rites and Customs of the Church*, 34.3.

17. Newman, *Rites and Customs of the Church*, 34.7, quoting Basil, *On the Holy Spirit*, 66.

18. Newman, *Rites and Customs of the Church*, 34.7.

19. As I have argued in chapter 5, the revival of Gothic architecture would influence the Aesthetic model of worship.

The present study, of course, is about the development of models of worship in America. As the Oxford movement and the Camden Cambridge Society crossed the Atlantic, more often than not they merged into one broad movement in the Protestant Episcopal Church. The influence in the United States was gradual but pervasive. In the early nineteenth century, most Episcopal churches were decidedly "low church." Episcopalians used the official prayer book, but Holy Communion was celebrated quarterly, clerical vestments were austere, and ceremony was kept to a minimum. Over the course of the century, under the influence of the Oxford and Cambridge movements, however, the seminaries of the Protestant Episcopal Church gradually adopted more and more Anglo-Catholic (meaning Gothic) art, architecture, and ceremonial elements. The priests who were trained in these schools brought those practices into local congregations, though not without controversy and suspicions of "Romanism."[20]

To summarize the story thus far: as different as each of these nineteenth-century movements may have been, the Restorationist movement, the Mercersburg movement, and the Oxford movement all sought to ground the worship of congregations in fundamental, universal patterns found in early church history.

The Catholic Liturgical Renewal in the Twentieth Century

During this time, the Roman Catholic Church was undergoing its own revaluation of public worship based on the recovery of historical sources. Protestants and even contemporary Catholics may find this a little hard to grasp, but before the mid-twentieth century, laity who attended a Catholic mass like the one my wife and I did in Vatican City did not have to pay much attention at all to what the priest was doing at the altar. The liturgy was in Latin, a language most of the congregation did

---

20. Not without cause, as some Episcopalians did indeed convert to the Roman Catholic Church under the influence of the Oxford Movement. For a personal account of conversion and the controversies engendered by the move toward Anglo-Catholic theology and practice, see, for example, Clarence E. Walworth, *The Oxford Movement in America; or, Glimpses of Life in an Anglican Seminary* (New York, NY: Catholic Book Exchange, 1895).

not understand. Roman Catholic priests presided at daily masses—that is, celebrations of the Eucharist—and laity were expected to attend mass weekly, but this did not mean frequent communion for most of the laity. Only the most pious Catholics communed more than a few times a year. When laity did receive a consecrated host (the communion bread) this was almost always *following* a mass, or *before* a mass, or even *during* a mass, from the reserved sacrament consecrated at a *previous* mass.[21] Most of the congregation sat or knelt at mass conducting personal devotions, such as praying the rosary.

Catholic and Protestant liturgical scholars in the late nineteenth and early twentieth centuries, however, began to re-examine evidence from the early church. They found that in the early church, all Christians in good standing were expected to commune at the weekly, Sunday (Lord's Day) Eucharist. The classic text that prompted much of the revision for full lay participation in the mass came from the *Apology* of Justin Martyr, writing from Rome around the year 160:

> And on the day called Sunday, all who live in cities or in the country gather together to one place, and the memoirs of the apostles or the writings of the prophets are read, as long as time permits; then, when the reader has ceased, the president verbally instructs, and exhorts to the imitation of these good things. Then we all rise together and pray, and, as we before said, when our prayer is ended, bread and wine and water are brought, and the president in like manner offers prayers and thanksgivings, according to his ability, and the people assent, saying Amen; and there is a distribution to each, and a participation of that over which thanks have been given, and to those who are absent a portion is sent by the deacons.[22]

Written before the development of standard Christian terminology, parts of Justin's description sound strange to modern Christian ears. For example, "memoirs of the apostles" meant the Gospels and perhaps the letters of Paul. Similarly, he referred to the Old Testament as the "writings of the

---

21. For a vivid description, see Bernard Botte, *From Silence to Participation: An Insider's View of Liturgical Renewal*, trans. John Sullivan (Washington, DC: The Pastoral Press, 1988), 2–3.

22. Trans. *Ante-Nicene Fathers*, vol. 1, https://www.ccel.org/ccel/schaff/anf01.viii.ii.lxvii.html?highlight=sunday#highlight, accessed July 1, 2010.

prophets." But Justin also wrote his *Apology* ostensibly for nonbelievers, and this called for descriptive rather than technical terms. The "president" or "presider" was the leader of the congregation, who in the early church probably would have been called "bishop" or "elder." The president was the one who preached the sermon, though Justin described this as the "instruction" or "exhortation" based on the scripture readings.

The presider offered the prayer "to the best of his ability," which probably meant extemporaneously. Yet in another of his writings, Justin gave an idea of the contents as giving thanks to God "for having created the world, with all the things in it for the sake of humankind, and for delivering us from the evil in which we were [born], and for utterly overthrowing the principalities and powers by Him who suffered according to His will."[23] Thus, while the presider did not read a prayer out of a book, neither did he or she simply make it up out of thin air. Moreover, this prayer was not really the prayer of the presider alone, since Justin made a point of saying that the congregation responds with "Amen," which means "so be it." In other words, the congregation participated by verbally agreeing with what the leader prayed on their behalf.[24]

In this simple text, liturgists of the Catholic Liturgical Renewal found the basic outline of a service of Christian worship in Rome in the mid-second century:

Gathering on Sunday

Scripture readings (Old and New Testament)

Preaching by presider

Congregational prayers[25]

---

23. Justin Martyr, *Dialogue with Trypho 41*, trans. Ante-Nicene Fathers, vol. 1, https://www.ccel.org/ccel/schaff/anf01.viii.ii.lxvii.html?highlight=sunday#highlight, accessed July 1, 2010.

24. Some of the paragraphs above are adapted from my book with Sara Webb Phillips, *In Spirit and Truth: United Methodist Worship for the Emerging Church*, second revised ed. (Maryville, TN: OSL Publications, 2008), 54–59.

25. Note, in a previous paragraph Justin also suggests that this congregational prayer concluded with a sharing of a kiss of peace. See *First Apology* 65: "Having ended the prayers [the intercessions], we greet one another with a kiss."

Offering of bread, wine (and water), for the Eucharist

Eucharistic prayer led by presider

The people give their "Amen"

Distribution of meal over which thanks has been given

Overall, as some liturgical historians would say, Justin described a two-part macro-pattern of "Word" (gathering for readings and preaching) and "Table" (setting a meal, giving thanks, and partaking), with the prayers of the congregation forming a central link between these two focal actions.[26]

Justin's bare outline of worship had long been known by scholars of the early church, but the rediscovery of some other long-lost early Christian liturgical texts further fanned the flames of liturgical renewal. The most important was the identification of an obscure piece of church order literature scholars identified as the *Apostolic Tradition* of Hippolytus of Rome, a bishop from the early third century.[27] Once that association was made, scholars thought they had authentic texts of very ancient ordination prayers and a detailed order of the Roman baptismal liturgy in the early third century. The ordination rite for bishop contained a eucharistic liturgy, including, remarkably, a long prayer of thanksgiving for the eucharistic meal:

> And when he is made bishop, let everyone give the kiss of peace, greeting him. And let the deacons bring the offering to him. And when he lays his hand on the offering with the presbyters, let him say, giving thanks:
>
> The Lord [be] with all of you.
> And let all the people say:

---

26. The classic description of the Word and Table macro-pattern is Gregory Dix, *The Shape of the Liturgy*, first published in 1945 (current edition New York, NY: Bloomsbury T & T Clarke, 2015), 36–47. Dix calls the "Word service" the Synaxis, a Greek term meaning "gathering," and argues that it was a Christian form of a Jewish synagogue service.

27. The association of this church order with Hippolytus and even the title, *Apostolic Tradition*, has recently been questioned by many liturgical historians. See Paul F. Bradshaw, Maxwell E. Johnson, and L. Edward Phillips, *The Apostolic Tradition* (Minneapolis, MN: Augsburg Fortress, 2002), 1–15.

> With your spirit.
>
> And he says:
> > Up, [with your] heart.
>
> And the people say:
> > We have [them] to the Lord.
>
> And he says, again:
> > Let us give thanks to the Lord.
>
> And the people say:
> > It is worthy and right.[28]

The order thus far in outline of this liturgy is:

Kiss of peace

Offering of the bread and wine for the eucharist

A three-part call and response between the newly ordained bishop and the congregation in which bishop asked permission to offer the thanksgiving.

Following the call and response, the *Apostolic Tradition* continues with the prayer for the Eucharist:

> We render thanks to you, God, through your beloved Child[29] Jesus Christ, whom in the last times you sent to us as savior and redeemer and angel of your will, who is your inseparable word, through whom you made all things and it was well-pleasing to you; you sent from heaven into the virgin's womb, and who conceived in the womb was incarnate and manifested as your son, born of the holy spirit and the virgin; who fulfilling your will and gaining for you a holy people stretched out [his] hands when he was suffering, that he might release from suffering those who believed in you; who when he was being handed over to voluntary suffering, that he might destroy death and break the bonds of the devil, and tread down hell and illuminated the righteous, and fix a limit and manifest the resurrection, taking bread [and] giving things to you,

---

28. Translation from Paul F. Bradshaw, et al., *The Apostolic Tradition*, 38, 40. Text amended for illustration purposes.

29. The use of the word *child* (or the Latin here could be translated as "servant") rather than *son* to refer to Jesus Christ is an indication of the antiquity of this prayer. We have other examples from the second century that use "child" as a modifier for Jesus, but not after the third century.

he said: "Take, eat, this is my body which will be broken for you." Likewise also the cup, saying: "This is my blood which is shed for you. When you do this, you make my remembrance," Remembering therefore his death and resurrection, we offer to you the bread and cup, giving thanks to you because you have held us worthy to stand before you and minister to you. And we ask that you would send your holy spirit in the offering of [your] holy church, [that] gathering [them] into one you will give to all who partake of the holy things [to partake] in the fullness of the holy spirit, for the strengthening of faith in truth, that we may praise and glorify you through your Child Jesus Christ, through whom [be] glory and honor to you, Father and Son with the holy spirit, in your holy church, both now and to the ages of ages. Amen.[30]

The *Apostolic Tradition* probably did not intend for the bishop to use these precise words. A later passage (*Apostolic Tradition* 9) says thanksgivings may be improvised so long as they are "orthodox." However, historians noted familiar elements and a familiar order in this prayer:

Order	Technical Terms for Reference
Opening call and response	Opening dialogue
Thanksgiving prayer	Thanksgiving
Account of the Last Supper	Institution narrative
Statement of remembrance of the saving work of Jesus	Anamnesis
Statement of offering	Oblation
Prayer for the descent of the Spirit	
Trinitarian doxology	Epiclesis
Amen (by the congregation)	Doxology
	Amen

Almost all of the ancient eucharistic prayers from the fourth century onward had these elements in the same order.[31]

---

30. Translation from Bradshaw, Johnson, and Phillips, *The Apostolic Tradition*, 38, 40. Text amended for illustration purposes. The text of this eucharistic prayer was adapted as Eucharistic Prayer II in the Roman Missal of 1970 and in Eucharistic Prayer B, Rite II of the 1979 *Book of Common Prayer*, to give two of many examples. It may be that this prayer from the early church has been more important in the twentieth century than it was in the third century!

31. W. J. Grisbrooke, "Anaphora," in *A New Dictionary of Liturgy and Worship*, ed. J. Gordon Davies (London: SCM Press, 1986), 10–17.

The Catholic Model

Beginning in the fourth century, eucharistic prayers further expanded to include the biblical acclamation "Holy, holy, holy" (*Sanctus*) and prayers of intercession for the world. A little later still, Western rites added the Lord's Prayer after the eucharistic prayer itself. And so on. The structure of the service of Word and Table was gradually evolving, and there were regional and even local differences. Nevertheless, liturgical historians were discovering an increasingly clear picture of the liturgical life of the early church. They found an amazing degree of coherence, so long as one did not focus too much on the local variations. And this discovery was thrilling.

The summit of liturgical renewal for Roman Catholics was the Second Vatican Council convened by Pope John XXIII at the beginning of the 1960s. Catholic liturgical scholars and theologians had already been preparing for reforms for several decades. Consequently, the first document the Vatican Council produced was the *Sacrosanctum Concillium*, or in English, *The Constitution on the Sacred Liturgy* (abbreviated as *SC*), and this changed the Catholic liturgy worldwide.[32] While *SC* refers to its work as a reform, it prefers the word *restoration*, implying that important practices that had been forgotten over the church's long history would be brought back into use, with attention to the participation of laity.[33] With *SC*, the Latin rite established by the Council of Trent during the Reformation in the sixteenth century would be restored based on precedents of the early church. In a break with long-standing practice, the reformed Latin rite would be translated into the vernacular languages of the world so that congregations could understand the liturgy and participate more actively. Moreover, Catholic laity began to commune during the actual mass rather than only from the reserved sacrament, and permission was widely given for laity to receive communion from the cup as well as from the bread, which had not been allowed under the liturgy of Trent. A full service of the Word, with abundant reading of

---

32. The English translation, http://www.documentacatholicaomnia.eu/03d/1963-12-04,_Concilium_Vaticanum_II,_Constitutio_%27Sacrosantum_Conciluim%27,_EN.pdf, accessed October 14, 2019.

33. We may note that this unintentionally echoes the concerns of Alexander Campbell and the Restorationists of the nineteenth century.

scripture and preaching, was restored to the regular Sunday mass, making the mass a service of Word and Table.

The Catholic Liturgical Renewal in Protestant Churches

The previous Roman Rite, established soon after the Council of Trent in the sixteenth century, had lasted with little alteration for over 450 years. But if the Roman church could change its worship, why not the Protestants? By the mid-twentieth century, Protestant liturgical scholars caught the wave of the ecumenical movement that followed in the wake of World War II (i.e., the World Council of Churches). They read the work of Roman Catholic, Eastern Orthodox, and Anglo-Catholic historical scholars in the Catholic Liturgical Renewal and began to join the emerging consensus on the importance of early Christian liturgical theology and practice.

A high point of the Protestant side of Catholic Liturgical Renewal is the *Baptism, Eucharist and Ministry* (*BEM*) document approved by the World Council of Churches (WCC) in 1982.[34] In order for the divided churches to achieve the visible unity they sought, theologians working with the WCC proposed a basic agreement on the theology and practice of baptism, eucharist, and ministry. While allowing for cultural and denominational differences, *BEM* proposed a fundamental unity of *telos* based on the principle of the cosmic, universal Lordship of Jesus Christ. Here, for example, is a statement regarding the Eucharist:

---

34. Founded in 1948, WCC is "a fellowship of churches which confess the Lord Jesus Christ as God and Saviour according to the scriptures, and therefore seek to fulfil together their common calling to the glory of the one God, Father, Son and Holy Spirit." Since its inception, the goal of WCC has been to overcome any barriers to shared witness and mission among the various Christian churches: "[WCC] is a community of churches on the way to visible unity in one faith and one eucharistic fellowship, expressed in worship and in common life in Christ. It seeks to advance towards this unity, as Jesus prayed for his followers, 'so that the world may believe' (John 17:21)." These statements are from "What Is the World Council of Churches?" at https://www.oikoumene.org/en/about-us, accessed August 11, 2019. The *BEM* document itself was no. 111 in a series of Faith and Order Papers going back to the earliest years of the WCC.

> The eucharist is the great sacrifice of praise by which the Church speaks on behalf of the whole creation. For the world which God has reconciled is present at every eucharist: in the bread and wine, in the persons of the faithful, and in the prayers they offer for themselves and for all people. Christ unites the faithful with himself and includes their prayers within his own intercession so that the faithful are transfigured and their prayers accepted. This sacrifice of praise is possible only through Christ, with him and in him. The bread and wine, fruits of the earth and of human labour, are presented to the Father in faith and thanksgiving. The eucharist thus signifies what the world is to become: an offering and hymn of praise to the Creator, a universal communion in the body of Christ, a kingdom of justice, love and peace in the Holy Spirit.[35]

The result of this ecumenical work is an amazing ecumenical convergence in the form of worship, at least in official books.[36]

Among Protestant liturgists, the Catholic Liturgical Renewal expressed a desire for worship deeper than the subjective approach that had come to dominate the Protestant approach to liturgy. Protestant reformers longed for a worship that had ontological depth. As I demonstrated in previous chapters, the Aesthetic Worship model looked toward aesthetic experience for this depth of reality. The Pentecostal model located this depth in visceral experience of the Holy Spirit. In the Catholic Liturgical Renewal model, that "something real" is the universal body of Christ that is essentially in continuity with the historic liturgical tradition of the ancient church. This is the church as it took shape in the period before the designation "Roman" Catholic made sense and long before the issues that prompted the Reformation became evident.

The Sunday liturgy, however, was not the only focus of the renewal. In addition to the Mass, *SC* also called for a restoration of the rites of Christian initiation (baptism, confirmation, and first communion), the liturgy of daily prayer, and the liturgical calendar. Protestant reformers followed

---

35. *Baptism, Eucharist and Ministry, Faith and Order Paper*, no. 111 (Geneva: The World Council of Churches), "Eucharist," par. 4. https://www.anglicancommunion.org/media/102580/lima_document.pdf, accessed August 8, 2019.

36. See Max Thurian and Geoffrey Wainwright, *Baptism and Eucharist: Ecumenical Convergence in Celebration* (Grand Rapids, MI: Eerdmans, 117).

this lead and also began to recover a number of patristic practices for baptism and the liturgical year in their official liturgical books.

Therefore, the Catholic Liturgical Renewal was not only a reform of Sunday worship; it was an essential reform of ecclesiology, that is, the theology of the nature, purpose, and meaning of "church." Fundamental to the logic of the Catholic Liturgical Renewal is understanding that the church is not merely an instrument to fulfill God's purpose in the world. Rather, the church as the body of Christ is "the expression of God's ultimate purpose itself."[37] In short, creation is the theater in which God's purpose is realized as church, which is the body of Christ in creation. The church as body of Christ is not merely a metaphor; rather, it is an ontological reality into which human beings are invited through baptism. In this ecclesiology, worship is not primarily the expressive work of individual Christians joining in a common task. Rather, to worship is to take part in the cosmic liturgy of the body of Christ that exists throughout eternity. Congregations do not make worship happen; rather, they join in what is already taking place among the angels and saints. To reference the epigraph of this chapter: "And so, with your people on earth and all the company of heaven we praise your name and join their unending hymn."

The *Telos* and *Ethos* of the Catholic Liturgical Renewal/Word and Table Pattern

Regarding Sunday worship, in broad strokes the Catholic Liturgical Renewal may be summarized thus:

Roman Catholics rediscovered scripture, preaching, and weekly communion of the laity.

Protestants rediscovered the Eucharist and weekly communion as the essential elements for Lord's Day worship.

---

37. Simon Chan, *Liturgical Theology: The Church as Worshiping Community* (Grand Rapids, MI: IVP Academic, 2006), 63.

Both Roman Catholics and Protestants rediscovered the patristic principle of the eucharistic liturgy as active participation of the laity in the body of Christ as their right and duty.[38]

Hallmarks of this model that draws on the practices of the early church can be summarized as follows:

An order of service that follows the order of Justin Martyr

Weekly preaching connected to generous reading of scripture

Intercessory prayers of the congregation for the world

The Lord's Supper as essential to the full Sunday service

A standard eucharistic prayer modeled on historic patterns

Weekly communion of the laity

The *telos* of this pattern is catholic worship—that is, participation in the universal body of Christ as the church has existed through time. The *ethos* intends to embody the classical/traditional/historical order in a local community at worship. A great strength of the Word and Table model is the way it allows Christians—like my wife and me in Italy—to participate in a common liturgical pattern across time and geography. A catholic worshiper can be at home in the service in any catholic congregation at worship anywhere in the world, as Sara found in St. Paul's Basilica. In this model, a Christian could recognize the universal pattern, even if the language, music, or art were local.

The catholic *ethos*, moreover, gladly embraces the cultural varieties of art, music, and architecture as these allow a congregation to join in worship with the church universal. The core pattern of liturgy is universal and foundational, but this pattern can only be manifest in specific, local communities. Each local community brings its culture, language, and art

---

38. As *SC* boldly declared: "Mother Church earnestly desires that all the faithful should be led to that fully conscious, and active participation in liturgical celebrations which is demanded by the very nature of the liturgy" (*SC14*). Protestant liturgical reformers fully embraced this aspiration.

to the universal praise of God. Cultural location is not trivial (just a matter of taste or usefulness as in the Revival, Sunday School, and Aesthetic patterns) but the necessary way a local church brings its native language, art, and music into the universal praise of God.[39]

The Catholic Liturgical Renewal model has historically been associated with printed texts, such as the *Book of Common Prayer*, or the *Roman Missal*. Nevertheless, there is actually much less emphasis on printed text than in Creative Worship or Traditional Worship, which has ad hoc printed prayers and responses for each service. In the Catholic Liturgical Renewal model, the ordinary prayers and gestures of the service are stable to allow them to be learned by heart, for at the heart of the Word and Table model is not a text merely to be read but a pattern to be fully enacted. That pattern is, as John Nevin proposed, the incarnate Son of God, Jesus Christ, in whom the church participates as members of his body. As the *Baptism, Eucharist and Ministry* document of the World Council of Churches states regarding the Eucharist: "In the eucharist, Christ empowers us to live with him, to suffer with him and to pray through him as justified sinners, joyfully and freely fulfilling his will."[40]

When a congregation engages a liturgy of Word and Table as participation in the living Christ, pastors and worship leaders focus on what praying these words and enacting these gestures *does* to the congregation more than the liturgy *means* in a personal sense. For if Christian worship really unites a congregation with the body of Christ throughout time and space (what it does), regardless of what any worshiper might think or feel at any given time (what it might mean to individuals), then worship is more than words in a book. Rather, it is the local incarnation of the universal body of Christ at prayer.

---

39. See, for example, the pastoral instructions on the liturgy for black Catholics concerning incorporation of the rich black cultural heritage of music, preaching, bodily expression, dress, and architecture in "'What We Have Seen and Heard.' A Pastoral Letter on Evangelization from the Black Bishops of the United States" (Congers, NY: St. Anthony Messenger Press, 1984), 30–32.

40. *Baptism, Eucharist and Ministry, Faith and Order Paper*, no. 111 (Geneva: The World Council of Churches), "Eucharist," par. 4. https://www.anglicancommunion.org/media/102580/lima_document.pdf, accessed August 8, 2019.

Assessment of the Catholic Liturgical Renewal/Word and Table Pattern

The chart at the end of this chapter demonstrates the convergence of liturgical practice across several denominations. But I should stress again that this is the model stated in the official liturgical books. The actual practice of local Protestants diverges greatly, as we have already seen in previous chapters.

Leaders in the liturgical renewal among Protestants have sometimes proposed an ideal model of Word and Table as the standard by which to critique the other patterns at their worst. Yet it is disingenuous to describe an imaginary fourth-century congregation at worship and use that as a standard for evaluating the crassest elements of the other patterns: the entertainment-saturated Seeker church, a poorly executed Creative Worship service, an elitist and stuffy Aesthetic church, or a cynically led, emotionally manipulative Pentecostal "prosperity church." That is, liturgical reformers have been guilty of using a fictional and ancient ideal of the Word and Table to damn the worst of the other models. Moreover, more recent historical research has shown that the notion of a fundamental universal practice in the patristic church is itself questionable.[41] Yet, even if we can establish such patterns, why should we assume that Christians in the twenty-first century must accept practices from the third or fourth century C.E.? We are not fourth-century Christians. We do not have fourth-century understandings of slavery or gender roles, to cite two very obvious examples. Perhaps some early liturgical practices are no longer contextually proper for contemporary Christians, such as requiring adult baptismal candidates to enter the font naked!

Sometimes denominational leaders have pushed the Word and Table model as yet another set of top-down regulations from denominational headquarters. Since congregations have received the model through denominational worship books, in practice Word and Table can become just another iteration of the Aesthetic Worship model: lovely prayers printed

---

41. See, for example, Paul F. Bradshaw, *The Search for the Origins of Christian Worship* (Oxford, UK: Oxford University Press, 1992).

in the pew hymnal. This happens when the official, published liturgy of a church is treated more as a written text to be read than a ritual of prayer and praise to be enacted. Indeed, I suspect that most Protestants think of liturgy as a printed text, either in a book or in a bulletin, rather than the historical form of the church universal.

Another problem is that the Catholic Liturgical Renewal/Word and Table model cannot work fully without the ontological ecclesiology that grounds it. Offering a service of Word and Table as a choice among a menu of options in a large congregation subverts this ecclesiology. Within its own model, Word and Table is not merely a choice among other models. It is the foundational liturgy of the one, holy, catholic, apostolic church. From the perspective of the Word and Table paradigm, when a congregation omits either Word or Table, they have drifted away from the deep tradition of the church. Since many Protestant clergy and laity, however, do not understand Word and Table as the basic, essential pattern of Sunday worship, most people understand Word and Table simply as one *option* among many.

For example, until 1989, many Methodists loosely followed a standard order of worship provided in their hymnal, and this order consisted of hymns, prayer, collection, scripture, and preaching—that is, a preaching service. Methodists celebrated the Lord's Supper quarterly, or at most monthly, and when they did, would *add* the ritual of the Lord's Supper to the end of this preaching service. In the *United Methodist Hymnal* of 1989, however, Word and Table is the standard order of worship for Sunday. If a congregation does not actually have the Lord's Supper, something essential has been left out. This is a major conceptual shift, though most United Methodist pastors and laity do not understand the significance of this shift. Consequently, Methodists continue to think of the Lord's Supper as an occasional addition to the preaching service. However, this subverts the way the Word and Table paradigm fundamentally works.

Finally, perhaps the biggest challenge to the Word and Table model is the requirement of "fully conscious, and active participation in liturgical celebrations which is demanded by the very nature of the liturgy." Unlike the Revival, Sunday School, or Aesthetic patterns, the Word and Table

The Catholic Model

pattern assumes that worshipers are active, baptized Christian believers who long to manifest their union with the body of Christ. Arguably, even the contemporary House Church pattern does not presume any deep level of conscious engagement with the universal body of Christ so long as the interpersonal commitment is deep. In many ways, the Catholic Liturgical Renewal/Word and Table model is closer to the Pentecostal model in the way participation entails the full offering of heart, mind, and body to the transcendent reality of God's presence. Full participation in a service of Word and Table requires a great deal of spiritual formation. This is why the Word and Table model presumes adequate religious training. Unlike a Seeker Service or a Creative Worship service, a worshiper has to know how to participate in Word and Table. This means that the Word and Table model cannot serve as the congregation's outreach to religious seekers because Word and Table is for already committed, baptized believers.

Despite these problems, the Catholic Liturgical Renewal/Word and Table pattern is the well to which churches continue to return in order to drink. This we see today as Seeker churches begin to practice Lent, Pentecostal churches discover that singing in tongues is not all that different from ancient liturgical chant, and House Churches become dinner churches centered on the Lord's Supper. Just as we saw in the testimony of Alexander Campbell, John Williamson Nevin, and John Henry Newman in the nineteenth century, some Protestants today continue to return to the biblical and patristic church to find a worship that is not arbitrary or merely subjective.

Nevertheless, the Word and Table pattern alone simply cannot be the only site of the church's evangelism, religious education, devotional practice, creative arts, or interpersonal emotional support. A vibrant congregation must do more than gather for worship once a week if it intends to make serious disciples of Jesus. Even with "fully active, conscious participation," the Word and Table pattern alone does not automatically form serious disciples of Jesus. Otherwise, most Anglo-Catholics would be better Christians than most Baptists. And that, it seems to me, is manifestly not true.

Chart: Ecumenical Convergence on Word and Table

Book of Common Worship (Presbyterian)	Lutheran Book of Worship	The United Methodist Hymnal	The Order of Mass (Roman Rite)
Call to Worship	Entrance Hymn	Greeting	Entrance Song
Prayer of the Day	Greeting	Hymn (or before Greeting)	Greeting
Hymn of Praise	Kyrie	Opening Prayer	Penitential Rite (confession)
Confession and Pardon	Hymn of Praise	Act of Praise	Kyrie
Peace	Prayer of the Day	Prayer for Illumination	Gloria in Excelsis (hymn of praise)
Hymn (more praise)	First Lesson	Scripture Lesson	Opening Prayer
Prayer for Illumination	Psalm	Psalm	First Reading
First Reading	Second Lesson	Scripture Lesson	Psalm
Psalm	Sung Gospel Acclamation	Hymn	Second Reading
Second Reading	Gospel Lesson	Gospel Lesson	Gospel Acclamation (sung)
Anthem	Sermon	Sermon	Gospel Reading
Gospel Reading	Hymn	Response (creed or other acts)	Homily
Sermon	Creed	Concerns and Prayers	Profession of Faith
Invitation	Prayers of Congregation	Invitation	Prayers of Intercession
Hymn	Peace	Confession and Pardon	Offering (bread, wine, other gifts)
Affirmation of Faith	Offering	Peace	Preparation of the Table/Prayer
Prayer of the People	Offertory Prayer	Offering	Great Thanksgiving

The Catholic Model

[Peace, if not done above]	Great Thanksgiving	Great Thanksgiving	Lord's Prayer
Offering	Lord's Prayer	Lord's Prayer	Sign of Peace
Invitation	Breaking of Bread	Breaking of Bread	Breaking of Bread
Great Thanksgiving	Communion	Communion	Communion
Lord's Prayer	Hymn	Post Communion Thanksgiving	Communion Song
Breaking of the Bread	Prayer	Hymn	Prayer after Communion
Communion	Silence	Dismissal with Blessing	Blessing
[post communion prayer]	Blessing and dismissal		Dismissal
Hymn			[ending processional hymn]
Charge and Blessing			

CHAPTER NINE
Conflated Worship

Coherence and Incoherence in Liturgical Order

Many of our churches are asking, "Can't we help our leanness and our barrenness with a liturgy?" I do not object to a liturgy more than I do to banners on a house, if it pleases men; but I would not regard it as the indispensable method . . . though I think the combination of a liturgy with Congregationalism is the mingling of foreign elements that do not go well together. It is a patch on the old garment; one or the other tears,—and it doesn't make any difference which; there is a hole.

—Henry Ward Beecher[1]

The pastor has convened the first meeting of his newly formed worship committee. He has carefully chosen the members to represent the demographic range of his congregation: older and younger generations; longtime members and a couple of newcomers; a member who is definitely more evangelical in perspective and a couple of persons who lean progressive.

"Thanks for agreeing to serve on this committee. As you all know, the leadership of our congregation has taken a survey of our members, and we discovered that over half of the congregation does not find our worship to be very engaging. The church council suggests that we need to make some changes to connect more with the needs of the congregation. Our task is to make suggestions for improvement. Let's brainstorm some ideas."

A man speaks up, "Well, that new church that started out at the old mall is growing like gangbusters. The preacher there never wears a robe. Maybe we need to be a little less stuffy." A member of the choir speaks

---

1. Henry Ward Beecher, *Lectures on Preaching*, second series (London: T. Nelson and Sons, 1874), 71.

up, "If we quit wearing robes, you'll lose half of the choir. They won't like processing in street clothes."

A middle-aged man speaks up, "I would love to try having a worship band instead of organ music every Sunday. I know that young people like the contemporary Christian music they hear on the radio. Maybe the choir could try. . . ."

He is cut short by the one teenager on the committee. "Honestly, I feel embarrassed when the church tries to sing that sort of music. That is *not* what *I* want."

Other suggestions follow randomly: "Can we have communion every Sunday?" "If we do that, can we at least change it up so we don't get in a rut?" "Can we make sure we have time to share prayer concerns?" "I remember when we used to ask everyone who had a birthday that week to raise their hand, and we all sang 'Happy Birthday.'"

And the pastor begins to panic. "I think I'm in trouble here."[2]

The Methodological Principles for Analyzing Worship Practice

This fictional scenario may be familiar to readers. I have experienced something similar myself. Our congregations, and particularly the most engaged members of our congregations, know about a wide range of worship practices through personal experience at other churches or religious meetings, through reading about them or seeing them on YouTube or on television, or even by hearing about them from others. Yet few pastors and even fewer congregational members recognize that worship practices usually originate in diverse patterns of worship that each have very different goals.

Recall that in previous chapters I developed a set of methodological principles for understanding and analyzing the diverse worship practices in Protestant congregations:

---

2. I proposed a very similar scenario in "How Shall We Worship?" *Worship Matters*, vol. 1, ed. E. Byron Anderson (Nashville, TN: Discipleship Resources, 1999), 23, and more expansively with Taylor Burton Edwards, "How (and Why) Shall We Worship?" available at https://www.wnccumc.org/resourcedetail/9296006, accessed December 6, 2019.

Principle 1: All worship follows patterns.

Principle 2: The patterns of worship function at two levels: the liturgical unit and the macro-pattern.

Principle 3: A macro-pattern of worship has a *telos* (goal) it aims to achieve.

Principle 4: Each macro-pattern has a particular *ethos* (character type or style) that fits with its particular *telos*.

Observation A: There are several identifiable character types in Protestant worship in the United States: Revival, Sunday School, Aesthetic Worship, Pentecostal Worship, Prayer Meeting, and Catholic Liturgical Renewal. The more recent manifestations of these patterns are Seeker Worship, Creative Worship, Traditional Worship, Praise Worship, House Church, and Word and Table.

Principle 5: Liturgical units are portable blocks of liturgical action.

Observation B: Typically, patterns of *telos/ethos* become conflated in contemporary practice.

Principle 6: The *telos/ethos* of various patterns are not interchangeable with each other and tend to clash when combined.

This chapter will explore Principles 5 and 6 and Observation B in more detail and add a seventh principle to the list. It also considers ways to avoid—or at least manage—the clash of *ethos* that typically arises when orders of worship combine liturgical units from different liturgical patterns.

Principle 5: Liturgical units are portable blocks of liturgical action.

As stated in Principle 2, patterns have two levels: the macro-pattern and the liturgical unit. Macro-patterns are aimed at particular goals, and each macro-pattern consists of distinctive liturgical units that serve that particular goal. However, the liturgical units of a macro-pattern also have their own identifiable shape and content. For example, a didactic, responsive call to worship comes from the Sunday School/Creative Worship pattern, but it is also a recognizable unit even apart from the Sunday School pattern. A connected set of praise songs forms the opening of the Pentecostal/Praise and Worship model, but it has its own distinct shape and content. A Revival service ends with an altar call, and that, too, has a distinctive form. Because they are formulaic, liturgical units can float free from their original macro-pattern, becoming portable blocks of liturgical action. The various liturgical units of the six dominant patterns constitute a large repertoire of available liturgical materials on which worship planners can draw for a particular service. Absent some strong controlling authority (such as the *Book of Common Prayer* of the Episcopalians or the Order of Mass of the Catholic Church), worship leaders may use this repertoire rather freely. And this gives rise to:

Observation B: Typically, patterns of *telos/ethos* become conflated in contemporary practice.

A Worship Order from an Urban Congregation

Let's look at a few examples of orders of service that employ—or conflate or mash up—a variety of liturgical units from different patterns.[3] This first case is the first page of a Sunday worship bulletin from an established, upper-middle-class, Anglo-American congregation of about 350 people. This congregation meets in a building with stained-glass windows and a large choir loft and pipe organ located high above the chancel stage. The building itself suggests that an Aesthetic Worship pattern would fit well in the space.

---

3. My examples all come from actual worship bulletins or orders of service I have collected. I have edited the materials to ensure that the congregations themselves will remain anonymous, and also to ensure that no copyright laws will be violated.

ORDER OF SERVICE[4]

CHURCH BELLS [Bells were sounded as the congregation gathered.]

ENTRANCE AND PRAISE [This title **in bold** marked the first block of the service.]

GATHERING [At this point, the associate pastor stood in front of the chancel and asked the congregation to observe a period of silence. He also gave a rationale for the silence. The rationale lasted a little more than one minute, while the actual silence lasted about twenty seconds.]

OPENING VOLUNTARY [Classical piece played on an organ]

WELCOME AND ANNOUNCEMENTS [A robed minister made several announcements from the pulpit. This concluded with the minister stating, "As we begin worship, let us share the peace of Christ," during which the congregation spoke to each other spontaneously, "Good morning," "Hi, how are you?" "Good to see you," etc. Some moved around from their seats to greet people.]

GREETING

>Prayer is the way we communicate with God who loves and cares for us.
>
>**We believe prayer is important, and we are thankful that God hears and answers our prayers.**
>
>Christ taught us to pray because God wants to answer our prayers and provide what we need.
>
>**May we be more persistent in our prayer, so God can have more opportunity to do for us what he wants to do!**

*PROCESSIONAL HYMN "Praise to the Lord, the Almighty"

>The cross and light precede us from the world into the sanctuary and from the sanctuary into the world. The cross symbolizes the triumph of Christ. The light signifies God's presence with us.
>
>[Actual words in the bulletin explaining the lighting of the candles. As the congregation sang, acolytes and a crucifer (who carried a processional cross) came

---

4. The lines in ALL CAPS are taken as they appear in the bulletin. My more descriptive comments are in brackets. An asterisk indicates congregation standing.

in quickly followed by the choir, which proceeded up to choir loft. Acolytes lit candles on the altar table. The crucifer stood in front of the pulpit, then placed the cross in a stand as the procession concluded.]

OPENING PRAYER [Led by a minister from the pulpit.]

O God, our heavenly Father, who loves us more deeply than even our own Mother or Father may love us: Teach us to pray believing in your desire to supply our needs, that we might receive your grace and experience your abundant love. We pray through your Son, Jesus, who revealed your love to us. Amen.

CHORAL CALL TO WORSHIP [A short classical setting of *Jubilate Deo*, sung by the choir.]

As listed in the bulletin, the contents of the Entrance and Praise block that begins the service has seven liturgical units originating from at least three different patterns—Aesthetic, Sunday School/Creative Worship, and Catholic Liturgical Renewal:

CHURCH BELLS **Aesthetic Worship**

OPENING VOLUNTARY **Aesthetic Worship**

GATHERING [admonition to silence]   The request for silence is a nod to **Aesthetic Worship**, but the lengthy teaching about the importance of silence is **Sunday School Worship**.

WELCOME AND ANNOUNCEMENTS   **Sunday School Worship**, particularly the friendship ritual aspect of the unit. However, the phrase "Let us share the peace of Christ" comes from the **Catholic Liturgical Renewal** worship, though in that model it is located either before or after the eucharistic prayer. The location at the beginning of the service suggests that this particular unit actually comes from the **Creative Worship** model, but it also had the egalitarian tone of the **Prayer Meeting**.

GREETING   The term "Greeting" is from the **Catholic Liturgical Renewal**, but the liturgical unit here is a didactic call to worship from the **Creative Worship** pattern rather than a liturgical greeting.

*PROCESSIONAL HYMN　　　　　　　**Aesthetic Worship**
OPENING PRAYER　　　　　　　　The phrase "Opening Prayer" comes from the **Catholic Liturgical Renewal**, but the awkwardly worded content of this prayer suggests it comes from a **Creative Worship** resource.
CHORAL CALL TO WORSHIP　　　**Aesthetic Worship**

I suggest that this service is a conflation or mash-up of the beginnings of an Aesthetic service, a Creative Worship service, and a Catholic Liturgical Renewal service:

The Beginning of the Service of Worship Compared with Three Different Models

EXAMPLE UNDER ANALYSIS	AESTHETIC MODEL	SUNDAY SCHOOL MODEL	CATHOLIC LITURGICAL RENEWAL
CHURCH BELLS	CHURCH BELLS		
OPENING VOLUNTARY	OPENING VOLUNTARY		
GATHERING			GATHERING
Teaching		Teaching/Lesson	
Silence	SILENCE		
WELCOME AND ANNOUNCEMENTS	CHORAL CALL TO WORSHIP	WELCOME AND ANNOUNCEMENTS	*ENTRANCE HYMN
*Sharing the peace		Sharing the Peace	
*GREETING			*LITURGICAL GREETING
Responsive reading		RESPONSIVE READING	
*PROCESSIONAL HYMN	*PROCESSIONAL HYMN	*PRAISE SONG	
OPENING PRAYER	[INVOCATION]	OPENING PRAYER	*OPENING PRAYER
CHORAL CALL TO WORSHIP			

* represents liturgical units present in various patterns, though not necessarily in the typical order of the patterns.

The reason this service felt as if it were starting over several times is because it conflates the beginning of three different worship patterns. Consequently, there are two different calls to worship—though one is incorrectly labeled "greeting." There is both a gathering and a welcome. The Aesthetic model is dominant, with a Sunday School/Creative Worship model laid over it and with a couple of nods to the Catholic Liturgical Renewal pattern found in the denominational worship book.

A liturgical mash-up of this sort creates a sense of incoherence in the service because the *telos/ethos* of the Aesthetic pattern is different from the *telos/ethos* of the Sunday School/Creative Worship pattern. Thus:

Principle 6: The *telos/ethos* of various patterns are not interchangeable with each other and tend to clash when combined.

In this case, the service begins with the Gothic effects of the church bells and classical organ music played very well. Then, the tone shifts abruptly. A very brief moment of silence brings the congregation back into a more contemplative mood (proper to the Aesthetic model), followed by the business meeting-like set of announcements. The subsequent fellowship ritual of members heartily shaking hands is rather boisterous, but then the order returns to a didactic tone in the responsive reading. The formal procession during the hymn, which interrupts the fellowship rite, displays the pomp and circumstance of the Aesthetic model. That we sit for the opening prayer immediately lowers the emotional energy of the congregation, and we settle in still further as the choir sings a choral call to worship. This opening block of liturgical actions seesaws between the sophisticated sensibility of the Aesthetic model and the didactic, more unpolished sensibility of the Sunday School/Creative Worship model. It is as if the service is having an argument with itself and can't decide what it wants to be.

I refer to such clashes of *telos/ethos* as "liturgical whiplash." Specifically, liturgical whiplash occurs when an order of worship that has been following one pattern suddenly shifts to a liturgical unit taken from a different pattern. For, while liturgical units are portable, they tend to keep something of the DNA of their original pattern. This is the sort of clash that

Henry Ward Beecher describes in the epigraph to this chapter. Beecher recognizes that trying to re-energize a complacent congregational worship service by adding bits of what he calls "liturgy" (and what I refer to as Aesthetic model) is to combine essentially incompatible forms of worship. I expand Beecher's insight about incompatible types of worship to include all of the various models of worship available.

A Worship Order from a Rural Congregation

Now for a more complete example of a conflated order of worship that I found in a printed worship program from a rural, African American congregation (United Methodist) with an average attendance of 100, an order of worship that ends with an altar call:

*[Items in **bold** and CAPITALIZATIONS appeared as such in the bulletin. Annotations in brackets are based on information provided by the pastor.]*

> Gathering—Silent Meditation [Recorded music played as some members of the congregation knelt at the chancel rail for prayer.]
> *Bringing of the Light—Acolyte
> *Processional Song [The pastor and a worship leader led the choir in a procession.]
> **Praise Service** [The worship leader led three upbeat songs, including a gospel chorus.]
> *Opening Prayer [An extemporaneous prayer led by the pastor]
> ***Call to Worship** [Led by the worship leader]
> Leader: Wait for the Lord, in whom we hope.
> **People: Worship the God of steadfast love.**
> Leader: Listen for Christ, who calls us here.
> **People: Open your hearts for the Spirit of God.**
> **Passing of the Peace (and greet visitors)** [Worship leader]
> **Parish Notices and Congregational Concerns** [Worship leader]
> *Hymn of Praise [Worship leader]
> *Affirmation of Faith—"The Apostles' Creed" [Worship leader]
> *Gloria Patri

Chapter Nine

OUR WORSHIP WITH TITHES AND OFFERING

Offering Selection—The Choir
*Offering Response [Sung by choir and congregation]
Scripture Lessons [Read by the pastor]
    Leader: This is the word of God for the people of God.
    People: Thanks be to God.
Selections—The Choir [One prepared anthem sung by choir]
The Sermon [The pastor]
Invitation to Altar Prayer and Christian Discipleship [The pastor]
*Invitational Hymn—The Choir [No one came forward during this hymn.]
*Closing Selection—The Choir
*Recessional [Acolytes extinguished the altar candles.]
*Benediction [The Minister offered this at the entry door, behind the congregation.]

Applying the method of analysis, I find distinctive liturgical units from at least four different patterns.

Aesthetic Worship units:	**Sunday School/Creative Worship units:**
Formal procession of the ministers and choir	Bringing in of the light
Parish notices	Call to worship
Hymn of praise	Passing of the peace/visitor greeting
Affirmation of faith followed by the Gloria Patri	
The offering sequence of units	
The scripture reading with congregational response	
Choir selection before the sermon	
Recessional	
Benediction	
Pentecostal Worship units:	**Revival units:**
Gathering with altar prayer	Invitation after sermon
Praise service	Invitational hymn
Extemporary opening prayer (at the conclusion of the praise service)	
Invitation to altar prayer after sermon	

218

As in the previous example, most conflation occurs in the opening sequence of liturgical units, and here is where I expect the congregation experiences the most liturgical whiplash. The Pentecostal-style altar prayer during the gathering is interrupted by a formal procession of choir and ministers. But the service returns to a Pentecostal *ethos* with the praise service and concluding extempore prayer. The most jarring whiplash (confirmed by the pastor himself!) takes place with the awkward transition from the vigorous extempore prayer led by the pastor to the more restrained responsive call to worship led by the worship leader. There is also a noticeable redundancy with the call to worship, since the congregation has quite obviously already been rather actively engaged in worship for a good fifteen minutes. Such redundancies are indications of a conflation of patterns. In this example, we find beginning units of the Aesthetic, Pentecostal, and Sunday School models jumbled together.

The passing of the peace (Sunday School *ethos*) re-energizes the congregation, but then the more formal parish notices prompts them to settle back down again, and their energy slumps. The hymn of praise that follows is much more subdued than the songs of the opening praise set. Indeed, the redundancy of placing another praise song here shows the conflation of the Aesthetic model with the Pentecostal model. Following the hymn of praise, the order has the Apostles' Creed followed by the *Gloria Patri*.[5]

From my survey of countless orders of worship, I have noticed that most obvious examples of conflation occur in the beginning sequence of a service. But a second "soft spot" for conflation is the concluding sequence, and indeed this particular worship service also showed noticeable conflation in the concluding liturgical units. Specifically, there is the mixing of concluding units from the Revival model (invitation) and Pentecostal

---

5. While historically the *Gloria Patri* would be located after a psalm or other scripture reading, *The Methodist Hymnal* of 1935, Order of Worship II put the *Gloria Patri* after the Apostles' Creed, and that is probably the source for this combination of units. This sequence continues to show up in United Methodist orders of worship, at least in the southeastern United States. Over the last fifteen years, I have surveyed numerous United Methodist worship bulletins provided by seminary students and pastors in my courses on public worship. Congregations that still employ the Aesthetic pattern tend to follow the sequence of Apostles' Creed/*Gloria Patri*, though none of the pastors or students had an idea why they followed this sequence! This includes at least one Korean United Methodist church located in a suburb of Atlanta, Georgia.

model (altar prayer) with the more formal recessional and benediction of the Aesthetic pattern.

Recall that the goal of the Revival model is conversion, and it employs emotional effects to elicit a strong response, especially at the end of the service with the altar call. Likewise, the Pentecostal form of the altar call tends to be rather intense in *ethos*. However, if a worship planner places an emotional altar call at the end of an artful and dignified Aesthetic service, it simply does not work. The congregation might recognize the altar call as an act of worship, but it is highly unlikely that anyone will spontaneously come forward. The congregation experiences a full-out Revival or Pentecostal altar call as a clash of style.

Yet Aesthetic/Traditional services often do end with a sort of altar call by calling it The Invitation of Christian Discipleship. Typically, congregations use this invitation to introduce newcomers seeking membership to the congregation. But rarely is this spontaneous. Even though a Revival altar call does not fit the Aesthetic model, Protestant congregations still hang on to a version of it and use it for a very different purpose. I account for this tendency to preserve liturgical units with the following principle we now add to our list:

Principle 7: Orders tend to conserve liturgical units that have become regular parts of public worship.

Liturgy as type of ritual practice is resistant to change and tends to conserve liturgical patterns and liturgical units.[6] This conservative principle means that it is generally easier to add something than to remove a liturgical unit or alter a pattern that is already in place. Orders of worship will grow as different pastors, choir directors, and worship planners who draw on the liturgical repertoire of American congregations add children's sermons, praise choruses, passing the peace, invitation to discipleship, or other liturgical units. But when a particular liturgical unit has been practiced for a long time, a congregation will likely accept it as a standard

---

6. According to the anthropologist Roy Rappaport, a defining characteristic of ritual is that it is more or less invariant. Rappaport says "more or less" because absolute invariability is neither desirable nor even possible. *Ritual and the Making of Humanity* (Cambridge, UK: Cambridge University Press, 1999), 36–37.

and expected part of their worship, "the way we've always done it." In many Protestant congregations the order of worship has become an attic in which more and more liturgical units are stored, both old and new.

If orders of worship are like attics, there are limits to how many liturgical units an attic can hold. Often the more recently added liturgical units are kept, while older liturgical units that were compatible with an older pattern of the congregation are removed. Yet even some older units will remain as a sort of relic of the past—sometimes meaningful, sometimes simply there. Returning to our second example, I asked the pastor of that church why he kept that awkward call to worship, even though the congregation did not seem to participate in this liturgical unit with enthusiasm. He responded: "You have to have a call to worship, don't you?" Actually no. For while a scripted call to worship is typical of Aesthetic, Sunday School, and Creative Worship orders, it is not part of the Revival or Pentecostal patterns. So a service does not have to have a call to worship if it clashes with the dominant model of the service. In this case, the order was preserving a unit that no longer served its purpose.

A Worship Order from a Suburban Congregation

Next up for our examination is an order of service from a suburban, predominantly white congregation (United Methodist) with a worship attendance of approximately 250.

```
PRELUDE            "Shine, Jesus, Shine"      Praise Team
WELCOME AND ANNOUNCEMENTS [Led by the worship
     leader]
*PASSING OF THE PEACE
*CALL TO WORSHIP   "This Is the Day"  [Call and response
     praise song led by the choir]
*OPENING PRAYER    [Led by worship leader]
*HYMN OF PRAISE    "I Love to Tell the Story"
*APOSTLES' CREED
*GLORIA PATRI
```

> CHILDREN'S MOMENT [Led by a layperson]
>   LITURGICAL DANCE [An adolescent dances to a recorded song.]
> PRAYERS FOR [sic] THE PEOPLE [The pastor offers a pastoral prayer.]
> THE LORD'S PRAYER
> PRAYER RESPONSE
> OFFERTORY [Organist plays a hymn arrangement, while ushers pass plates.]
> *DOXOLOGY
> ANTHEM   Chancel Choir
> SCRIPTURE READING [One lesson read by pastor/preacher]
> MESSAGE [Pastor/preacher]
> HOLY COMMUNION [Using the Invitation, Confession/pardon, and Great Thanksgiving of "A Service of Word and Table II" from the *United Methodist Hymnal*. The congregation comes forward to commune by intinction.]
> *SONG OF RESPONSE [Congregation sings hymn.]
> *BENEDICTION
> POSTLUDE [Organist plays classical piece.]

Once again we find units from several different worship patterns here. The service begins with a single rousing praise song, led by a praise band, which is a liturgical unit from the Seeker Service model, particularly when it is followed by a welcome by a worship leader.

The first moment of whiplash occurs with the unit announcements, which shifts the emotional energy of the service from praise and communal interaction to the emotional feeling of a business meeting.

Energy picks up again with the passing of the peace, a fellowship ritual during which worshipers move around the pews to say hello to each other. This boisterous liturgical unit comes to an end when the choir begins a call and response chorus, "This Is the Day," that was popular among youth groups in the late 1960s and 1970s. These liturgical units fit quite well with the *ethos* of a Sunday School assembly.

After the chorus comes the hymn of praise, and here the service more or less begins again, this time as an Aesthetic model service. The Apostles' Creed and *Gloria Patri* follow next, also in the Aesthetic model. The children's moment and the liturgical dance shift back to the Sunday School/ Creative Worship model. The next several units seem to be from the Aesthetic model, until we arrive at the "message." This use of that term—rather than "sermon"—for preaching is a nod to the Revival/Seeker Service model of worship, though in this particular case the "message" was not particularly evangelical or seeker-friendly.

Following the message comes a service of Holy Communion, and the congregation uses most of "A Service of Word and Table II" from the *United Methodist Hymnal* but skips The Peace, Offering, and Lord's Prayer, since those have already taken place earlier in the service. Finally, there is the concluding benediction.

Since the service concludes with Holy Communion, it might seem that the overall structure of this service is "Word and Table." However, a comparison of this order with the more complete order found in "A Service of Word and Table I" (*United Methodist Hymnal*) shows a good bit of rearranging of liturgical units.

Chapter Nine

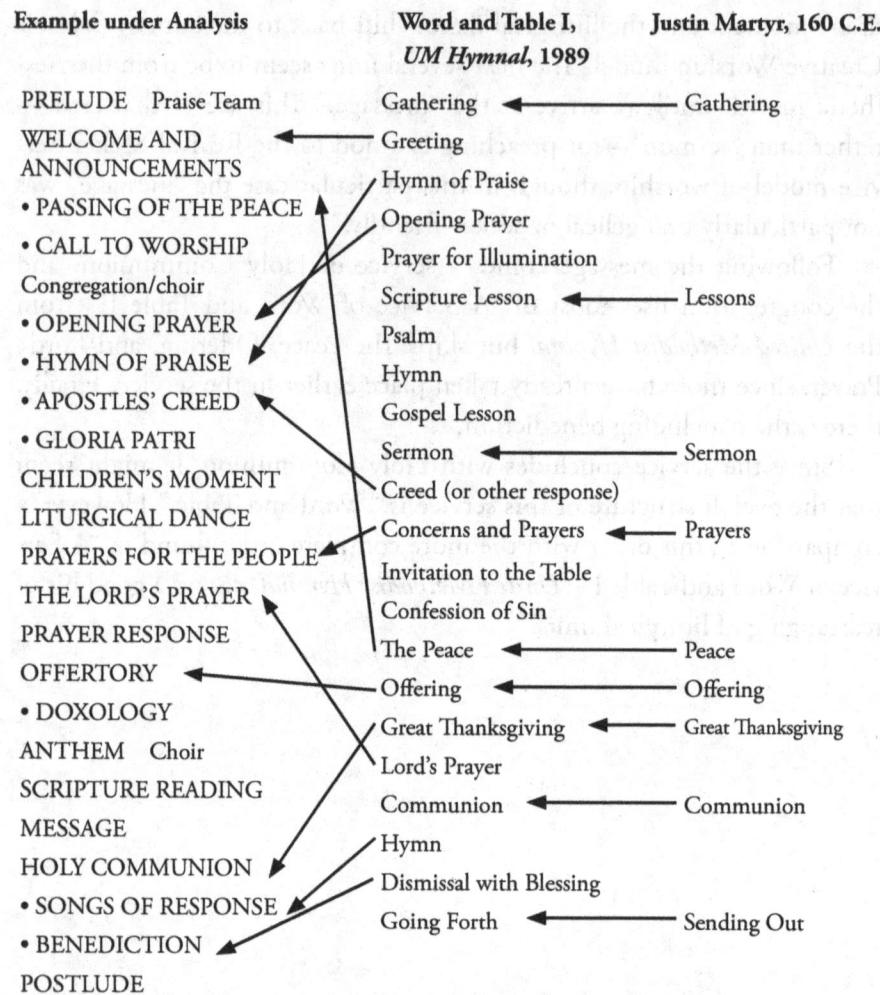

The United Methodist Word and Table service lines up with the classic structure of Word and Table in the early church as described by Justin Martyr, though it fills it out by adding several elements (hymns, creed, confession, etc.) and expanding others (more scripture readings, psalm, prayers, Lord's Prayer at the end of the Great Thanksgiving). Even though many liturgical units of the Word and Table order are found in the service we are analyzing, they have been put into a quite different order. How might we account for this rearrangement?

Conflated Worship

Let's compare this order of service with the "Order of Worship II" from *The Methodist Hymnal* of 1935, a hymnal used by The Methodist Episcopal Church, South, the denomination that preceded *The United Methodist Church*.

Example under Analysis	*The Methodist Hymnal*, 1935 Order of Worship II
	Let the People Kneel or Bow in Silent Prayer upon Entering the Sanctuary
PRELUDE Praise Team ←———————	The Prelude
WELCOME AND ANNOUNCEMENTS	
* PASSING OF THE PEACE	
*CALL TO WORSHIP ←———————	The Call to Worship
[Sung by congregation]	Hymn
*OPENING PRAYER ←———————	The Invocation
*HYMN OF PRAISE ←———————	The Anthem; or Chant
	Responsive Reading
*APOSTLES' CREED ←———————	The Apostles' Creed
*GLORIA PATRI ←———————	The Gloria Patri
CHILDREN'S MOMENT	Lesson from the Holy Scriptures
LITURGICAL DANCE	
PRAYERS OF THE PEOPLE ←———————	The Pastoral Prayer
THE LORD'S PRAYER	The Offering
OFFERTORY ⎤	The Offertory
*DOXOLOGY ⎦←———————	The Presentation of Offerings
ANTHEM Choir ←———————	Hymn
SCRIPTURE READING	
MESSAGE ←———————	The Sermon
HOLY COMMUNION	Prayer
	The Invitation to Christian Discipleship
*SONG OF RESPONSE ←———————	Hymn or Doxology
*BENEDICTION ←———————	Silent Prayer or Benediction
POSTLUDE ←———————	The Postlude

Notice how many of the elements in the order we are analyzing correspond to this Aesthetic model order from 1935! The liturgical unit that has been reordered is the reading of scripture, which has been placed before the sermon. And Holy Communion has been added in the slots previously occupied by the prayer and the invitation to Christian discipleship. Despite the addition of Holy Communion, the fundamental pattern of this service is the Aesthetic model as found in *The Methodist Hymnal* of 1935.

Conflated Orders and the Problem of Coherence

So far, we have examined orders of worship that import diverse liturgical units into an overarching Aesthetic/Traditional model. But the conflation of incompatible liturgical units also occurs within other models. One late December, I attended a Seeker Service with a large, urban congregation that also had a large, very traditional mainline Protestant service at another venue on its campus. The service began as a light came up on an artificial snow-filled stage set that looked very much like a televised Christmas variety show. The music took off with a rousing rendition of "Jingle Bell Rock," led by a highly polished stage band. A worship leader took the stage to give a very brief welcome, which was followed by a Christmas carol, which the band played in upbeat tempo as the congregation sang along. The band stopped abruptly when a worship leader returned to the stage. She announced that we were in the season of Advent and invited a family up on the stage to light the Advent wreath that I only then noticed was located stage right. The parents with their three children stood around the wreath, holding crumpled pieces of paper. The mother read a short piece about the "Shepherd's Candle," while the oldest child lit the third candle. The father awkwardly read a prayer, said an amen, then mumbled "O come, O come, Emmanuel." The parents guided their children offstage as the worship leader thanked them and commented to the audience, "It's good to be reminded about Advent." A soloist attempted to bring the service back into the flow of the Seeker service model with a Christmas-themed song by a well-known contemporary Christian artist, but the energy in the room had long since dissipated. The Advent wreath devotional, a liturgical unit from the Sunday School model, caused so much liturgical whiplash that the service could barely recover.

Awkward conflations of patterns show up in the worship of congregations across the denominational spectrum, and it is almost always because liturgical units have been imported from worship models with a different *telos* and *ethos*—much as the conflicting recommendations for change in the chapter's opening vignette illustrated. In the case above, the unpolished Sunday School exercise of lighting the Advent candle clashed with the theatricality of the Seeker model. Learning about Advent through a domestic ritual may serve the *telos* of the Sunday School, which aims to build Christian character. But it does not serve well the *telos* of the Seeker model, which aims to entice the unchurched to take a second look at Christianity.

Sometimes the clash is less obvious. Consider the use of a projected "countdown clock." The countdown clock originated in sporting events and New Year's Eve celebrations and then was adapted to arena rock concerts. Then some Seeker churches adopted the practice as a theatrical way to build anticipation for the service. Some large Pentecostal churches have also recently adopted the countdown clock to begin worship. However, a hard-start beginning evoked by a countdown clock inevitably subverts the gradual soft start of a Pentecostal model service with worshipers joining in prayer or song as the congregation gradually convenes.

Or consider this: an Episcopal congregation near my home has started printing the collects in a worship bulletin for the congregation to recite along with the priest as a way to engage the congregation in the prayers. Unison reading of printed prayers is a didactic practice of Sunday School worship. However, in the implicit Catholic model of the *Book of Common Prayer*, congregational participation comes through hearing the prayer and giving affirmation with the congregation saying amen as a call and response. Reading in unison turns this aural participation into a didactic exercise. And at least one member of that congregation has shared with me that she finds the new practice off-putting.[7]

Yet conflation of liturgical units and even worship models does not necessarily result in incoherence of order. Indeed, the history of Christian liturgy is filled with examples of borrowing of liturgical units or ritual orders. We see this in the importation of prayers and liturgical actions from the Gallican liturgical books into the Roman Rite in the early Middle Ages or, more recently, the adoption of Syrian liturgical patterns by Protestants in the twentieth century. My Methodist students are usually surprised to discover that the Great Thanksgiving of the services of Word and Table in *The United Methodist Hymnal* and *Book of Worship* follows the structure of the eucharistic prayer in the Eastern Orthodox *Liturgy of St. John Chrysostom* rather than the Western order of the Roman Rite.

Moreover, while for the sake of clarity I have presented the six patterns of *telos/ethos* as distinct models, in actual use the models are very porous. For example, the Revival and Pentecostal pattern both have roots in the frontier camp meeting, and they have a similar structure. But they have a somewhat different set of liturgical units. The Aesthetic pattern developed in part as a refinement of the exercises of the Sunday School pattern, and this shows up in the way the Aesthetic model sometimes strings together its liturgical units and also in the way Sunday School units continue to show up in the Aesthetic/Traditional order of worship. Sunday Schools and Revivals share a reliance on novelty. And small, particularly rural, Protestant congregations gravitate toward the intimacy of the Prayer Meeting because they are already small groups, even when they ostensibly engage Aesthetic, Sunday School, or Revival liturgical units. Aesthetic and Catholic Liturgical Renewal patterns tend toward formality of performance. Furthermore, having an order of service with diverse liturgical units does not necessarily indicate that a congregation will experience the service as incoherent. Any order practiced long enough will be

---

7. It may be surprising to those outside the tradition that the prayer book tradition of Episcopalians and Anglicans requires almost no congregation unison reading of prayers. It does call for unison saying of some prayers, such as the Lord's Prayer or the confession of sin. But these standard prayers along with most congregation responses are quickly learned by regular repetition.

the expected pattern of a congregation and therefore resistant to change. The conflated order will become the default mode of the congregation—the way worship happens out of habit.

Compatibility among the Six Models

My observations, along with the anecdotal evidence I have collected from students, pastors, and worship leaders, suggest that a conflated order of service will have coherence to the degree that it has a single overarching pattern of *telos/ethos*. Such an order will likely exhibit a strong character, even though it may have some minor character flaws. The many books by Robert Webber on "ancient-future" and "blended worship," for example, argue explicitly for the incorporation of the best of contemporary worship practices into a basic order grounded in the Word and Table pattern going back to the early church.[8]

Additional characteristics of the models suggest why some conflations seem to work, or at least are inconsequential to the overall coherence, while other combinations cause liturgical whiplash.

The experience of liturgical flow is dominant in some orders. Pentecostal/Praise worship facilitates the experience of flow through music and immersive experiences of prayer, while Catholic Liturgical Renewal worship achieves flow through participation in a fixed liturgy. At the other extreme, Sunday School and Creative Worship models tend to be episodic, and they give less attention to flow as to an immersive experience. Flow, however, is a fragile psychological state. Combining a high-flow Pentecostal praise set with a responsive, written call to worship will break the flow of the song set. In such a mash-up, the Sunday School model will dominate. But a written call to worship, even if it did not employ sophisticated language, probably would not overwhelm an Aesthetic/Traditional order because Aesthetic worship is also episodic and less dependent on an extended experience of flow.

---

8. See, for example, Robert E. Webber, *Ancient-Future Worship: Proclaiming and Enacting God's Narrative* (Grand Rapids, MI: Baker, 2008); and *Planning Blended Worship: The Creative Mixture of Old and New* (Nashville, TN: Abingdon Press, 1998). In this last book, Webber offers many concrete suggestions for how to do this in ways that facilitate liturgical flow.

The printed-text liturgical units of the Sunday School/Creative Worship and Aesthetic/Traditional patterns tend to subvert the theatricality of the Revival/Seeker pattern, the interpersonal intimacy of the Prayer Meeting/House Church pattern, and the exuberance of the Pentecost/Praise and Worship pattern. And when the prayers and rituals of the Catholic Liturgical Renewal pattern are used as ad hoc Sunday School or Aesthetic liturgical units, they become mere worship resources rather than a participation in the universal worship of the saints and angels.

Sincerity (or at least the appearance of sincerity) is extremely important for the Revival, Pentecostal, and Prayer Meeting models. Sincerity is less important for Sunday School, Aesthetic, and Catholic Liturgical Renewal models.[9] The theatricality of Revival and Seeker worship requires excellence in performance, as does the visual and aural beauty of Aesthetic pattern services. But the Prayer Meeting is less concerned with formal excellence, and Sunday School/Creative Worship often revels in the awkward attempts of unpolished worship leaders. In fact, for some people polished performance mars the perception of sincerity. "That's just a performance" essentially means "That was not sincere."[10]

Finally, the Pentecostal and the Catholic Liturgical Renewal patterns share a profound recognition of worship as participation in the divine life through the power of the Holy Spirit. For these two patterns, worship is not primarily an instrumental means to something else, be it the conversion of sinners, religious education, spiritual maturity, or Christian fellowship, though worship may achieve all of these objectives as a byproduct. Nor is worship something constructed as an expression of human commitment and aspiration. Rather, to worship God is to partake in the reality of God. In the Catholic model, the bread and wine do not merely remind the believer about Jesus: they really are the body and blood of the Lord offered to all who commune. In the Pentecostal tradition, speaking in tongues really is praying in the language of angels. And the reality of

---

9. On the tension between sincerity and ritual, see Adam B. Seligman, Robert P. Weller, Michael J. Puett, and Bennett Simon, *Ritual and Its Consequences: An Essay on the Limits of Sincerity* (New York, NY: Oxford University Press, 2006).

10. Matthew Lawrence Pierce, "Redeeming the Performance: The Question of Liturgical Audience," *Liturgy*, vol. 28, no. 1 (2013): 54.

such worship cannot be simulated as an exercise. I think this is why we see the conflation of Pentecostal and Catholic models of worship in Africa and Asia, and in the United States in the Catholic Pentecostal movement.

Worshiping Well

We have, then, six dominant models of *telos/ethos* that can be combined in countless ways. The method I have been developing accounts for the rich diversity of Protestant worship in the United States, and the method also suggests how to diagnose character flaws in worship arising from the conflation of incompatible models. But coherence in the character of worship is not enough. We also want worship to be compelling. And here I will add one item to the list of methodological principles:

Observation C: Almost anything done well will be more compelling than almost anything done poorly.

It is not enough to study worship, understand worship, and plan worship. Good worship leaders will also pay attention to the conduct of worship. If worship is not well led, it is unlikely that the congregation will be actively engaged. That said, there is a second point we must add to this observation:

Each model generates its own standard of excellence.

Returning to the game metaphor I employed in chapter 1, the criteria for excellent plays will depend on the specific rules and goals of a particular game. A "good pitch" in baseball is radically different from a "good pitch" in football, though both involve throwing a ball for another player to catch. Leading a Revival well is not the same as leading a Prayer Meeting well because each of these models has a distinctive goal and character.

In conflated orders of worship, the criteria of excellence tend to become muddled. We see this when a fine sermon preached at the early traditional service falls flat at the contemporary service. And this is why I suggest that a conflated service needs a single overarching model of *telos/ethos*. Absent an overarching model, leaders will have difficulty establishing the standard of excellence needed to understand how to lead the service well. One way to know if a particular liturgical unit belongs in an order of service is to ask this simple question: Can this act of worship be done well in this order of worship? If the answer to this question is not a clear *yes*, that liturgical unit probably doesn't belong. My anecdote about the Advent wreath devotion at the Seeker Service is a case in point.

Finally, good worship must be compelling, whatever pattern of worship the congregation follows. As I have observed, almost anything done well will be more compelling than something done poorly. This means that competent performance of liturgical leadership is a necessary skill. And competent performance will corelate to the pattern of *telos/ethos* being performed.

And so, we now arrive at a complete list of the Principles of Method for analyzing liturgical order for coherence of goal, character, and liturgical flow.

Principles of Method, Complete

Principle 1: All worship follows patterns.

Principle 2: The patterns of worship function at two levels: the liturgical unit and the macro-pattern.

Principle 3: A macro-pattern of worship has a *telos* (goal) it aims to achieve.

Principle 4: Each macro-pattern has a particular *ethos* (character or style) that fits with its particular *telos* or goal.

Observation A: There are several identifiable character types in Protestant worship in the United States: Revival, Sunday School, Aesthetic Worship, Pentecostal Worship, Prayer Meeting, and Catholic Liturgical Renewal. The more recent manifestations of these patterns are Seeker Worship, Creative Worship, Traditional Worship, Praise Worship, House Church, and Word and Table.

Principle 5: Liturgical units are portable blocks of liturgical action.

Observation B: Typically, patterns of *telos/ethos* become conflated in contemporary practice.

Principle 6: The *telos/ethos* of various patterns are not interchangeable with each other and tend to clash when combined.

Principle 7: Orders tend to conserve liturgical units that have become regular parts of public worship.

Observation C: Almost anything done well will be more compelling than almost anything done poorly. Each model generates its own standard of excellence.

Patterns in Protestant Worship

Revival	Sunday School	Aesthetic	Pentecostal	Prayer Meeting	Catholic Liturgical Renewal
Preliminaries Greetings Testimonies Music Message Altar Call	Opening exercises Devotional reading Theme of the day Program Announcements Dismissal	Anglican prayer book Introit, collect, etc. Lessons Offertory Sermon Classical music/hymns	Revival pattern with "praise worship" for preliminaries. Speaking in tongues "Settling" down before "message" Altar call open for various responses	Singing Scripture reading Personal testimony Extemporaneous prayer Confession of sin Sharing of personal concerns Closing hymn	Gathering/greeting Scripture readings Sermon Intercession Offertory Thanksgiving Communion Dismissal
Goal: Conversion of the individual	**Goal:** Christian character	**Goal:** Culturally sophisticated worship	**Goal:** Spiritual union	**Goal:** Interpersonal encounter	**Goal:** Participation in the universal body of Christ
Character: Novelty Audience-driven Emotional effects Professionalism	**Character:** Didactic Novelty and tradition Worship as exercise Control by leader	**Character:** European aesthetic Prayer book language Ostentatious	**Character:** Ecstatic enthusiasm Genuine praise Embodied participation Patterns by heart	**Character:** Egalitarian Personal sharing Emotional intimacy	**Character:** Catholic orientation Based in ancient history Patterns by heart

Conflated Worship

Similar to: Theater	Similar to: Gymnasium	Similar to: Classical concert	Similar to: Rock concert	Similar to: Support group	Similar to: Military training
Seeker Service	Creative Worship	Traditional Worship	Praise and Worship	House Church	Word and Table
Preliminaries Music Greetings Congregational song Performed song Skits/multimedia Message [response open]	No set pattern Often very "print" oriented Requires reading skill Exclamation points! Printed directions!	Choral introit Call to worship Responsive reading Lesson(s) Anthem Prayer Offertory Sermon Benediction	Much like Seeker pattern but with more congregational participation, use of gestures (raising hands, etc.) Song set at beginning Intense prayer in congregation	Sharing of joys and concerns Personal prayer Close-knit fellowship Conversational	Gathering Prayers/praise Lessons Sermon Intercession/response Offertory Great Thanksgiving Communion Dismissal

CHAPTER TEN

Worship Patterns Online

The medium, or process, of our time—electric technology—is reshaping and restructuring patterns of social interdependence and every aspect of our personal life. It is forcing us to reconsider and reevaluate practically every thought, every action, and every institution formerly taken for granted. Everything is changing—you, your family, your neighborhood, your education, your job, your government, your relation to "the others." And they're changing dramatically.

—Marshall McLuhan, 1967[1]

Dave Coverly/Speedbump.com[2]

---

1. Marshall McLuhan, Jerome Agel, and Quentin Fiore, *The Medium Is the Massage: An Inventory of Effects* (Corte Madera, CA: Gingko Press, 2001, original pub. 1967), 8. N.B. The title of this book has the word "Massage" even though McLuhan is associated with the catchphrase, "The medium is the message."

2. Reprinted with permission of Dave Coverly/speedbump.com.

Chapter Ten

In March 2020, as I was anticipating receiving the edited copy of the manuscript for this book from Abingdon Press, the coronavirus pandemic was beginning to spread in the United States. State governments issued "stay-at-home" orders, and congregations scrambled to figure out how to "do church" without meeting in person. For more than a decade, some groups of Christians have attempted to establish various types of fully "online churches." These range from congregations in the virtual world of *Second Life*, in which persons relate to each other through personal "avatars" in simulated environments,[3] to more conventionally organized congregations in which people engage with each other through synchronous worship and prayer activities. Many more conventional congregations had been using various forms of online media for years, including livestreaming worship services and posting video recordings of some parts of these services on YouTube or other media sites. But the majority of congregations used online media only as a supplement to their in-person worship and fellowship activities. In a matter of days in March as the states began issuing stay-at-home orders, the vast majority of Christian congregations in the United States became fully "online churches" in a massive social experiment born of necessity.

Initial reports from congregational leaders suggest that more people are viewing livestreams of their services or watching posted video than had attended in-person services. Moreover, some of my pastoral contacts say that many former or inactive members are responding to these digital worship offerings. It is much too soon to know if this will continue for the long run. Nevertheless, anecdotal evidence suggests that given so much initial success, many congregational leaders plan to continue to offer digital forms of worship for their congregations, even after their congregations begin returning to in-person worship.

Recall that at the end of the previous chapter, I rounded out the discussion with the following:

---

3. For a list detailing religious communities in Second Life, see https://secondlife.com/destinations/belief (accessed June 15, 2020).

Observation C: Almost anything done well will be more compelling than almost anything done poorly. Each model of worship generates its own standard of excellence.

This also applies to various forms of online media, requiring a further observation:

Observation D: The medium in which worship is offered generates its own standard of excellence. The standard of excellence of the medium will determine to a large degree its compatibility with a particular model of worship.[4]

Worship and Broadcast Media

The broadcasting of religious programming goes back to the earliest days of radio in the 1920s. Tona Hangen's account of religious broadcasting from its origin until the 1960s describes how mainline Protestants, Catholics, Fundamentalists, and Pentecostals all jockeyed for a place in this new media landscape. While the mainliners and Catholics had an early edge in the use of radio, by the post–World War I era, the Fundamentalists and Pentecostals were monopolizing the airwaves. There is a certain irony that the groups most associated with a rejection of modern science embraced radio with enthusiasm. That Fundamentalist preachers, Evangelical revivalists, and Pentecostal faith healers found adherents through the radio would have been unimaginable only fifty years earlier.[5]

---

4. The Rev. Dr. David Gambrell, associate for worship in the Office of Theology and Worship of the Presbyterian Church (USA), heard a presentation I gave on my models of worship typology. As I was finishing this chapter, he sent me an email with this comment on the ways churches are engaging online media during the pandemic: "I was in an online staff meeting this morning thinking about the various approaches people are using for digital worship, and it occurred to me that your schema probably has some bearing on the platforms people choose: YouTube for aesthetic value, Zoom for small group intimacy, Facebook/social media for evangelism" (June 17, 2020, used by permission).

5. Tona J. Hangen, *Redeeming the Dial: Radio, Religion, and Popular Culture in America* (Chapel Hill: University of North Carolina Press, 2002).

Chapter Ten

One reason Fundamentalists and Pentecostals found success through the radio is that their styles of worship and preaching were especially compatible with a medium that keeps worshippers' attention through the use of entertaining music and dramatic suspense. In short, the standards for an engaging radio program were the standards for a good religious radio program, and the models of worship most compatible with those standards of excellence found a hospitable place. As Hangen notes:

> The drama embedded in revivalism—the enacting of a conversion or reliving of one's own past conversion—became another kind of American entertainment form. With the same reassuring regularity with which a radio drama detective solved the crime, a radio serial hero saved the day, or a radio game show contestant won a cache of valuable prizes, all within the tidy and familiar confines of a time slot to which listeners could "tune in next time," radio revivalism unfailingly brought its listeners around to the same conclusion in every program.[6]

I noted in previous chapters that the Pentecostal model shares with the Revival model a disdain for any tradition that does not immediately engage a congregation, and that both of these models gravitate to emotionally charged preaching. Pentecostal worship, as I described it, is even more visceral and embodied than Revival preaching, and yet Pentecostal radio preachers and faith healers quickly found a way to make radio worship feel nearly as embodied as worship with a physical congregation. The phrase "Put your hand on the radio" has become a satirical cliché among modern critics of Pentecostalism. Yet radio faith healers saw this as a tangible "point of contact" with the preacher, and indeed, by putting one's hand on a radio, a person could feel the voice of the preacher through the vibrations of the loudspeaker.[7] In this way, radio was made to be compatible with the embodied character of Pentecostal worship.

The rise of television broadcasting followed a similar trajectory. Some wealthy, large, mainline churches began to televise their worship services,

---

6. Hangen, *Redeeming the Dial*, 152.

7. Anderson Blanton, *Hittin' the Prayer Bones* (Chapel Hill: University of North Carolina Press, 2015), 182.

though at first this entailed little more than installing one or two fixed video cameras to capture the worship service as it took place. Just as Fundamentalist, Evangelical, and Pentecostal preachers have dominated religious radio, so also have they dominated the television, and they did this by adapting their televised worship to the new visual form of entertainment. Whereas mainliners felt constrained by the 57½-minute format of the one-hour slots offered by mainstream television stations, the Evangelicals and Pentecostals overcame this obstacle by establishing their own television networks. Moreover, mainline religious broadcasts were dull by comparison with the more dramatic and overtly entertaining programs produced on these more recent Christian networks. As with radio, the standards for a good, entertaining television program were the same standards of excellence for a successful religious television program, and forms of worship with a *telos* and *ethos* most compatible with those standards have been more successful.

The influence has also flowed in the other direction. For example, back in the 1960s, the small, rural Methodist congregation of my childhood put together a very somber Christmas pageant every year. By the time I had become a youth pastor in the 1980s, such programs had given way to comedy, even as they tried to maintain a serious core of gospel message, along the lines of the popular children's novel, *The Best Christmas Pageant Ever*.[8] Religious pageants and other Sunday school skits became "sitcoms." Preachers, too, began to adapt church announcements and even sermons to some of the conventions of the opening monologue of a late-night TV show.

Underneath all of this is the story of the Revival and Charles Finney's new approach to religion, which we examined in chapter 3. Recall that, for Finney, the cardinal sin of ineffective religion was boredom! As I noted in that chapter, if one accepts that Christianity is essentially a message detached from any traditional practice, it is difficult to refute his embrace of novelty to attract and keep attention.

---

8. Barbara Robinson, *The Best Christmas Pageant Ever* (San Francisco, CA: Harper & Row, 1971).

Chapter Ten

Worship Patterns and Internet-Based Media

During the pandemic of 2020, as churches began to move all of their services and fellowship activities online, they quickly began to learn new standards for engaging productively with their congregations. Internet-based media share some of the same bias toward entertainment and drama to attract and keep attention. (Readers may think of the clickbait advertising on the web that entices viewers to click through a long chain of photos and text—and ads!—in order to find out what happened at the end of the story.)

Even so, there are also significant differences that affect how churches are engaging online media. First of all, in recent years the internet has become more accessible and its production less expensive than radio or television. Certainly, some people still do not have access to computers or internet resources, and older folks may not have the inclination or ability to engage fully with online church. Yet the internet is becoming increasingly democratic; almost anyone with a smartphone camera can produce a video recording or join in a virtual meeting.

Second, because internet media have the capacity for synchronous interaction among groups, this creates new possibilities. For example, Pentecostal preachers have conducted faith healings over radio or television, and for Pentecostals this is very much a sacramental practice, broadly understood. Mainline Protestant congregations, on the other hand, have had little interest in conducting their sacramental rites through broadcast media. In recent years, some Protestant congregations began experimenting with conducting Holy Communion through the internet, though most mainline Protestant traditions resisted online Communion. The United Methodist Council of Bishops, to cite one example, pronounced an official moratorium on the practice in 2013. Nevertheless, during the pandemic of 2020, many United Methodist bishops urged their congregations to break the moratorium, with a promise to restore it once the pandemic had been contained—though not without controversy among some pastors who continue to support the moratorium. Likewise, the Presbyterian Church (USA) endorsed the practice of online Communion during the pandemic, though similarly not without controversy. The interactive capacity of computer media has made such a dramatic shift imaginable and therefore possible during an extended time when congregations were not allowed to meet in person.

Internet media come in three broad forms: livestream, posted video (Facebook, YouTube, Vimeo), and real-time interactive formats (Zoom, Google Meet, Skype); and each of these forms has its own standards of excellence. Live video streaming is much like a television program, and in recent years as "smart" televisions can connect to the internet, many people are watching livestreamed worship on a wide-screen television, which allows for a more "immersive" experience of viewing. This medium favors big productions that have the video production values of a television program, with multiple camera angles and well-produced sound quality.[9]

Livestreaming has the advantage of the participatory excitement of joining in an event as it unfolds. According to a 2017 market survey of online engagement, "one in five [respondents] said watching live streaming video makes them feel as if they are a part of an event."[10] The survey does not comment on how the production quality of livestreamed video affects the experience, though my own participation in numerous online streaming worship services from a wide variety of congregations suggests that the quality of product matters greatly. I've read numerous anecdotal reports of congregations that conduct livestreaming worship by using a single stationary video recorder to capture a service as it unfolds in real time.[11]

Many of these reports also suggest that although viewers begin to watch these live-capture services, they soon lose interest, or they will log on to the service at about the time they expect to hear the sermon. While some congregations are reporting a larger total viewership online than

---

9. Livestreamed worship does create some issues with copyright, especially around the posting of video for later viewing. I suspect that one of the reasons megachurches rarely post recordings of entire worship services on their websites is to avoid posting copyrighted songs.

10. https://www.emarketer.com/Article/Some-Live-Streaming-Video-Already-Constant /1016137, accessed June 26, 2020.

11. I acknowledge that I am employing a great deal of "anecdotal evidence." At the time I am writing this chapter (June 2020), I have found very little scientific data on viewership or church usage since the beginning of the pandemic in the US in March 2020.

they would have received at in-person service alone, this report does not mean the everyone who logs in attends the entire service. That is hardly surprising. One can imagine how viewers would quickly tire of watching a football game, a livestreamed concert, the Rose Bowl Parade, or any similar live event if it did not include multiple camera angles and commentary. A stand-alone camera may mimic the single location from which an individual watches from bleachers, standing on the street, or sitting in a pew, but this single camera cannot capture the visceral experience of actually attending these events. To approximate the experience of engagement requires a great deal of sophisticated production.

I suggest that worship patterns that aim to produce experiences of "flow" (notably the Revival/Seeker model and the Pentecostal/Praise and Worship model) are more conducive to livestreamed worship, especially as they feature stage bands, worship sets, and very practical "messages" as the core features.[12] Congregations that employ an Aesthetic model may have some success if their production values are high, though listening to a congregation sing a traditional hymn or recite a responsive reading is, frankly, not very interesting in a video production.

Another form of online media used by church is streaming video on demand. In this format, specific parts of the service are prerecorded (introductory words, announcements, music, readings, sermon, etc.) and then posted on a video hosting platform with a link embedded in the congregation website or Facebook page. While some congregations use the on-demand format for video archives of their livestreamed sermons, many are now using this format to put together longer and more complete services of worship that are prerecorded by a variety of individuals from a variety of locations. This has proved to be quite popular during the pandemic

---

12. Sam Han, in his account of the technological expertise of a megachurch satellite congregation, makes this observation: "The worship pastor is responsible for all of the technical ins and outs of the church. At Bright Church, New York, this turns out to be quite a bit, as much of the worship service, which Bright Church across the board calls 'experience,' is wholly reliant upon the smooth functioning of various technologies." Han goes on to note: "It is no wonder that Bright Church adamantly calls their worship services 'experiences.' As Jeremy Sitz, Bright Church's Head of Innovation, relayed to me, 'It is intentional. It's not service. We're trying to help you experience God.'" Han's observations also apply to their video streams of these "worship experiences." *Technologies of Religion, Routledge Research in Information Technology* (New York, NY: Routledge, Taylor & Francis, 2016), 58–59.

when readers, minister, and music leaders have no option but to make their recordings without gathering together in one place. My wife, who pastors an urban congregation, has employed this medium for her church. Each week her staff collects short video entries from various members of the staff and congregation (offering a prayer, reading a lesson, leading a song, and so forth). The worship service is then produced by editing these discrete liturgical units into the complete service, which is officially released to the public on Sunday morning. The standard of excellence for this type of video production is the television variety show. A variety show is episodic, with each particular part standing more or less alone as its own complete piece: an interview, a comedy skit, commercials, a monologue, a musical performance. This online medium fits best with the character of the Aesthetic/Traditional model or the Sunday School/Creative Worship model, both of which are made up of strings of very distinct liturgical units.

The more highly interactive videoconferencing formats such as Zoom and Google Meet were developed to facilitate business meetings. They also have screen-sharing capabilities, which allow posting of graphic materials or texts, and they have the capacity for recording meetings that may be edited and posted later for on-demand access. Because they allow participants to see faces up close during group interaction, they work well with the democratic intimacy of the Prayer Meeting/House Church model. An excellent teleconference is one in which people participate actively in discussion. A teleconference does not work well for group singing or group recitation, as small group leaders are quickly discovering.

Some congregations have employed a combination of these various media, with parts of the worship service streaming live, parts of the service prerecorded (for instance, a musical performance), and the final segment of the service moving to a teleconferencing link for group prayer or for a more interactive service on "online communion." Ostensibly, this has the potential to incorporate the best features of each format: the excitement of the live broadcast, the polish of the video set piece, and the interactive intimacy of the small group teleconference. My own experience with such services is that the mix of live and recorded video flows well but that the transition to the teleconference provokes the feeling of "liturgical whiplash" that I describe in chapter 9 (p. 219–22).

The one model I have not associated with online media is the Catholic Liturgical Renewal model, though I did touch on this topic with the brief note on the controversy concerning the possibility of "online Communion." I do not want to wade too far into that controversy here, though it is fair to say that Christian traditions that lean toward the catholic end of the ecclesial scale have been much more resistant to the possibility than those that skew toward the congregational side. Some Catholic congregations (and some Episcopalians and Lutherans too) do of course stream video of their services, including the Eucharist, and encourage viewers to watch such services and pray along with them, as a sort of devotional practice. Indeed, not a few Protestants have been known to watch the Christmas Eve Mass broadcast from the Vatican (or at least have it on in the background while they are finishing up wrapping gifts, as we have done in my house!). Yet, as far as I know, no one (Protestant or Catholic) is encouraged to put bread and wine in front of the screen, pray the prayers along with the Pope, and receive these elements as the Eucharist. Even if someone were to do that, it would not actually be the Church's Eucharist as it is understood within the Catholic Liturgical Renewal model, no matter how personally meaningful the experience may be to that individual. In short, for the Catholic Liturgical model, Communion is not first of all an "experience" but a concrete, real practice. And online Communion is not merely a bad practice, it is essentially impossible. Since the Eucharist is a fundamental component of the Catholic Liturgical Renewal/Word and Table model, no form of video worship can actually fulfill the *telos* of that model, no matter how effectively it is conducted or produced. During the pandemic of 2020, Catholic Liturgical Renewal congregations are, therefore, "fasting" from the Eucharist as they pause in-person gathering, even as they are exploring new devotional and small group practices of prayer and scripture reading through online social media and in domestic settings.

I suggest that once the pandemic has subsided and the churches that survive are able to reflect on their strategies for dealing with the crisis, we will discover that our experiments with online worship have raised fundamental theological questions of the nature and organization of the church: What is a congregation? What is the meaning and purpose of ordination? What is church order? What is the mission of the church? What is the Church Catholic, and how is it found (or not found) in the local congregation? And does the internet promote genuine catholicity or a false catholicity, or is it capable of producing both depending on how it is employed? Once congregations are able to return to in-person worship, we will likely find that our experiments of necessity will have changed both our expectations of worship and our concrete practices.

As I write the conclusion to this chapter, I have no idea how churches will address such problems. For in addition to the coronavirus pandemic, many white Americans have (finally?) reached a critical awareness of our centuries-old social disease of white supremacy and systemic racism. White Christians have implicit and sometimes explicit responsibility for the racism epidemic, and addressing this disease will require a seismic change, especially in the culture of white congregations in America. All of this has come to a head just as I was hoping to send my copyedited manuscript back to Abingdon Press, leading me to violate a fundamental principle of good writing: "Do not bring up a new topic in the conclusion of an essay!"

Rather than insist that some conventions simply do not hold true anymore, I will appeal a deeper principle that God revealed to John the Elder on Patmos long ago: "Behold, I make all things new." In this moment of crisis for the Church of Jesus Christ, let that be our hope and prayer.

Conclusion

Good Worship?

Ring the bells that still can ring
Forget your perfect offering
There is a crack in everything
That's how the light gets in

—"Anthem" by Leonard Cohen

"Good service, Pastor."

"Thanks."

Countless pastors receive such a comment each week after worship, and accept it as a compliment, a word of gratitude, or perhaps just an awkward greeting. But what does it mean to have a "good service"?

Across the landscape of Protestant congregations in the United States, six major patterns influence the content and practice of worship. These patterns arose to meet different concerns. They point to different goals, and they have acquired distinctive styles or character. A Revival aims at the gut to provoke religious conversion. A Sunday School aims at the mind to educate for Christian character. An Aesthetic service tries to elevate the cultural and spiritual refinement of worshipers, while a Pentecostal service seeks a euphoric, decidedly unrefined encounter with the Holy Spirit. Prayer Meetings strive for interpersonal intimacy, while Catholic Liturgical worship joins with the universal song of the saints and angels throughout the cosmos.

Consequently, to understand what qualifies as a "good service," we would need to ask, "Good to what end?"

We typically don't ask such questions or worry about the goal or character of worship when it seems to be going well and when our members say "Good service, Pastor." We only begin to worry when worship seems to fail for some reason. But few members of our congregations understand how worship actually works, just as I don't really understand the intricacies of how the engine in my car works! I only become interested in the engine when something goes wrong—and even then I rely on a mechanic to diagnose the problem and fix it. In much the same way, when worship fails to engage a congregation, its members will necessarily rely on pastors and worship leaders to diagnose and repair what has gone wrong. I hope that the method for analyzing worship I have developed will assist you in both diagnosis and repair.

And yet there is more to "good worship" than having a well-oiled machine. To be sure, anything done well will be more compelling than anything done poorly. But that maxim does not consider whether the "thing" being done is worth doing in the first place. Even a theologically deficient order of worship might be compelling if it is done well, while a theologically rich service can fail to be compelling if it is led poorly.

The method I have developed in this book does not provide a theological assessment of the six models. I have made some theological observations all along, but mostly I have stayed at the level of description. I have tried to show the implicit, and often unconscious, default modes of thinking that shape the content and practice of worship. By doing so, I hope I have brought them to awareness so that you can evaluate these default modes of thinking—to become aware of the rules of the games you and I are playing (to return to my sports metaphor).

But even though I have tried to give more or less equal attention to the six patterns, it would be wrong to assume that they are equivalent as overarching models for public worship of God on the Lord's Day. Nowhere am I suggesting that congregations simply choose a model and try to do it well. A well-led Revival should evangelize, a Sunday School worship should educate, Aesthetic Worship should inspire with the riches of Christian art, Pentecostal Worship should open us to the power of the Spirit, and Prayer Meetings should enable us to share the blessing and burdens of fellow believers. Healthy congregations need all of the above: evangelism, education, art, spiritual power, and intimate fellowship.

Conclusion

The Word and Table model is different from the other five because it does not approach worship as an instrument to achieve its goal. Instead, Word and Table is essentially participation in the worship of saints and angels across time and space. Rather than make worship happen, in the service of Word and Table we join in what already is taking place. Or, as Robert Webber puts it, "We enter into the heavens around the throne of God to join the communion of saints in that place of eternal worship."[1]

As participation with the saints in glory, Word and Table also has the capacity to avoid the weaknesses of the other patterns: the individualism of the Revival, the consumer mentality of the Seeker Service, the unwieldy didacticism of the Sunday School assembly, the wordiness of Creative Worship, the class bias of Aesthetic Worship, and the nostalgia of Traditional Worship. Word and Table shares with Pentecostal Worship a desire to worship in obedience to the Spirit, but it is able to avoid the chaotic excesses that can happen when Pentecostal Worship breaks free from the traditions of the historic stream of the church universal.

That said, the worship of the church this side of glory will always fall short of the perfection to which we aspire. Still, we strive to be obedient to the awe-inspiring and fearful task of serving God and the world as faithful disciples of Jesus Christ.

And so for the altar call: Friend, will you allow the light that breaks through the cracks of our imperfect worship to shine forth to all the world?

---

1. *Planning Blended Worship: The Creative Mixture of Old and New* (Nashville, TN: Abingdon Press, 1998), 21.

www.ingramcontent.com/pod-product-compliance
Lightning Source LLC
Chambersburg PA
CBHW011749220426
43669CB00022B/2957